THOMAS HARDY:
TOWARDS A MATERIALIST CRITICISM

GEORGE WOTTON

Thomas Hardy: Towards a Materialist Criticism

GILL AND MACMILLAN

BARNES & NOBLE BOOKS
Totowa, New Jersey

Published in Ireland by
Gill and Macmillan Ltd
Goldenbridge
with associated companies in
Auckland, Dallas, Delhi, Hong Kong,
Johannesburg, Lagos, London, Manzini,
Melbourne, Nairobi, New York, Singapore,
Tokyo, Washington
© George Wotton, 1985
7171 1361 2
First published in the USA 1985 by
Barnes & Noble Books,
81 Adams Drive,
Totowa, New Jersey 07512
ISBN 0-389-20564-8

Library of Congress Cataloging in Publication Data:

Wotton, George.
  Thomas Hardy, towards a materialist criticism.

  1. Hardy, Thomas, 1840–1928—Criticism and interpretation.   I. Title.
PR4754.W66 1985   823′.8   85–749
ISBN 0-389-20564-8
Print origination in Ireland by Computertype Limited
Printed and bound in Great Britain by
Biddles Ltd, Guildford and King's Lynn

For Pam with love

Contents

Preface

'Every exploiting class', Sebastiano Timpanaro has written, 'always needs a discourse on "spiritual values"'. This book is in the nature of a critical engagement with one such discourse— 'Literary Criticism'. It is not, however, a generalized polemic against varieties of literary critical or theoretical positions, rather it concentrates on a specific and concrete instance, namely the production and reproduction of the novels of Thomas Hardy. My aim has been to historicize Hardy's writing and, by regarding it as a social event rather than an ideal object, to contribute to an understanding of the function of imaginative writing not only in the process of cultural/ideological production but also in reproducing the actual relations of production in class society.

But if Hardy's writing has a history so too does the discourse which treats it as an object of knowledge, and if this book is the product of a struggle against one critical tradition it is also quite clearly produced out of another. Yet to put it in these terms is to point to a major difficulty. When, as a mature student at the University of Essex, I acquired in 1972 a copy of Pierre Macherey's *Pour une théorie de la production littéraire*, I found the concept of literary production a profound shock to my received Leavisite ideas about 'Literature', no less of a shock, indeed, than Marx's theory of social production was to my idealist notions about 'Life'. Both revealed my real ignorance concerning what I had long taken for granted as self evident truths about those two idealist categories and I understood for the first time that the effect of my own education and upbringing, of my trained responses—as an 'individual'—to 'Life' and 'Literature' had been to depoliticize me as a person. I had become a kind of ideological automaton, the very epitome of Matthew Arnold's 'classless alien'. If this realization brought a sense of having to start afresh, to find a new beginning, it also brought a realization of the singular absence of a 'place' from which to start. The absence of an indigenous theoretical critical tradition produced an acute sense of disorientation. From where was one to take one's bearings? As Terry Eagleton noted in the Preface to *Criticism and Ideology*, 'Any English Marxist who tries now to construct a materialist aesthetics must be painfully conscious of his inadequacies ... to intervene from England is almost automatically to disenfranchise oneself from debate. It is to feel acutely bereft of a tradition, as a tolerated house-guest of Europe, a precocious but parasitic alien.' Published in 1976 perhaps the greatest value of that pioneering work is the way it articulates the nature and extent of that historical isolation and alienation. It may seem to some a strange irony that the material place, the actual site of that new beginning was the 'improbable institution' (Eagleton's term) of the University of Oxford. And yet it was the very improbability of *that* institution situated in a city where the structure of class division is so dramatically and visibly present in the radical separation of the great industrial complex of the car factory from the ideological apparatus of the University, that the contradictions and crises of the period were sharpened and focused.

While this country did not experience an upheaval comparable to that which shook France in 1968 in some respects the year 1972 came nearest to it. Two events in particular occurred in that year the far reaching effects of which are being violently felt as I write these words twelve years later. I refer to 'Bloody Sunday' when British paratroopers shot and killed thirteen people in Londonderry and to the 1972 miners' strike. To some it appeared that the social foundations upon which the dreaming spires of the improbable institution rested were indeed crumbling. A senior advisor to the Heath government wrote of this time, 'many of those in positions of influence looked into the abyss and saw only a few days away the possibility of the country being plunged into a state of chaos not so very far removed from that which might prevail after a minor nuclear attack,.'* Between Bloody Sunday and the flying pickets of 1972

*Brendan Sewill, quoted in David Thompson, *England in the Twentieth Century*, Pelican Books, p. 317.

and the Brighton bombing and the pitched battles between police and miners' pickets of 1984 the economic crisis has deepened and the social and political contradictions have become more acute. Nowhere has the impact of this critical period been felt more than in the educational system. Every level and every area of the system has been profoundly affected and none more so than the humanities the role and function of which have undergone radical reappraisals both on the right as well as on the left. In this situation 'English Literature' has again become the site of bitter ideological and political struggles. The difference between now and ten years ago is that an English Marxist no longer feels disenfranchised from debate. A long historical silence has been shattered by all those who have struggled in many ways and in many places over the past decade to develop, in theory and in practice, a materialist under-standing of cultural production.

While this book emerges out of that common struggle it is also stamped with a peculiarly personal imprint bearing as it does the marks of my own attempt to break with what Louis Althusser once called the language of ideological spontaneity. If the result of that personal struggle is a certain awkwardness, even crudity, then for that I alone am responsible. But in so far as one of the most formative influences on its production has been the practical activity of teaching literature in the Humanities depart-ment of Hatfield Polytechnic my indebtedness to other people is such that my own contribution has sometimes seemed to me to be almost marginal. This is a matter not only of theory but also of practice, particularly those innumerable situations both in the classroom and out of it where the issues raised here have been the subject of debate. The generation of ideas in such practical situations is always in a way communal, produced out of the necessities of the moment and to all those, both students and teachers, who have been part of that productive process, this book stands as a tribute. I would, however, like to thank those of my co-workers with whom I have been most closely associated at Hatfield Polytechnic, Gill Davies, Graham Pechey, Jean Radford and Judith Thompson. To them I am particularly indebted as also to Terry Eagleton, Paul O'Flinn and Peter Widdowson whose rigorous criticisms contributed to the shaping of this book.

Introduction

The most startling thing about *The Great Tradition* is not the cavalier dismissal of 'the good little Thomas Hardy' from the realm of 'Literature' but just how much, in writing his book, Leavis felt—*knew*—he could take for granted. It is as though every evaluation he makes is prefaced by a rhetorical absence, an unspoken 'we all know, don't we, what is meant by life, art, consciousness, Literature?' That this silent assumption is of the utmost importance is evident from the fact that what we are all deemed to know and to take for granted as shared knowledge are the twin propositions upon which, even now, the scholastic practice of criticism is based. The first of these propositions concerns the *a priori* nature of 'Literature' and the second the evaluative function of criticism itself. Thus, emphatically, Leavis declares that 'The great English novelists are Jane Austen, George Eliot, Henry James and Joseph Conrad', and he establishes the domain of his study as 'the field of fiction belonging to Literature', a field in which 'some challenging discriminations are very much called for'.[1] It is not the value judgments themselves that a materialist criticism must call into question, but the 'self evident' truths upon which they are founded. And here we are confronted by the problem of meaning for when criticism ceases to be based on what could justifiably be called 'common sense', on that assumed understanding of something called 'Literature', then what is called for is no longer discrimination but definition.

In what ways then does a criticism grounded on materialist principles differ from criticism grounded in 'common sense'? To begin with, a materialist criticism rejects the distinction between 'fiction' and 'Literature' which is based on procedures of evaluation, and replaces it by a distinction between writing and literature based on concepts of production. Here the word literature does not signify, as in Leavis's text, an object, the pre-existent domain of the discourse of criticism, but a *social relation*, the product of the social exchange between writing and criticism. From a materialist perspective Leavis's term 'Literature' signifies those texts which have undergone a determinate productive process in the ideological discourses of criticism which use the techniques of discrimination, evaluation, separation and elaboration to distinguish and elevate them from the various forms of 'imaginative' writing in general. The object of study for a materialist criticism, however, is not, as with Leavis, 'Literature', but the relations between history, ideology, writing and criticism. And the aim of a materialist criticism is not evaluation or the discovery of meaning or significance in the 'literary text' but an understanding of the historical conditions of the production of writing and the ways in which literature operates in the process of reproducing the relations of production of class society.

Furthermore, to think in materialist terms and in order to break with the idealist notions of writing as creation or reflection we should think of writing actively as labour[2] and language and ideology as the materials upon which that labour is expended, bearing in mind that while writers are undeniably the producers of their texts, they do not themselves produce the linguistic and ideological materials with which they work. Once the act of writing is thought of as a labour expended upon something, something which is not determined by the writer and which exists independently of him or her, then the nature of the relation between writers and what they produce is changed from one of private ownership to one of social process. The same also holds for the consumers of writing and their activity for as every reading of a text is a reproduction in the light of historical, ideological, linguistic and experiential factors which differ from those of the writer, the consumption of writing is simultaneously also a production. Literary criticism is a particular form of reading in which writing is consumed in certain determinate ways. In this productive consumption the writing is continually elaborated, 'constructed' and reproduced in the image of its meanings. It is not that the text is altered, rather it is ideologically activated, put to productive use.

As they appear in a materialist criticism then, writing and literature are conceptually different terms and cannot be distinguished from one another by evaluation as could Leavis's 'fiction' and 'Literature'. They are, rather, separate moments in a determinate productive process comprising an articulation between the historical moment of production of writing and the subsequent moments of consumption/reproduction which entail the ideological activation of writing by the discourse of criticism. However, the concept of production does not refer only to the separate moments in the production-consumption cycle of literature but also to the productive capacity of writing itself. There are two distinct but related elements here. The first involves what I shall call the aesthetic project which has to do with what the producer of the writing wants his or her product to do, that is, the ideological effect the writing is intended to produce. While this first element is a matter of ideological production and is bound up with the writer's intention, the second is a matter of a production of the ideological which is quite independent of intention. What I am suggesting is that writing produces a *scenario* of the ideological and that the 'view' of ideology which is thus produced is not a product of the writer's consciousness and is quite different from what the writer 'wants us to see'. It is therefore important to distinguish between the aesthetic project, the ideological problematic upon which that project rests and the 'view' of ideology produced by the writing, and to understand that a knowledge of these does not reside in writing but is itself a product of materialist criticism.

Briefly, the aesthetic project of Hardy's writing can be identified as the production of an *insight* into the true realities of life and the ideological problematic upon which this project is based is centred on the idea of knowledge being an act of discovery of a pre-existent reality which might be expressed by the formulation 'knowing as seeing'. Seeing here takes on a meaning which is much more than simply looking, for it is a definite *act* which every individual subject 'endowed with the faculty of "vision" … exercises either attentively or distractedly'.[3] This idealist and empiricist mutation has significant ideological consequences in that the real social contradictions in class society are transformed into problems of individual perception. Class struggle is idealized into conflicting points of view, sights and oversights in vision, everything becoming a matter of the individual subject's true or false acts of seeing. Thus in Hardy's writing class and gender conflicts appear as conflicts of perception in the multifarious acts of seeing of the characters who inhabit Wessex. By endowing the imaginary world with a richness and complexity which resembles the real world (but does not reflect it) the writing produces the possibility for an infinite number of acts of sight to take place involving not only the characters but also the writer and the readers. However, it was not Hardy's intention that a true mode of perception be found *in* the writing but that true perception, the insight into the real, be produced *by* the writing in the consciousness of the subject who attentively peruses it. In this way production (writing) determines consumption (reading) by casting the reader in the role of seer. This determination operates in such a way that Hardy's language appears as the 'bearer' of the seen, involving the reader in a complex network of points of view. Many of Hardy's so-called stylistic infelicities are due to this peculiar use of language which strives not so much to produce an image of a character or a scene as to set up a determinate relationship between seer and seen in order that 'the real' be made visible. It is in the endless diversity of these subject-centred perceptions of the world, in the difference between the points of view of an infinite number of individuals that the writing achieves its ideological effect namely that of transforming social class and gender conflicts into conflicting points of view.

However, a materialist criticism does more than simply enable us to identify the writing's aesthetic project, it enables us to grasp the productive nature of writing itself. In the present case what materialist criticism enables us to see is that by evoking a mode of perception which turns a whole world into an object of contemplation for the individual consciousness, Hardy's writing produces an image of an ideological mode of appropriating reality. Quite independently of the writer's intention the writing produces a *scenario* of ideology in action, ideology actually functioning as the acts of sight of perceiving subjects. In this *scenario* of conflicting points of view what individuals see is dependent on how they are ideologically addressed and constituted (interpellated) as subjects in and by ideologies of class and gender. While these ideologies are themselves a part of the means of production for Hardy's writing, the writing does not simply reflect or represent them but actually puts them into contradiction. It does this in two main ways. First, by confronting the sovereignty of the subject—which the subjective mode of perception signifies—with a totally different way of seeing dependent on the community of the working people of Wessex; second, by confronting those ideological discourses which spoke of 'the progress of civilization and the improvement in the moral sentiments of mankind'[4] by a structure of perceptions in which 'womankind' is perceived as 'mankind's' lesser Other. In Hardy's writing the harmonizing ideological discourses of the Victorian bourgeoisie are brought into head-on conflict with the alter-ideology of women as the *sexus sequior*, the inferior, or in its genteel Victorian version, weaker sex. As Göran Therborn has suggested, in the relations of power and domination 'the alter-ideology of the dominating subjects is translated into attempts to mould the dominated according to the rulers' image of them'.[5] Time and again we find that it is precisely such images which intervene into the individual's vision of an harmonious conjunction of consciousness and being to distort and disrupt a desired unity. In Hardy's writing these images are put into play by a specific structure of perceptions.

These ideological considerations should not, however, obscure the fact that a materialist criticism starts out from the premise that the production of Hardy's writing is rooted in, and emerges out of, the contradiction between an historical process and an historical moment. That is, as I shall show, the contradiction between the long process of the separation of the producer from the means of production, which constituted the basis of the development of capitalism in Britain, and the effects of the Great Depression on the economic and social structure of the counties of south-west England in the last quarter of the nineteenth century. But this is not to say that Hardy's writing 'reflects' history. History is not writing's raw material; the primary material upon which the labour of writing is expended is not the conflict between the relations of production and the material forces of production, but the ideological forms in which people become conscious of that conflict and 'fight it out'. In Hardy's case the ideological forms are those of his class of origin and those of the intellectual grouping to which he gave the name 'the thinking world'.[6] While there are certain similarities between the contradictions inherent in the *class situation* of the small producer or petty bourgeois in terms of its inherent instability as a transitional class, its very existence guaranteed only by a compromise between the antagonistic classes between which it is uneasily situated, and the *ideological* compromise formation elaborated in the ideological discourses of 'the thinking world', there is a radical difference between the experiential knowledge and customary forms of the one and the utopian idealism of the other, between the harmony of 'hearts and hands' and the harmony of being and consciousness.

The aesthetic project of Hardy's writing, however, is determined by the latter, by that unique conjunction of discourses which were elaborated in the terms of an idealist philosophy, an empiricist theory of knowledge, an altruistic ethics, an undogmatic theology and a reformist politics. This peculiar ideological compromise formation expressed both the reformist will of the traditional intellectuals, expressed in the utopian desire to change society by weakening its antagonistic extremes and transforming them into harmony, and the hope for the progressive development of the identity between social being and social consciousness. This ideological formation might well be designated by the term used by D. G. Ritchie, that is, Idealist Evolutionism.[7]

Hardy gave a personal expression to each of these ideological positions. As an 'Intrinsicalist' he expressed his belief that the true political principle was a compromise, writing in *The Life of Thomas Hardy*: 'Conservatism is not estimable in itself, nor is Change, or Radicalism. To conserve the existing good, to supplant the existing bad by good, is to act on a true political principle, which is neither Conservative nor Radical.'[8] He gave his religious beliefs the particular form of the Idea of the Universal Will, the It, becoming conscious of Itself, a form of idealism which replaced 'the old Transcendental Ideals' with the 'Idealism of Fancy'.[9] We find his altruistic views contained in his belief in evolutionary meliorism and in his 'doctrine' of the Universe growing 'sympathetic', a belief reinforced by the law of evolution which, he wrote, 'shifted the centre of altruism from humanity to the whole conscious world collectively'.[10] Philosophically he inclined to the Kantian compromise between materialism and idealism, his perception of reality being determined by the empiricist problematic of knowledge which he expressed as the search for the essence of the real in apparent reality.

In so far as Hardy believed that the function of the artist was to draw aside the veil of the apparent, he defined himself as a seer whose art was not concerned with the mirroring of reality or the expression of ideas, but with seeing into the structure of the real. Such perception, arrived at through the operation of the 'imaginative reason', he believed to constitute the true function of art and was true realism. He wrote that 'the seer should watch the pattern among things which his idiosyncracy moves him to observe, and describe that alone. That is, quite accurately, a going to Nature; yet the result is no mere photograph, but purely the product of the writer's own mind.'[11] This is the imaginative reason at work, an intervention on the writer's part, an act of 'disproportioning—(i.e. distorting; throwing out of proportion)—of realities', to show more clearly the features that matter in these realities'.[12] Through this intervention Hardy believed that true art *produced the effect* of essential reality, writing that 'Art is the secret of how to produce by a false thing the effect of a true.'[13] This 'reality effect' is produced by 'true Art's' ability to draw aside the veil of the apparent and allow the clear sighted reader a vision of the truth and is the basis of the aesthetic project of Hardy's writing.

There is, however, a crucial and determining link between the production of Hardy's writing and its reproduction in the discourse of criticism which has ensured a remarkable ideological continuity over the period of a hundred years since the publication of the first novels. This is due to the fact that those critical discourses which have produced Hardy's writing as Literature are themselves determined by the same empiricist and idealist problematic as that which determined Hardy's own aesthetic project. Through its revelation of the truth, criticism 'realizes' Hardy's 'moments of vision' through its own special procedures. There is, in consequence, an homology between the contradictory modes of perception in Hardy's writing and the conflicting 'critical' perceptions in the discourses of aesthetic ideology, that is, between the writing's aesthetic project and the ideological intentions of criticism. Time and again the original aesthetic project and the ideological intentions of criticism become fused in the process of consumption/reproduction: 'Hardy is both realist and symbolist, which is to say that by being intensely and imaginatively realistic, he passes beyond realism to discover the archetypal form, the timeless categories, implicit in an immediate context, a context which consequently becomes the symbolic utterance of a larger meaning.'[14]

There is thus a coherence between the ideological comprom-ise formation I have referred to as Idealist Evolutionism, the aesthetic project of Hardy's writing and the critical enterprise of aesthetic ideology. However, the relation between these and the writing itself is *not* one of identity. Whereas writing puts the ideological into contradiction, the discourse of criticism effaces contradiction by excluding it. The product of the exchange bet-ween writing and the discourse of aesthetic ideology is writing cleansed of its contradictions. In order to assert its mastery over writing, criticism subjects it to a specific consumption/repro-duction process ideologically activating it in certain deter-minate ways and preparing it for future consumption as a uniquely 'free' discourse which allows an endless diversity of subject-centred perceptions to take place. Thus the conflicts in the structure of perceptions in Hardy's writing are reproduced in the discourse of aesthetic ideology in the free play of an infinite variety of 'critical' points of view.

It has proved difficult for feminist and Marxist criticism to break with the traditional forms of bourgeois aesthetics. The relation between 'theory' and 'criticism' has turned out to be rather uneasy as is evidenced by the way the two have been quite rigorously held apart appearing either in completely separate works or, where an application of one to the other has been attempted in a single work, separated by the device of 'theoretical' and 'critical' chapters. This difficulty is not simply a formal matter. Whereas criticism as customarily practised is an ideological discourse, theory attempts to be a (non-ideo-logical) understanding of that discourse. The difficulty arises not when talking of F. R. Leavis, but when being confronted with having to say something about *Jude the Obscure*. Faced with that necessity 'theory' inevitably dissolves into 'criticism' and what a feminist or Marxist then actually says about *Jude* appears remarkably similar to what a 'bourgeois' critic says, but from a different 'point of view'. This is inevitable while it is only the players who have been changed and not the rules of the game. What I am suggesting is that the formal structures of bourgeois criticism impose areas of silence, do not allow certain things to be said and that in order to say these things materialist criticism must actually have a different form to attain its objectives.

What the present work attempts is an exploration of the relations between the production of Thomas Hardy's writing and the social production of 'Thomas Hardy'. To this end the book is divided into three parts. The first deals with the conditions of production of Hardy's writing and involves a consideration both of the historical and social as well as the aesthetic and ideological factors involved in that production. The second part is concerned with the relations between ideology and writing elaborated in the concept of the structure of perceptions which informs Hardy's novels. The third and final part concerns the relation between Hardy's writing and aesthetic ideology, the ways in which 'Thomas Hardy' has been produced as 'Literature' and the social and ideological function of that production. I am well aware of the limitations of this project, of what it leaves out. But I hope those who feel with Francis Mulhern that '"Literary criticism" as it is mainly practised in England is in reality the focal activity of a discourse whose foremost general cultural function is the repression of politics'[15] will read it sympathetically as one attempt among others to combat that repression.

As the concept of ideology plays such an important part in this book it remains, finally, to say a word about the meanings I attach to the term. It should be borne in mind that in what follows I want to emphasize the materiality of the ideological sphere, to stress the material social existence of ideology and to reject outright the idealist notion that ideology is a 'false consciousness'.

In his essay on the Italian painter Leonardo Cremonini, Louis Althusser has written that '"culture" is the ordinary name for the Marxist concept of the *ideological*'.[16] This is, arguably, too close an identification, but we can certainly see what he means in a passage such as the following:

Taking now the point of view of identification, the reader must remind himself as the author has constantly to do, of how much is here embraced by the term *culture*. It includes all the characteristic activities and interests of a people: Derby Day, Henley Regatta, Cowes, the twelfth of August, a cup final, the dog races, the pin table, the dart board, Wensleydale cheese, boiled cabbage cut into sections, beetroot in vinegar, nineteenth-century Gothic churches and the music of Elgar.... And then we have to face the strange idea that what is part of our culture is also part of our *lived* religion ... bishops are part of English culture, and horses and dogs are part of English religion.[17]

It seems a moot point whether this passage, which embraces the institutions, practices, beliefs, cultural objects, 'consciousness' of a class society is a definition of culture or the ideological. Althusser's own definition of ideology is that of a 'system of representations ... perceived-accepted-suffered cultural objects' which negotiate the '*lived* relation between men and their world'.[18] The two are very close and yet there is a difference, a dissimilarity which may itself be ideologically and culturally determined in so far as a discourse which speaks of 'culture and society' is 'fighting it out'[19] in a different way from one which speaks of 'ideology and the social formation'. Nevertheless, I think that the juxtaposition is helpful and would agree with Göran Therborn that the concept of culture is useful alongside a broad definition of ideology.[20] Indeed, it is Therborn's 'broad definition' I would adopt as a working hypothesis. He writes that ideology refers

to that aspect of the human condition under which human beings live their lives as conscious actors in a world that makes sense to them in varying degrees. Ideology is the medium through which this consciousness and meaningfulness operate...[It] includes both everyday notions and 'experience' and elaborate intellectual doctrines, both the 'consciousness' of social actors and the institutionalized thought-systems and discourses of a given society.[21]

Therborn adds an important rider to this proposition: 'To conceive of a text or an utterance as ideology is to focus on the way it

operates in the formation and transformation of human subjectivity.... To understand how ideologies operate in a given
society requires ... that we see them not as possessions or texts
but as *ongoing social processes.*'[22]

Implicit in these propositions is the concept of the sphere of
the ideological as a site of struggle, an arena of continuous
contestation where class and gender conflicts are fought out.
Furthermore, in such a formulation ideologies are seen to exist
not as elaborated discourses (although discourse is an element of
the ideological), but as dynamic social processes. However provisional this definition may be it also has the virtue of stressing
the social and material aspect of ideology (its existence in institutionalized thought-systems—church, school, court of law and so
on) while retaining the importance of human consciousness and
experience. This is crucial for any consideration of Hardy's
writing deeply rooted as that writing is in ideological and cultural conflicts.

With regard to this last, Raymond Williams, ever sensitive to
the experiential forms of ideological struggle, has written in his
essay on Hardy of the 'conflicts of desire and possibility' of those
who live in the 'border country' between custom and education.[23] In so far as the opposite of customary is taken here to be
educated, the opposition is structural, part of a definite ideological process. This dichotomy, central to Hardy's writing, also
informs much of Raymond Williams' own work where he traces
the historical disintegration of the 'knowable community'. It is
also to be found in Gramsci who writes of that aspect of
education which fosters new conceptions of the world which
challenge 'the conceptions that are imparted by the various
traditional social environments which can be termed folk-
loristic'.[24] Historical and geographical considerations must
figure prominently in any understanding of this aspect of the
ideological affected as it is by differing states of development of
the forces and relations of production as well as by those
material determinants associated with locality or region.

This is where culture and ideology flow into one another
for we are dealing here with customs, traditions, modes of
behaviour, practices, rituals, beliefs and superstitions which
form part of an unarticulated, customary 'way of life' of a
community. But as one of the major functions of the ideological

formations of a dominant class is to universalize that class's own interests and represent them as the interests of the generality, they repress and dominate such customary cultural/ideological formations. Individuals often experience this ideological conflict as a sense of radical displacement. This displacement is not, however, the result of a willed social mobility but of an historical process of separation. And it is with a consideration of that historical process that a materialist criticism of Hardy's writing must begin.

PART ONE

The
Conditions of Production
of
Hardy's Writing

1

The Radical Separation

In his perceptive essay on Hardy, Raymond Williams writes that 'work enters his novels more decisively than in any English novelist of comparable importance'[1] and he emphasises the point that the social forces of Hardy's writing are deeply based in the rural economy of Wessex, 'in the system of rent and trade; in the hazards of ownership and tenancy; in the differing conditions of labour on good and bad land and in socially different villages'.[2] While this is undoubtedly a correct emphasis, it does raise the question as to how to understand the rural economy of that place at that time and the labour it sustained. On the face of it this appears to be a relatively simple matter of local rural history but it is not enough simply to identify the historical period to which a body of writing relates and treat it as a kind of scenic 'backdrop' against which the writing is 'set'. This suggests both that the relation between Hardy's writing and history is passively reflectionist and that the history is itself a *tableau vivant* of some 'timeless order'. I believe Hardy's writing can only be understood once the history to which it alludes has been fully grasped as a dynamic on-going process.

In the nineteenth century the rural economy of Dorset and its neighbouring counties was grounded in and largely dependent upon an agriculture which in many respects was considerably less advanced than in other parts of the country. The reason for this relative backwardness was that Dorset was only very slowly affected by the scientific and technical developments of the agricultural revolution of the late eighteenth and early nineteenth centuries due to the fact that it was primarily a sheep rearing, cattle grazing and dairy farming area. This form of agriculture had extremely important economic and social effects in that it tended to maintain a relatively high proportion of independent small scale production in the form of farms, small holdings, allotments, small industries and numerous rural trades.[3] Throughout the nineteenth century this mode of production sustained that 'interesting and better-informed class'[4] of small producers right up until the period of the Great Depression. This crisis which started in 1873 and continued into the middle of the 1890s had a catastrophic effect on small scale production in Dorset. Not only did it kill off many small industries and force large numbers of farmers to sell land in order to survive, but whole occupational groups virtually disappeared. The artisans and small business people Hardy mentions in his novels — the carpenters and the smiths, the masons and the shoemakers, the hucksters and the higglers—went the way of 'the many little village officials, the viewers of fields, the letters of cattle, the common shepherd, the layward, the chimney sweepers [who] lost their employment and with it the plots of land they had held in payment of their services'.[5] Above all it was working small land-ownership which was most drastically affected. The *Victoria History of Dorset* records that just before the Great Depression in 1871 (the year of Hardy's first published novel, *Desperate Remedies*) 200,000 acres in the county were farmed by their proprietors but that by 1906 this acreage had fallen to 43,296 and that Dorset, 'which at one time was pre-eminently the county of the yeoman', had seen 'this most useful class of men almost extinguished within its borders'.[6] Those who survived faced the ever present threat of falling into destitution because, as Marx pointed out, 'the maintainance or loss of the means of production on the part of small producers depends on a thousand contingencies, and every one of these contingencies or losses signifies impoverishment'.[7] Those who could not preserve their independence in this precarious situation either had to join the ranks of the rural proletariat, move to the towns or emigrate.

What happened in Dorset in the last quarter of the nineteenth century should not be seen in isolation nor should Dorset and the south-western counties of England be regarded as a 'back water' set apart from the 'main stream' of history. Hardy's novels *do* relate to the history of a locality, but that history cannot be thought of only in terms of a changing rural economy, or a changing way of life, or even of 'the social crisis in which Hardy lived'[8] although quite clearly these are involved. To understand that *local* history we must think in terms of the historical process of transformation which was the very basis and pre-condition of capitalist production relations, the genesis of which Marx first analysed in *Grundrisse* where he wrote:

> The inner construction of modern society, or, capital in the totality of its relations, is ... posited in the economic relations of modern landed property, which appears as a process: ground rent—capital—wage labour.... We therefore always find that, wherever landed property is transformed into money rent through the reaction of capital on the older forms of landed property ... and where, therefore, at the same time agriculture, driven by capital, transforms itself into industrial agronomy, there the cotiers, serfs, bondsmen, tenants for life, cottagers etc. become day labourers, wage labourers, i.e. that *wage labour* in its totality is initially created by the action of capital on landed property, and then, as soon as the latter has been produced as a form, by the proprietor of the land himself. This latter then himself 'clears', as Steuart says, the land of its excess mouths, tears the children of the earth from the breast on which they were raised, and thus transforms labour on the soil itself, which appears by its nature as the direct well-spring of subsistence, into a mediated source of subsistence, a source purely dependent on social relations.[9]

Far from suggesting a 'timeless order', the term rural England signifies the site of a radical transformation, the production of new economic and social relations, a mode of production which depends on a radical separation between wage labour and capital. This separation took the form of a massive accumulation of property on the one hand, and on the other the transformation of the rural worker into a propertyless wage labourer. 'Nowhere', wrote Marx, 'does the antagonistic character of capitalist production and accumulation assert itself more brutally than in the progress of English agriculture.'[10]

Unlike the case in that of all previous social formations, the capitalist mode of production presupposes the labourer as a free labourer, that is, the seller of his own labour power. But more than that it presupposes:

> the complete separation of the labourers from all property in the means by which they can realise their labour. As soon as

capitalist production is once on its own legs, it not only maintains this separation, but reproduces it on a continually extending scale.... The immediate producer, the labourer, could only dispose of his own person after he had ceased to be attached to the soil and ceased to be the slave, serf, or bondman of another.... The expropriation of the agricultural producer, of the peasant, from the soil, is the basis of the whole process. The history of this expropriation, in different countries, assumes different aspects, and runs through its various phases in different orders of succession, and at different periods. In England alone ... has it the classic form.[11]

The main social consequences of this history of expropriation were the gradual decomposition of the old feudal relations of production, the virtual disappearance of certain social groups and the progressive proletarianization of the rural workers. This process of transformation, however, did not begin with the inception of modern agriculture in the middle of the eighteenth century. As Marx points out, 'the revolution in landed property, from which the changed mode of production starts as a basis, has a much earlier date'[12] and, indeed, is inseparable from, if not synonymous with, the enclosure movement which started in England in the twelfth century, developed rapidly between 1450 and 1640, slowed down until the middle of the eighteenth century and then gathered momentum again after 1750. Between 1760 and 1830, for example, some three and a half thousand Enclosure Acts were passed enclosing over five million acres of common land.[13] While the long process of enclosure of the commons destroyed the English peasantry[14] the later enclosure of the wastes[15] deprived the land worker not only of land but also of habitation and fuel, so that in effect the English rural worker was dispossessed as ruthlessly as the North American Indian:

> Enclosure (when all the sophistications are allowed for) was a plain enough case of class robbery, played according to fair rules of property and law laid down by a parliament of property-owners and lawyers ... [it] was the culmination of a long secular process by which men's customary relations to the agrarian means of production were undermined. It was of profound social consequence because it illuminates, both

backwards and forwards, the destruction of the traditional elements in English peasant society.... The loss of the commons entailed, for the poor, a radical sense of displacement.[16]

'To the enclosure of the common', George Sturt observed, 'more than to any other cause may be traced all the changes that have subsequently passed over the village.'[17] Sturt writes of the transformation of a domestic into a commercial economy where 'every hour's work acquired a market value',[18] a situation in which everything had to be bought rather than home produced, gathered or gleaned, a situation in which co-operation became the competition in the market of free labourers. 'Not now may their labour be a bond of friendship between them; it is a commodity with a market value, to be sold in the market.'[19]

The corollary of displacement was immiseration, and, from the end of the Napoleonic Wars on, the condition of the rural working class was truly appalling. 'Of all the animals kept by the farmer', commented Marx, 'the labourer, the *instrumentum vocale*, was thenceforth the most oppressed, the worst nourished, the most brutally treated.'[20] Traditionally passive, it is a measure of the rural workers' suffering that they resorted at last to violent action. 'The Swing riots, in 1830,' wrote one observer, 'revealed to us by the light of blazing cornstacks, that misery and black mutinous discontent smouldered quite as fiercely under the surface of agricultural as of manufacturing England.'[21] It would be a mistake, however, to believe that the conditions which provoked the Swing riots relate merely to the early part of the century, for although the period between the repeal of the Corn Laws and the depression of the 1870s is considered to be English agriculture's golden age, the various contemporary reports on the wages, housing, diet, health and general condition of rural workers all attest to conditions of the most dire distress. Nor did matters improve once the mid-Victorian boom came to an end:

The continual emigration to the towns, the continual formation of surplus-population in the country through the concentration of farms, conversion of arable land into pasture, machinery, etc., and the continual eviction of the agricultural population by the destruction of their cottages, go hand in hand. . . . The packing together of knots of men in scattered little villages and small country towns corresponds to the forcible draining of men from the surface of the land. The continuous superseding of the agricultural labourers, in spite of their diminishing number and the increasing mass of their products, gives birth to their pauperism. Their pauperism is ultimately a motive to their eviction and the chief source of their miserable housing which breaks down their last power of resistance, and makes them mere slaves of the land proprietors and the farmers. Thus the minimum of wages becomes a law of Nature to them.[22]

Although this 'law of Nature' applied to Britain as a whole, it affected certain areas with greater severity than others, and none more so than the West Country. Indeed, if ever Hobbes's description of the state of man as solitary, poor, nasty, brutish and short were applicable, then it was to the condition of the 'peasantry' in south-west England throughout the nineteenth century where, as E. G. Wakefield wrote, the 'peasant' was neither a freeman nor a slave, but a pauper.[23] Significantly the loudest 'voice of distress' emanated from the county of Dorset:

Every year imparts to the infected body of England some more formidable symptom of mortality, engendered by the parent evil, *pauperism*. . . . The voice of distress echoes from the extremes of the British Islands. . . . The note is pealed in Lanark, pinched with hungry wretchedness; or the cry comes from Lancashire, from Gloucester, Sussex, Norfolk, Cambridge, Hants, Notts, Berks till the chorus is swelled to its full volume of distress by the deep groans of Dorset, where the wages of the labourer are five shillings a-week, and where committals for crime have recently increased, from three hundred to three thousand three hundred.[24]

Much the same things were bring written a quarter of a century later even after the period of greatest prosperity. 'There is no doubt' wrote F. G. Heath, 'that the very worst phase of our agricultural system—in so far as it relates to wages, cottages, and to the general treatment of the peasantry—is to be observed in the West of England.'[25] Heath also drew the readers' attention specifically to the agricultural workers of Dorset who have 'long

had the reputation of being the most wretched of all the
labouring classes in England',[26] and he quotes an article from
the *Daily Telegraph* on 'peasant life in Dorset'. This article, which
appeared in the year *Under the Greenwood Tree*[27] was published,
stated that the labourer:

> stands a good chance, provided he be faultless as a labourer,
> and properly deferential as an inferior, of having a hundred-
> weight or two of firewood delivered at his door in the cold
> weather. Piddletown, it will be seen, depends a great deal on
> the grace of its suzerains. When they smile benevolently it
> stops a certain degree shorter of starvation than when they
> have to frown reprovingly. What might happen if in a
> moment of supreme displeasure they were to withdraw their
> pigstraw and firewood, the most vivid imagination in Piddle-
> town cannot conceive.[28]

Anyone who attempted to interfere with the power of these
'suzerains' was dealt with by means of the law, social ostracism,
abuse and even threats of personal violence. That such conditions and such poverty continued throughout the nineteenth
century is confirmed by the reports of the National Agricultural
Labourers' Union as well as by the *Victoria History* which records
that even in 1892 money wages in Dorset were as little as ten
shillings a week.[29]

In the West Country in general and in Dorset in particular the
condition of the rural worker had not changed significantly by
the beginning of the present century. Despite a small increase in
wages, the condition of workers was not improved by the general
decline in agriculture after 1873 and the effects of continuing
rural depopulation. Rider Haggard, for example, commented
that 'as yet … employers could hardly be said to have tempted
the labourers to remain by means of adequately increased
wages, shorter hours, or other advantages'[30] and he concluded
that the farm labourer was still at the 'very bottom of the social
scale'.[31] Whatever Haggard's ideological intention, we can only
conclude from his study that the condition of the labourers in
Dorset was still, at the end of the nineteenth century, among the
very worst in the country and that the process of 'clearing' the
land continued.[32]

The driving force of this process of 'clearing'—the forcible draining of people from the land—derives from the tendency of the capitalist mode of production to destroy the specificity of labour by reducing all forms and sorts of labour to labour in general, simple labour, and transforming the rural producers into free labourers who possess only their labour power which they must sell, if they can, on the open market. Labour is regarded by capital, not as a particular kind of labour, a specific skill or activity based upon knowledge and experience, but as labour pure and simple, abstract labour, which lacks 'all the characteristics of art'[33] and is merely material activity. This means the negation of the (semi-artistic) artisanal mode of production where the main concern is the quality of the product, the particular skill of the worker and the specific nature of the work. 'The principle of developed capital', writes Marx, 'is precisely to make special skill superfluous, and to make manual work, directly physical labour, generally superfluous both as skill and as muscular exertion: to transfer skill, rather, into the dead forces of nature.'[34] With the introduction of machinery (the dead forces of nature) on a large scale the worker is transformed into a simple, monotonous productive force which does not have to use specific physical or intellectual faculties.[35] The progressive division of labour has the effect not only of simplifying labour and turning the worker into a detail worker responsible for one operation in the productive process, but also of separating physical from mental work, agricultural from industrial labour and the country from the town.[36]

To summarize this general process we can say that the change to the capitalist mode of production depended upon the dissolution of the feudal mode of production, the dissolution of the relations of personal dependence which characterize the social relations of production of the Middle Ages.[37] This process has as its historical basis the transformation of the rural worker (the peasant, yeoman, artisan, small producer, etc.) into a propertyless wage labourer, the capitalization of ground rent and the rise of the tenant farmer, the necessary preconditions for large-scale commodity production.[38]

However, this general process is by no means an even one, for although it consitutes the necessary basis for the historical transformation to the capitalist mode of production, it is also the area in which survivals are most likely to occur. 'Although this transformation in the countryside', writes Marx, 'is the last to push towards its ultimate consequences and its purest form, its beginnings there are among the earliest.'[39] This means that in certain areas pre-capitalist modes exist alongside and *at the same time as* the capitalist mode of production. 'Within a single society, such as the English, the mode of production of capital develops in one branch of industry, while in another, e.g. agriculture, modes of production predominate which more or less antedate capital.'[40] Thus, 'classical landed property reappears in modern small-parcel landownership'.[41] Within the economic unit such survivals relate to a pre-capitalist mode of production, and what characterizes the social relations of production here are relations of personal dependence. These relations continue to exist in 'the patriarchal industries of a peasant family'.[42] The small producer, the yeoman farmer, the artisan had the capability, unlike the propertyless wage labourer, of producing *within the family unit* products which were not commodities. In such a situation the different kinds of labour such as tending sheep or cattle, maintaining essential plant and tools, general repairs, making clothes, brewing beer and cider, baking bread, making butter and cheese, gathering fuel, raising and slaughtering pigs and preparing the resultant produce, in fact the entire range of practical skills and various forms of work involved in the process of home production for home consumption, were in themselves direct social functions because they were functions of the family unit.

Another characteristic of labour in such a mode of production is to be found in its relations with the wider community. Despite the fact that the small producer or the artisan produce commodities, their production does not fall under the capitalist mode because the owner of the means of production and the direct producer (the labourer) are united in one person: 'the means of production become capital only in so far as they have become separated from labour and confront labour as an independent power'.[43] In consequence of such relations of production there is an absence of commodity fetishism, there is no necessity 'for labour and its products to assume a fantastic form different from their reality'.[44] This is the basis of what Raymond Williams has called the knowable community, and despite his obsession with 'the decline and fall of the Hardys, Hardy's personal history, with all its connections with, and interrelations between, labourers, artisans, working small landowners and small producers, relates precisely to this mode of production.[45]

It should not be forgotten that this mode of production did not exist by itself or in isolation, but alongside and at the same time as the more developed form, and that in consequence it was inherently unstable. This instability was due to the fact that separation appears as the *normal* relation in capitalist society where the capitalist as such is only the function of capital and the labourer a function of labour power. Economic development, writes Marx:

> distributes functions among different persons; the handi-craftsman or peasant who produces with his own means of production will either gradually be transformed into a small capitalist who also exploits the labour of others, or he will suffer the loss of his means of production ... and be transformed into a wage labourer. This is the tendency in the form of society in which the capitalist mode of production pre-dominates.[46]

If the social relations which small-scale production tended to maintain were a crucial determinant, their inherent instability was no less important in the production of Hardy's work.

Hardy's writing then, is rooted in a unique historical conjuncture which is comprised of three distinct but related elements. The first is an historical *process* namely, the separation of the direct producer from the means of production, that process which entailed the dispossession of the rural workers, their transformation into propertyless wage labourers, 'naked individuals'. This process was the basis of the general conditions which enabled the development of the capitalist mode of production and was of several centuries duration. The second is an historical *contradiction*, namely the survival of certain relations, modes of production and elements of modes of production which pre-date the capitalist mode, but exist alongside it in a peculiarly complex and transitory state as non-developmental survivals of historically superseded forms. The third is an historical *period*, that 'watershed between two stages of capitalism',[47] the crisis known as the Great Depression which, in the last decades of the nineteenth century, rapidly destroyed those survivals. As the site of these conflicting meanings, Wessex, far from alluding to 'a time-less order', or a nostalgia for a distant 'organic community', alludes to a classic case of uneven development in the history of British capitalism. But between that history and the writing itself lies a complex ideological formation.

2

The Discourses of Hegemony

What I have called the radical separation which characterizes the relation between wage labour and capital and which determines the whole character of the capitalist mode of production and the relations of domination and exploitation which depend upon it, constitutes that 'absence' which cannot be mentioned by ideology. Around that absent centre are woven the various universalizing and eternalizing discourses which speak not of separation, exploitation and struggle, but of the General Interest, Equality, Freedom, Progress, Civilization, Culture and the Common Good, those ideological discourses which efface contradiction, render it invisible. Furthermore, ideology represents capitalism and the rule of the bourgeoisie as being without end because, by giving an historical intention (free competition) a natural justification, it makes contingency appear eternal.[1] 'The assertion that free competition equals the ultimate form of the development of the forces of production and hence human freedom', wrote Marx, 'means nothing other than that middle-class rule is the culmination of world history.'[2] And as the social formation is represented in ideology as an homogeneous 'society', it appears to be one of endless possibilities in so far as it is not only eternal but also without internal barriers, a totality in which individuals/subjects may, if they so desire, freely develop their individuality to the fullest extent. As the ideological 'space' of society is boundless, there can be no category of exclusion; everyone is a citizen of this ideological world of freedom, equality and the general interest. As Palmerston said in his speech during the Don Pacifico debate in the House of Commons in 1850:

> We have shown that liberty is compatible with order; that individual freedom is reconcilable with obedience to law. We

have shown the example of a nation, in which every class in society accepts with cheerfulness the lot which Providence has assigned to it; while at the same time every individual of each class is constantly striving to raise himself in the social scale —not by injustice and wrong, not by violence and illegality, but by preserving good conduct, and by the steady and energetic execution of the moral and intellectual faculties with which his creator endowed him.[3]

It is not *society* which hinders the subject's free development, for society is constantly reforming itself to ensure 'the progress of civilization and the improvement in the moral sentiments of mankind',[4] perpetually developing itself 'with the utmost possible fullness and freedom'.[5] In this sense the terms bourgeois and society are synonymous because the bourgeoisie represents itself 'as an organism in continuous movement, capable of absorbing the entire society, assimilating it to its own cultural and economic level'.[6]

It would not be possible, however, to extrapolate from the foregoing the existence of a single monolithic ruling-class ideology in the nineteenth century if only because of a unique peculiarity of the capitalist formation in Britain which has a profound influence on the realm of the ideological. In effect the British ruling class was divided into two major groups which represented respectively the interests of landed property and the interests of industrial capital, and in so far as it is upon 'the different forms of property' that 'an entire superstructure of distinct and peculiarly formed sentiments, illusions, modes of thought and views of life'[7] depend, this division had its inevitable political and ideological reflex. But, because it was an internal division rather than one between two distinct classes, it resulted in what might be called the 'inwardness', even the self-absorption of the ruling classes. 'We speak of two interests of the bourgeoisie', Marx observed, because despite its 'feudal coquetry and pride of race' large landed property had been rendered thoroughly bourgeois by the development of modern society, and while the Tories imagined themselves to be 'enthusiastic about monarchy, the church and the beauties of the Old English Constitution', history had proved them to be 'enthusiastic only about ground rent'.[8] In the same vein one might add that the Liberals were just as enthusiastic about dividends as the Tories were about rent. However, this separation of the different forms of property ownership, its division between two groups within the ruling class, has the effect of maintaining and institutionalizing at the political and ideological levels a peculiar form of 'class division'.

On the political level this division became institutionalized in the two party system. Herbert Spencer observed that Tory and Liberal stood for 'two opposed types of social organization, broadly distinguishable as the militant and the industrial—types which are characterized, the one by the *régime* of status ... the other by the *régime* of contract'.[9] On the ideological level this internal division took the form of an endlessly prolonged and endlessly prolongable debate (in itself a reflex of the 'parliamentary' system) between the representatives of 'tradition' and the representatives of 'progress'. To both parties a concept of continuous history was crucial. On the one hand history conceived as a process of differentiation and evolution, 'a line of progress with a logic akin to destiny',[10] was the ideological reflex of the growth and development of the economic and political power of the representatives of capital, the '*régime* of contract'. On the other hand, history conceived as tradition, as a record of dynastic and cultural continuity, was the ideological reflex of the continuation of the economic and political power of the representatives of property, the '*régime* of status'. Matthew Arnold captured this sense of the continuous in the sobriquet he used to designate the aristocracy in *Culture and Anarchy*, namely the Barbarians, a term which suggests a line of descent that stretches from Atilla to the Duke of Westminster.

The ideological reflex of the class struggles in which the bourgeoisie was involved in the nineteenth century is born and in the main by two broad ideological currents which I shall call, simply for the sake of identification, the discourse of the Inevitable and the discourse of Possibility. The first of these, the discouse of the Inevitable which revolved about the concepts of progress and the advance of civilization, propagated the myth of the eternal and was centred on Man's destiny. The second, the discourse of Possibility, which revolved about concepts of tradition and culture, propagated the myth of the universal and was centred on the human essence. Again, very broadly, we may identify the first with the *régime* of contract and the second with the *régime* of status. This is not to say, of course, that anyone who spoke of progress was a manufacturer or that only aristocrats believed in the virtues of tradition. As Marx pointed out, there is no necessary 'social' equivalence between the representatives of a class or group and the class or group they represent, that, indeed, they may be 'as far apart as heaven from earth' in their 'education and their individual position'. What gives them the status of representatives is that they identify themselves politically and ideologically with a particular class or group and that they are, in consequence, 'driven, theoretically, to the same problems and solutions to which material interests and social position drive the latter practically'. This is, in general, 'the relationship between the *political* and *literary representatives* of a class and the class they represent'.[11]

The appearance of Charles Darwin's *On the Origin of Species* in 1859 can be taken as the pivotal moment in the discourse of the Inevitable in that it provides an index of the ideological continuity from the Philosophical Radicals of the early part of the century to the Social Darwinists of the latter part and because what was later referred to as Darwinism really pre-dated Darwin by half a century. Darwinism, as Bertrand Russell pointed out, was a 'global free competition, in which victory went to the animals that most resembled successful capitalists'.[12] In chapter three of *On the Origin of Species* Darwin wrote that his theory was 'the doctrine of Malthus applied with manifold force to the whole animal and vegetable kingdoms'.

Published in 1789, Malthus's *First Essay on Population* was in effect a biological vindication of capitalism and a 'proof' of the invalidity of socialist theory which marked the beginning of a movement to interpret human action in biological terms, a movement which steadily gained ground throughout the nineteenth century and was modified and developed in the light of Darwin's theory of evolution. In this theory the bourgeoisie found one of the ideological means whereby it could constitute itself as the ruling class through the myth of the inevitable, the preordained growth, development and change of the social organism as a whole. This transformation of historical reality into natural inevitability has the effect of eternalizing the economic laws of capital by making them appear as the natural laws of a higher necessity. In this ideological world 'it doesn't matter what ends men may think they pursue, in fact the cause of history is determined by an impersonal process over which they have no control'.[13] This 'impersonal process' deprives individuals/subjects of their class determination in that they appear to be subject not to economic laws governing the relations of production in a capitalist social formation, but to natural laws governing Man's destiny in the general evolution of civilization. Thus, wrote Malthus, 'a degree of misery is the necessary and inevitable result of the laws of nature' which human institutions could 'mitigate but never remove'.[14]

And half a century later when the industrial bourgeoisie, brimming with confidence after their defeat of the working class and the interests of landed property,[15] claimed for themselves the role of leaders of civilization and for the society they were fashioning in their own image the title of 'Workshop of the World', Herbert Spencer declared the law of the survival of the fittest to be that civilization's principle determinant. He wrote in *Social Statics* that the 'poverty of the incapable, the distress that came upon the improvident, the starvation of the idle, and those shoulderings aside of the weak by the strong, which leave so many "in shallows and in miseries", are the decree of a large, far seeing benevolence'.[16] Spencer saw history as the working out of natural law, a process of evolution from the hordes of primitive tribes to the complexity of bourgeois society. But this process was the result of an unknown and unknowable force, a kind of cosmic division of labour which operated on the material world producing the ever greater variety, coherence, integration, specialization and individuation of modern civilization. As John Burrow has observed of Spencer's Synthetic Philosophy, it was an attempt 'to apply a formula of evolution whose central idea was the development from simple to complex, purporting to be derived from the fundamental laws of matter and motion, to every kind of phenomenon throughout the universe'.[17] Thus liberal bourgeois society (along with its economic and political doctrines of *laissez-faire*) became part of the inevitable working out of fixed and immutable natural laws. Men were simply the subjects of this metaphysical power, simply the agents through which It worked via 'the beneficent working of the survival of the fittest',[18] and social changes were 'brought about by a power far above average wills. Men who seem the prime movers are merely the tools with which it works.'[19] In this ideological discourse the laws of a liberal capitalist economy appear, as Marx rightly claimed, as overwhelming natural laws that irresistibly enforce their will over the agents of production and confront them as blind necessity.[20]

But against this 'mechanistic' myth of the eternal inevitability of the progress of civilization stood the discourse of Possibility which was concerned not primarily with Man's destiny but with the human essence. 'Against mechanism', Raymond Williams has written, culture or as it was earlier called by Coleridge, cultivation, 'offered a different and superior social idea.... Grounding itself on the idea of "the harmonious development of those qualities and faculties that characterize our humanity", this general condition, Cultivation, could be taken as the highest observable state of men in society, and the "permanent distinction and occasional contrast" between it and *civilization* (the ordinary progress of society) drawn and emphasized.'[21] Once again we find that the function of this ideological discourse was to efface the reality of class society by rendering individuals 'classless'. Matthew Arnold was quite specific on this point stating that the 'social idea' of culture sought to 'do away with classes'[22] by which he meant not that culture seeks to do away with class society but that it seeks to transform class members into 'class aliens', to give them the status of classless individuals/subjects. Arnold was insistent that the bourgeoisie, the 'natural educators of the masses, would be 'very greatly profited by the action of the state'[23] in this task, and in *Culture and Anarchy* he attempted to show the dominant class how to universalize itself by equating the conditions of its existence with culture in general.

No one knew better than Arnold the ideological shortcomings of the industrial bourgeoisie, the 'philistines', or that their utilitarian philosophy was not adequate to an hegemonic class. 'Now', wrote Arnold, 'is the moment for culture to be of service, culture which believes in making reason and the Will of God prevail'.[24] Coming as it does at the end of the period of mid-Victorian prosperity, *Culture and Anarchy* stands on the brink of the transition from industrial to monopoly capitalism which was to bring progressive state intervention and control, and from this point on the 'voice of the deepest human experience'[25] increasingly found its utterance not in the established church but in the expanding state education system. And since culture was the manifestation of the 'best self' rather than the 'class self', and since its appreciation and even its creation was to be open to all, it was both 'classless' and 'universal'. It was in this universal discourse that the apostles of culture, and especially literary culture, were to find confirmation of their individuality, their freedom, their equality, above all, their common humanity.

Arnold's ethical concern for the common good through the pursuit of perfection touches on another important strand in the discourse of Possibility namely that of the neo-idealist philosophy which came to prominence in the last decades of the nineteenth century and which constituted a bold attempt to systematize a reformist ideology into a totalizing philosophical system which Melvin Richter has called 'a combination of theology with the ideological defence of the then existing order'.[26] Perhaps the most remarkable aspects of British Idealism were its close relation to theology and its emphasis on active altruism. As Richter points out:

> The most prominent spokesmen for British Idealism were all sons of Evangelical clergymen within the Church of England. It was an essentially religious concern which first brought Green, Bernard Bosanquet, and F. H. Bradley to the study of philosophy.... In Green's hands, Idealism became a vehicle of reform, thus reflecting certain aspects of Evangelicalism and Christian Socialism.... Green believed that he had found in Idealism a profound truth ... how to reconcile right thought with right conduct. At the heart of his own teaching is the exultation of an integral and ever active altruism. Through continued and purposeful striving, there may be released progressively, if never completely, a type of character and an organisation of society which is altruistic, subordinating personal pleasures to the common good.... Philosophical Idealism, as Green presented it, combined many of the most characteristic assumptions of his age.... It argued that the very existence of art, morality, religion, and even science itself constituted evidence that reality is something more than the arbitrary interpretation of facts perceived by the senses.[27]

Just as in eighteenth-century France the philosophers' appeal to reason as the sole judge of everything in existence was, in Engels's words, 'nothing but the idealized understanding of the middle burgher, who was then evolving into the bourgeoisie'[28] so in England at the end of the nineteenth century the philosophers' appeal to the benificent development of Reason was the 'idealized understanding' of the late Victorian bourgeoisie elaborated into a teleological discourse of continuous becoming which gave it the ideological guarantee of its own historical inevitability.

This sense of historical inevitability is inseparable from the radical transformation which British capitalism was undergoing in the last decades of the nineteenth century. Unquestionably the 1870s and 1880s 'were an age of universal catastrophe for agriculture'[29] and the period of the Great Depression saw such an alarming decline in the older basic industries that the Royal Commissioners reported in 1886 that 'the diminution in the rate of profit obtainable from production, whether agricultural or manufacturing, has given rise to a widespread feeling of depression among the producing classes'.[30] But this was also the period of the new imperialism: 'If it were necessary to give the briefest possible definition of imperialism', wrote Lenin, 'we should have to say that imperialism is the monopoly stage of capitalism'.[31] The effects of capital's development to a higher stage were dramatic for while the manufacture and export of goods was typical of the old capitalism 'when free competition held undivided sway ... typical of the latest stage of capitalism, when monopolies rule, is the export of capital'.[32] Certainly this was the case in Britain where the period was marked by a stagnation in the export of goods but a huge expansion in British foreign investment.[33] Perry Anderson comments on this period: 'With the agrarian depression of the 1870s the traditional base of the landowning class collapsed. Thus, just at the moment when the "atavistic" values of the landed aristocracy appeared mortally threatened, imperialism rescued and reinforced them.'[34] Thus, out of these transformative crises the sense of continuity was not only strengthened but given new impetus and direction. But allied to this was the urgent necessity to develop also a sense of social cohesion, of national unity.

The ideology of a united nation state at the head of a vast and expanding empire had a potent appeal to all classes. Furthermore, the demands of imperialist expansion produced a necessity for social reform for, as Lord Rosebery said, 'An empire such as ours requires as its first condition an imperial race, a race vigorous and industrious and intrepid.... In the rookeries and slums which still survive an imperial race cannot be reared.'[35] It was with this reformist and melioristic aspect of the ideological formation that the new idealism was associated for as Simon has pointed out, the movement of thought 'which linked imperialism with a new veneration for the state found its theoretical justification' in the neo-idealism of T. H. Green and Bernard Bosanquet who reacted against the 'atomistic, highly individualist utilitarianism of J. S. Mill and Herbert Spencer, [and] stressed instead the realisation of individuality through society, and advanced a new concept of the organic nature of the state as embodiment of the people's will'.[36] Green's reformist altruism, together with his desire to recast Christianity in the form of an 'undogmatic theology' and his concept of history as the unfolding of objective reason, constitutes the most coherent elaboration of what I have called the discourse of Possibility. It is, however, in its implicit emphasis on the sovereignty of consciousness that its importance for our present considerations lies.

3

The Ideology of the Thinking World
and the Production of Wessex

In what relation did Hardy stand to these ideological currents? *The Life of Thomas Hardy*[1] enables us to answer that question with some precision. Many critics have been frustrated by this biographical work because it appears to be so singularly un-revealing. Unlike Rousseau's proclaimed intention 'to display to my kind a portrait in every way true to nature',[2] Hardy's *Life* refuses the confessional mode and avoids a display of those intimate personal details which would provide the critic with the key to unlock the door to the secret inner chamber of the writer's work and character. Yet *The Life* is profoundly re-vealing in so far as Hardy constructed a personal history which is not so much the record of a life as the production of a world-view.

In *The Life* Hardy tells us of his own and his family's long and intimate connection with the Church; he tells us of his prolonged study of religious texts, his delight in the poetry of the Bible and church music, his continuing church attendance. We know that he worked at church restoration, that his first novel had a religious theme and that he married a deeply religious woman. He tells us that as a child he played at being a parson and that in his mid-twenties he 'nourished a scheme of a highly visionary character ... the idea of combining poetry and the church— towards which he had long had a leaning'.[3] Nowhere, however, is there any mention of a belief in God or indeed of a crisis of a loss of faith. Indeed, far from suggesting such a loss, Hardy wished us to understand that he had never believed in God (which stretches one's credulity) although he had assiduously sought him all his life, writing a few months before his fiftieth birthday: 'I have been looking for God for fifty years, and I think that if he existed I should have discovered him. As an external personality, of course—the only true meaning of the word'.[4] He made it quite clear that his 'philosophy' did not include a belief in God in the traditional Christian sense stating that the only 'reasonable meaning' of God was 'the *Cause of Things*, whatever that cause may be'.[5] Hardy wanted to avoid any suggestion of a belief in those 'old transcendental ideals',[6] those 'dogmatic superstitions read every Sunday'[7] but he did not thereby deny an ultimate 'Prime Cause or Invariable Antecedent' to which he gave the name 'It'.[8] The Christian God—the external *personality*—has been replaced by the *intelligence* of the First Cause. The whole movement is contained in the words 'First Cause omniscient, not omnipotent'[9] that is, the replacement of the old concept of God as all-powerful by a new concept of universal consciousness. The 'tribal god, man-shaped, fiery-faced and tyrannous'[10] is replaced by the 'Unconscious Will of the Universe' which progressively grows aware of itself and 'ultimately, it is to be hoped, sympathetic'.[11] Hardy claimed this idea for himself and maintained that the name for this Universal Subject (the It) was his own invention, but as Lenin pointed out about the idealist inventions of the late nineteenth century, 'It is immaterial what these abstractions are called: whether Absolute Idea, Universal *Self*, World Will…. One must be blind not to perceive the identical idealist essence under these verbal cloaks…. In plain language this is called God.'[12]

Hardy went to great lengths in *The Life* to avoid any suggestion of a loss of faith, suggesting rather a continuous development of a rational idealism, an idealism which could find a religious expression and even a 'liturgical form'[13] in what he called 'an Idealism of Fancy'.[14] He clarified his views in the Apology he wrote to *Late Lyrics and Earlier*:

> … poetry, pure literature in general, religion—I include religion, in its essential and undogmatic sense, because poetry and religion touch each other, or rather modulate into each other—are, indeed, often but different names for the same thing…. It may indeed be a forlorn hope, a mere dream, that of an alliance between religion, which must be retained unless the world is to perish, and complete rationality, which must come, unless also the world is to perish, by means of the interfusing effect of poetry—'the breath and finer spirit of all knowledge; the impassioned expression of science'.[15]

The interesting thing about this declaration is that in its explicit association of poetry/literature with an undogmatic religion, and in the expressed hope for an alliance between such an undogmatic theology and rationality, it reads very much like an attempt to effect a reconciliation between the different positions Matthew Arnold and T. H. Green took over the question of the basis for a replacement for Christianity. These two major ideologues both acknowledged the scientific critique of Christianity and the necessity for a viable alternative and they also agreed on the role the State should play in taking over the moral leadership of society. Where they disagreed, however, was over the foundation upon which the alternative to Christianity was to be laid, Arnold believing that it should be poetry/literature, and Green an idealist metaphysics.[16] The resolution of this conflict is exactly captured in Hardy's term the Idealism of Fancy suggesting as it does both Green's emphasis on an idealist metaphysics and Arnold's emphasis on the poetic imagination as a basis for a post-Christian religion.

If Hardy took care that the 'future should know only what he wanted it to know', this is only a 'most deliberate deception'[17] from the biographer's point of view. The importance of *The Life* does not lie in the fact that Hardy was consciously trying to conceal the secret and determining facts of his life (social or sexual), but that in it he gives us a world-view in which the real contradictions of his position are reconstituted on an imaginary level, presented as a coherent discourse which excludes those contradictions. He presents the passage from the religion of his youth and early manhood to the idealist philosophy of his maturity as the conflict-free progression of a single unifying process of discovery of the truth that consciousness is the real subject of historical development.

In *The Archaeology of Knowledge* Michel Foucault has written:

Continuous history is the indispensable correlative of the founding function of the subject.... Making historical analysis the discourse of the continuous and making human consciousness the original subject of all historical development and all action are the two sides of the same system of thought. In this system, time is conceived in terms of totalization and revolutions are never more than the moments of consciousness. In various forms, this theme has played a constant role

since the nineteenth century: to preserve, against all decentrings, the sovereignty of the subject, and the twin figures of
anthropology and humanism. Against the decentrings
operated by Marx—by the historical analysis of the relations
of production, economic determinations, and the class
struggle—it gave place, towards the end of the nineteenth century, to the search for a total history, in which all the differences of a society might be reduced to a single form, to the
organization of a world-view, to the establishment of a system
of values, to a coherent type of civilization.[18]

Hardy attempted to cast his *Life* in the mould of just such a
totalizing discourse, a synthesis of those ideological currents to
which I have referred, 'a generalized form', in his own words, 'of
what the thinking world has gradually come to adopt'.[19] This
consisted of a combination of reformist politics (evolutionary
meliorism), idealist philosophy, a covert Deism (the It), a belief
in inevitable progress and a fundamental altruism in the concept of the universe becoming not only conscious but 'sympathetic', tempered by an anti-materialist pessimism which, in
Sebastiano Timpanaro's works, 'attributed to "nature" (i.e. to a
secular version of the "inscrutable decrees of Divine Providence") the iniquities and sufferings for which the organization of
society is responsible.'[20]
However, the determining absence which informs the
structure of Hardy's autobiography is class conflict in so far as the
history of the Thomas Hardy who appears here is that of one of
Matthew Arnold's 'classless' intellectual 'aliens' who 'are
mainly led, not by their class spirit, but by a general *humane*
spirit'.[21] As the bearer of that ideology the Thomas Hardy of *The
Life* appears as the classless spokesman for 'humanity' at large
and that is why we cannot confuse *The Life* with the cycle of
novels, cannot equate the elaboration of a philosophy with the
writing. They are totally separable because Hardy's writing is
not the expression of an ideology, rather it is articulated in relation to the ideological, to what Foucault calls the 'discourse of
the continuous'. Hardy's writing produces a conflict between
that original ground where consciousness is *not* the subject of all
historical development and action, namely Wessex, between
that and the sovereignty of consciousness, the reign of ideas

which is articulated in *The Life* and which alludes to those ideological currents I have designated as the discourse of Possibility and the discourse of the Inevitable. The fundamental distinction between the writing and *The Life* is that in the novels the sovereignty of the subject is not only 'shown' but *contested.*

Hardy's writing is not an elaboration or a depiction of the discourse of the continuous, it is not a fictional representation of that straight and unbroken line on which the centred history of Man is written. It is the product of a labour of transformation which, situated between history and ideology, between the radical separation to which it alludes and those ideological 'readings' of that process, readings which make not the material struggles of classes but human *consciousness* the subject of all historical development, produces a space where it is possible to see what those ideological discourses strive incessantly to efface, namely that they are not endless, classless, universal, all-embracing but finite, partial, historical, limited and partisan. For Wessex is the site of discontinuities, beginnings and ends and boundaries, of the contingent and the particular and the accidental, and while it is produced out of those very ideological currents, it delimits them. In Wessex the 'classless' myth of the universal and the myth of the eternal are, to use Macherey's term, put to the test of the written word.

And this brings us to the crucial question of the status of Wessex itself. I suggest thinking of Wessex not as a 'place' but as a whole complex of relations which go to make up the 'world' of Hardy's writing. Of course Hardy drew on his own experience of rural Dorset, on local history and legend, on local topography, on the environment in general and upon the lives of his family, relations, friends and acquaintances in order to fashion the images of Wessex and the characters who 'inhabit' Wessex. But it would be as inappropriate to ask of Hardy's writing 'was it really like that?' as it would be to ask of one's dreams if they were a true representation of waking reality, for there is no identity between Wessex and history. Wessex has its own reality which is not immediately determined by the historical and geographical reality of Dorset.

If Wessex were nothing more than the reflection of a certain social/historical situation—the demise of the 'peasantry', the impact of urban on rural society, the end of an era, the immiseration of the workfolk, or simply social change—then all its reality would exist outside it in the real history of which it was simply the reflection, and Hardy would be merely the historian of these changes. Such views of Wessex emphasize the similarity, identity or coherence between writing and its historical moment. Similarly, if Wessex is perceived as 'the country' (and Hardy as a rural novelist), or an anthropological enclave (and Hardy as a regional novelist depicting the folkways, traditions and language of the region) similarity, verisimilitude is stressed and Wessex becomes merely the fictional representative of Dorset. And if, on a grander scale, Wessex is seen as the 'background' against which, or the 'stage' upon which, the conflicts between Man and Nature, free will and destiny, Man and fate, individual consciousness and the It take place, or as the 'environment' in which the Darwinian struggle is fought out, it is reduced to the status of a mythical landscape before which the *dramatis personae* enact their dramas. All critical commentaries which perceive Wessex as either the reflection of the real or the mythical setting in which the drama of mankind's predicament in the universe is played out, determined as they are by an empiricist or idealist problematic which conceives writing as the product of the author's consciousness, deprive Wessex of its reality.

A materialist view of Wessex is that it is neither a mechanical reflection nor an idealist creation, but a system of reality which is produced out of a combination of elements—the time, place, relations and means of production—involved in the productive process of writing itself. First there is the historical fact of the destruction of the small producer, that long process of the separation of the workers from their means of production. Secondly there is the unique combination of time, place and relations of production—Hardy being born at that time in that place and as a member of that class—which situates Hardy in relation to that historical process. Thirdly there are the ideological 'readings' of that history determined on the one hand by the various customary and experiential ideological formations of Hardy's class of origin, and on the other by the ideological discourses of 'the thinking world'. Finally, there is the aesthetic project itself, conceived as the revelation of an essential reality through the writing (production) of a non-realistic world where the real is made vividly visible.

But Wessex cannot be conceptualized apart from its 'inhabitants'. I have suggested that we think of Wessex as a complex system of relations and it is quite clear from Hardy's writing that one of the most important of these is that relation between individuals and their world mediated by work. Hardy divides the working people of Wessex into two distinct groups. He used the term workfolk to designate the general labourers, and the 'better informed class' to include artisans, small producers, tradesmen and 'skilled countrymen' 'who formed the backbone of village life'.[22] Far from being minor characters of peripheral importance to the 'central drama' (which could really be enacted without them), their presence is constitutive because *all* Hardy's characters exist in relation to the experiential knowledge and customary forms of their world. Even those who appear to have little direct relation to that world have no reality apart from it in so far as it is precisely in their relation to that working relationship—the extent to which they are in harmony with or alienated from it—that their reality lies. But that reality is itself conditioned by one of the conflicting ideological readings of the history of radical separation which is determined by Hardy's class position.

In class society the age old conflict between town and country becomes a weapon in the class struggle. The real accretion of wealth and power by the industrial and financial bourgeoisie is masked by the myth of urban, particularly metropolitan 'superiority'. In the nineteenth century this claim of superiority (of sophistication, culture, education, worldly wisdom, manners, dress and so on) went hand in hand with the fostering of the myth of the inept and unsophisticated rural worker (recognized at a glance as 'Hodge') with his risible, inarticulate speech and boorish manners. Such caricatures masked the real exploitation of the country by the towns, namely the reduction of the rural areas to vast labour reserves. The ideology of superiority had a material existence in the stereotypes of popular urban culture, in jokes, songs, cartoons, music hall turns, all of which fostered prejudice against the 'innate' deficiencies of the rural working classes. The West Country farm workers who leer cretinously at us out of the pages of *Punch* dressed in smocks, a straw in their mouths, were always obsequious, deferential and barely articulate yokels who could never give a direct answer to an educated question. Such 'humorous' stereotypes not only hid real class divisions and conflicts but also had the important function of impeding working-class solidarity by fostering regional prejudices.

Far from the Madding Crowd opens with the evocation of just such an ideological perception of the countryman as Hodge:

> When Farmer Oak smiled, the corners of his mouth spread till they were within an unimportant distance of his ears, his eyes were reduced to chinks, and diverging wrinkles appeared round them, extending upon his countenance like the rays in a rudimentary sketch of the rising sun.... He wore a low-crowned felt hat, spread out at the base by tight jamming upon his head for security in high winds, and a coat like Dr Johnsons ... and boots emphatically large.... Mr Oak carried about him, by way of watch, what may be called a small silver clock ... [which] was as a necessity pulled out by throwing the body to one side, compressing the mouth and face to a mere mass of ruddy flesh on account of the exertion, and drawing up the watch by its chain, like a bucket from a well.[23]

This is the image of the countryman instantly recognizable to the urban middle-class reader as 'Varmer Giles' but the very literariness of the language and the Gargantuan imagery reveals the parodic intent. This ideological view is the novel's point of departure from which we are progressively distanced by the gradual revelation of the 'real' Gabriel Oak. In accordance with the aesthetic intention the concealing veil of apparent reality —that of the undifferentiated mass, the class of labourers— is stripped away to reveal the essential diversity behind appearance. It is in the terms of such an experiental revelation that Angel Clare gets to know the workfolk at Talbothays Farm:

> The conventional farm-folk of his imagination—personified in the newspaper-press by the pitiable dummy known as Hodge—were obliterated after a few days' residence. At close quarters no Hodge was to be seen.... His host and his host's household, his men and his maids, as they became intimately known to Clare, began to differentiate themselves as in a chemical process.... The typical and unvarying Hodge

ceased to exist. He had been disintegrated into a number of varied fellow-creatures—beings of many minds, beings infinite in difference ...[24]

Hardy never attempted to 'show' the condition of the working class in nineteenth century England in the manner of such writers as Gaskell, Kingsley, Disraeli, Dickens or Gissing. In his novels there are no scenes of the poverty, misery and degrada- tion of the rural workers which might stir the middle-class conscience to sympathy and pity, but in 1885 he did write a de- fence of the rural worker in his essay 'The Dorsetshire Labourer'. In this he specifically rejects the view of the workers as part of an indistinguishable horde of country boobies living in poverty and misery whose only hope was the workhouse and the grave, stressing instead their individuality and rich linguistic traditions. For Hardy the real tragedy of the rural workers was not their poverty or living conditions but the alien conformity which was being imposed upon them as they were progressively transformed from 'workfolk' to 'labourers'. In Hardy's view they were becoming more and more like the undifferentiated mass which he had observed with horror in the city, that 'mon- ster whose body had four million heads and eight million eyes'.[25] But this essay is not a revelation, let alone an analysis, of the real conditions of existence of the rural working class but an attack on the ideology of urban superiority, an attack mounted from a specific ideological position. In effect Hardy replaces the ideological view, which was fostered by the urban bourgeoisie, of the rural worker as Hodge, by a rural petty bourgeois view of the loss of individuality brought about by the imposition of urban 'civilization'. Twenty years later, in a letter to Rider Haggard, he made essentially the same points again stressing that the material improvements in the labourers' conditions had been accompanied by the disappearance of village tradition which was 'absolutely sinking, had nearly sunk, into eternal oblivion'.[26]

   In both 'The Dorsetshire Labourer' and the letter to Hag- gard, Hardy reflects on the contradictory results of 'progress', the effects of material and scientific development on the people of Dorset. In his view the material benefits to the rural workers were far outweighed by the loss of individuality, of tradition and sense of place. But the effects of historical change on the better informed class were more dramatic, for here there were no benefits to balance the losses. For Hardy the most important, the most valuable characteristic of the social structure which was being destroyed by the new relations of production was differentiation. His perception of his own class of origin was precisely not as a class but as a collection of individuals whose essential characteristic was their difference from one another. Within the continuities of environment and tradition, local history and folklore each member of the group had a place as an individual. But now these people were being transformed into something qualitatively different from what they had been. Torn out of their rural environment, turned out of their natural courses like water forced to flow uphill by machinery, and driven by necessity to the towns they 'degenerate into anarchists, waiters on chance'.[27] Hardy really saw this as a process of proleterianization, the transformation of the *individual* worker into the *undifferentiated mass* proletariat, a transformation which, in his view, was both degrading and dehumanizing, and a change from the community as a collective, 'an aggregate of countless units'[28] each with his or her own individuality and peculiarities, to that 'organic whole ... having nothing in common with humanity'.[29] From this position, determined by the ideology of his class of origin, Hardy's view is not one of historical development but historical degeneration.

This means that the 'inhabitants' of Wessex are not the representations or reflections of their counterparts in history but constitute part of a complex *perception* of history, a perception which is grounded in that ideological view of the radical separation. What I am suggesting is that the world of Wessex is neither a reflection nor a 'fiction' but a production which has its own mode of reality. This reality is not the creation of the writer's consciousness but is the product of the contradiction between the aesthetic project and the conflicting ideological formations to which I have referred. In order to understand Wessex as a system of reality I want to look at the relations between the workfolk and the better informed class, at their relations to the world they inhabit and at the way in which their definition (what they are) is determined by what they do and how they do it. I shall begin by looking at the better informed class and at the mode of production which they represent, for it is here that the specific significance attached to labour and experiential knowledge in Hardy's writing is realised.

4

The Aesthetic Project and the Community of Labour

I have suggested that one of the determining factors in the production of Hardy's writing is the aesthetic project of writing an imaginative world into existence which would reveal the 'true realities of life'.[1] In the aesthetic project history is conceived as the discourse of the *apparent* and imaginative writing as the discourse of the *real* so that the relation between writing and history appears as one of revelation. Thus the reader is meant to find in Wessex a vision of the real which lies *behind* the apparent. In *The Well-Beloved*, Jocelyn Pierston makes a reference to a speech made by John Bright in 1858 in which he said that 'palaces, baronial castles, great halls, stately mansions do not make a nation. The nation in every country dwells in the cottage.' In Hardy's view this is an allusion to the 'true reality' which written history masks. But that reality is not a 'natural' or 'given' reality, it is an ideological reality expressive of the material interests and social position of the rural small producer.[2] In this Hardy is very much the literary representative of his class or origin and in Miller Loveday and his mill he gives us an image of the immemorial continuity of this class whose history, like its culture, is unwritten, an historical continuity reaching back beyond the Norman Conquest to Anglo-Saxon times:

> Miller Loveday was the representative of an ancient family of corn-grinders whose history is lost in the mists of antiquity. His ancestral line was contemporaneous with that of De Ros, Howard, and De La Zouche; but, owing to some trifling deficiency in the possessions in the house of Loveday, the individual names and intermarriages of its members were not recorded during the Middle Ages, and thus their private lives in any given century were uncertain. But it is known that the

family had formed matrimonial alliances with the farmers not
so very small, and once with a gentleman-tanner ... at every
stage backwards [Mr. Loveday's] sires and gammers thus
doubled and doubled till they became a vast body of Gothic
ladies and gentlemen of the rank known as ceorls or villeins,
full of importance to the country at large, and ramifying
throughout the unwritten history of England....

Overcombe Mill presented at one end the appearance of a
hard-worked house slipping into the river, and at the other of
an idle, genteel place, half-cloaked with creepers at this time
of year, and having no visible connection with flour.[3]

This passage constitutes one of those nodal points in Hardy's
writing where the unity of allusion to recorded history (De Ros,
Howard, De La Zouche) and the imaginary history of Wessex
(Miller Loveday and his ancestors) reveals the 'real' history of
England. The ironic tone of this revelation indicates the
ideological position from which Hardy is writing. The presence
in recorded history of those names depends on land *ownership*.
The *apparent* history of England is thus nothing more than the
record of the private lives of the large owners of property, a
record which conceals the *real* but unwritten history of the Lovedays and the class they represent.

But the 'house of Loveday' represents not only the unrecorded
history of the labour of the Lovedays but Overcombe Mill itself
which is firstly a place of work (the 'hard-worked house') and
secondly a place of residence ('an idle, genteel place'). The
image thus represents not only the continuity of life and labour
of a specific group 'full of importance to the country at large,
and ramifying throughout the unwritten history of England',
but also the *unity* of life and labour. Overcombe Mill signifies a
relationship which is completely different from that signified by
those country houses 'built for enjoyment pure and simple'[4]
about which 'the old-fashioned stranger instinctively said,
"Blood built it, and Wealth enjoys it"'.[5] More than this, the mill
is also part of the environment, an integral part of the landscape
itself.

In the introduction to *The Scarlet Letter* Nathaniel Hawthorne
wrote that 'long connection of a family with one spot, as its place
of birth and burial, creates a kindred between the human being

and the locality, quite independent of any charm in the scenery or moral circumstances that surround him. It is not love, but instinct.'[6] It is that sense of instinctual connection, 'kindred', between individual and place that Hardy called the beauty of association. In Wessex, landscape has no significance in itself but only in terms of its human connections. The same is also true of the 'things' with which it is full. 'The beauty of association', wrote Hardy, 'is entirely superior to the beauty of aspect, and a beloved relative's old battered tankard to the finest Greek vase.'[7] What was important for Hardy was the *sign* of the relation between people and their environment so that an object or mark 'raised or made by man on a scene is worth ten times any such formed by unconscious Nature. Hence clouds, mists, and mountains are unimportant beside the wear on a threshold, or the print of a hand.'[8] Thus 'places' and 'things' have a specific relational significance in Wessex, like the doorway of the Dewy cottage in *Under the Greenwood Tree* which 'was worn and scratched by much passing in and out, giving it by day the appearance of an old keyhole'[9] or the large two-handled mug from which the workfolk drink in *Far from the Madding Crowd:*

> cracked and charred with heat ... furred with extraneous matter about the outside, especially in the crevices of the handles, the innermost curves of which may not have seen daylight for several years by reason of this encrustation thereon—formed of ashes accidently wetted with cider and baked hard.[10]

In the imaginative world of Wessex 'places' and 'things' do not reflect real things, objects or locations, rather they signify certain ideological relations which are expressive of the experiential and customary formations of the workfolk and the better informed class. In this sense Wessex can be thought of as an ideological landscape, an image of what Vološinov has called the shared spatial and ideological purview which constitutes the ideological world of its inhabitants signifying a community of assumed value judgments. But it also signifies (as Overcombe Mill in *The Trumpet-Major*, Talbothays Farm in *Tess of the d'Urbervilles*, the woods in *The Woodlanders*, the Great Barn in *Far from the Madding Crowd* show) the natural condition of production to which the working people relate as to their own inorganic being. 'The barn was natural to the shearers, and the shearers were in harmony with the barn',[11] writes Hardy in *Far from the Madding Crowd,* and like Overcombe Mill the Great Barn at Weatherby represents a functional continuity:

> One could say about this barn, what could hardly be said of either the church or the castle, akin to it in age and style, that the purpose which had dictated its original erection was the same with that to which it was still applied. Unlike and superior to either of those two typical remnants of mediaevalism, the old barn embodied practices which had suffered no multilation at the hands of time. Here at least the spirit of the ancient builders was at one with the spirit of the modern beholder. Standing before this abraded pile, the eye regarded its present usage, the mind dwelt upon its past history, with a satisfied sense of functional continuity throughout —a feeling almost of gratitude, and quite of pride, at the permanence of the idea which had heaped it up.... For once mediaevalism and modernism had a common standpoint. The lanceolate windows, the time-eaten arch-stones and chamfers, the orientation of the axis, the misty chestnut work of the rafters, referred to no exploded fortifying art or worn-out religious creed. The defence and salvation of the body by daily bread is still a study, a religion and a desire.... So the barn was natural to the shearers, and the shearers were in harmony with the barn.[12]

In *Capital* Marx defines the term economy as a system of social relations and he shows that the capitalist mode of production is the only one in which the specific form of the social relations is mystified, or fetishised to use his term, into a form of a relation between products themselves—'social relations between things'.[13] The whole of chapter twenty-two of *Far from the Madding Crowd* from which the above quotation comes 'reveals' the economy to be precisely a system of social relations, but of relations between people not things. The text proclaims labour, production, to be the basis of social existence. But the barn embodies a mode of production in which time is not the measure of value, in which useful articles were not produced for the *purpose* of being exchanged, that is, not for the realization of surplus value, but as use values 'for the defence and salvation of the body'. But in Hardy's writing the barn and what it represents is perceived as 'the real', the embodiment of 'the permanence of the idea which had heaped it up'. The mode of production which the barn embodies is seen as an ideal. Again we find that history, as represented by castle and church (the recorded history of De Ros, Howard, De La Zouche), is construed as the veil which conceals the essential reality, embodied by the barn, of the productive labour of the working people of Wessex. The aesthetic project is to remove that veil, to set aside apparent reality in order to reveal the 'deeper' reality of those practices which have suffered no mutilation at the hands of time, the sustaining pre-capitalist productive relations of the small producer. For this reason we find the labour in Wessex is never abstract, general labour, it is always specific. It is labour conceived as *property*, not merely as the source of property, and as such it represents the living unity of the individual and his or her world as opposed to the separation inherent in the social relation in which labour power is a commodity. Here Wessex represents an abstraction in so far as from the historically antagonistic relations of the 'peasant' and capitalist modes of production, a specific relation is selected and designated as the *essential* relation which constitutes the harmonious resolution to the historically antagonistic relations of production of 'mediaevalism' and 'modernism'. That is the relation which presupposes the worker as proprietor or at least in which the proprietor works. In other words, it represents those relations which are dissolved by the capitalist mode of production. Consequently we find that in Wessex proprietorship is a matter of the individual possession of the instruments of labour. This presupposes the craft of artisanal mode of production where labour itself is still half artistic, half end-in-itself, a mastery of specific skills and where even the small capitalist remains a master-journeyman.[14] Even the comparatively well-off self-made men, the employers of labour like Henchard in *The Mayor of Casterbridge*, Melbury in *The Woodlanders*, Crick in *Tess* are skilled men who work alongside their employees.

In *Desperate Remedies*, Edward Springrove senior exemplifies the harmonious relation between individual and labour, between artist and artisan. Although Springrove is an employer he is himself part of the community of labour. Inn keeper, farmer, cider-maker, this 'poet with a rough skin' was 'an employer of labour of the old school, who worked himself among his men'.[15] However, not all the better informed class are employers or even self-employed. Throughout the novels skilled workmen become self-employed or even employers or fall from that position into the ranks of the rural workers. But this is not a crucial distinction in Wessex. What counts is the expressive nature of skilled labour. In Stephen Smith's father in *A Pair of Blue Eyes* we have an image of the typical Wessex artisan.

John Smith—brown as autumn as to skin, white as winter as to clothes—was a satisfactory specimen of the village artificer in stone. In common with most rural mechanics, he had too much individuality to be a typical 'working-man'—a resultant of that beach-pebble attrition with his kind only to be experienced in large towns, which metamorphoses the unit Self into a fraction of the unit Class. There was not the speciality in his labour which distinguishes the handicraftsmen of towns. Though only a mason, strictly speaking, he was not above handling a brick, if bricks were the order of the day; or a slate or tile, if a roof had to be covered before the wet weather set in, and nobody was near who could do it better. Indeed, on one or two occasions in the depth of winter, when frost peremptorily forbids all use of the trowel ... he had taken to felling and sawing trees. Moreover, he had practised gardening in his own plot for so many years that, on an emergency, he might have made a living by that calling. Probably our countryman was not such an accomplished artificer in a particular direction as his town bretheren in the trades. But he was, in truth, like that clumsy pin-maker who made the whole pin, and who was despised by Adam Smith on that account and respected by Macaulay, much more the artist nevertheless.[16]

This is more than merely a comparison between town and country. Hardy is alluding here to two totally antithetical economic relations, comparing the different forms of labour determined by the artisanal and capitalist mode of production. John Smith is a village artificer, a craftsman whose economic character lies precisely in the *specificity* of his labour not its 'speciality'. Here labour has not lost all the characteristics of art;

it is not a purely abstract activity as is one of the eighteen different operations involved in the manufacture of Adam Smith's pin.[17] What characterizes the labour of the 'typical "working-man"' is that it has been developed into mechanical activity, merely material activity in Marx's term, activity pure and simple, regardless of its form.[18] Unlike a member of the working class of the urban areas 'where limitation is all the rule in labour'[19] John Smith, like Jude Fawley, is 'an all-round man, as artisans in country-towns are apt to be'.[20] 'Strictly speaking' John Smith was a mason, a worker in stone, but as well as being skilled in that particular craft he could also lay bricks and tile a roof, fell and saw timber and grow crops on his small-holding. In the practice of these skills John Smith realized his individuality. In these specific labours he manifested his essential Self, in and through them he existed as a separate, defined and definable individual among other individuals, similarly defined, in his group.

In Wessex the contradictory relations between wage labour and capital are evoked by images of the contradiction between Self and Class. The progressively abstract nature of *labour* characteristic of a particular stage in the development of the forces and relations of production is evoked by an image of the progressively abstract nature of the *labourer* brought about by the 'beach-pebble attrition with his kind ... which metamorphoses the unit Self into a fraction of the unit Class'. Hardy's own class view and the ideological centring of the Self meant that he could not see the potential of that historical 'metamorphosis'. There is, in consequence, no awareness in Hardy's writing of the possibilities for working class solidarity, knowledge and action which being 'a fraction of the unit class' engenders.

It might be helpful to follow these ideological motifs through a single novel in order to get some sense of their structural coherence. If we look at *The Woodlanders*, for example, we find that the distinctions between the *native* inhabitants of Hintock are not distinctions of class but distinctions of individuality. The woodlanders are distinct from one another not only as the oak is distinct from the elm, but also as each oak or elm is distinct from every other oak and elm. To see them simply as trees is analogous to seeing the rural workers as Hodge, and is indicative

of an alien vision. In this respect the woods are analogy of the
social structure of Wessex, a structure which is defined in terms
of contiguity and difference but not separation. It is a structure
in which each individual thrives or withers, grows straight or
crooked, is sound or diseased in an entirely unique way but a
way which is totally different from the enclosed, self-centred
individualism of bourgeois society. It is a structure in which the
reality of being and doing is a matter of the common perception
of a shared material existence in which 'I' can realize itself only
on the basis of 'we', a commonalty which is evoked by the social
contiguity of the characters who inhabit the world of work. This
contiguity operates on two planes. Economically it works
'vertically' in terms of a hierarchy of the socio-economic
standing of each character in the community. Ideologically it
works 'horizontally' in terms of the shared experiential and customary forms of the community. The vertical is the plane of the
'I' and the horizontal that of the 'we', and the point where these
two planes intersect accords the individual his or her place in the
community. Any attempt to separate the 'I' from the 'we' leads
to a loss of contact with the unspoken value judgments of the
community.

In Little Hintock the timber, bark and copse-ware merchant
George Melbury is driven by a passion to obliterate a social
slight he received when young at the hands of the parson's son. A
poor boy himself, he is determined that his children would never
be made to feel socially inferior through lack of education. This
driving passion to acquire money to educate his children
together with his native skill and energy eventually elevate him
to the position of 'chief man of business' in Little Hintock. The
much less affluent Giles Winterborne is totally unlike Melbury
in character. Quiet, dreamy, somewhat abstracted and careless
of personal success, he has none of Melbury's driving energy.
Yet this 'young yeoman'—'woodsman, cider merchant, apple-
farmer'—through family connection and 'a partnership based
upon an unwritten code, by which each acted in the way he
thought fair towards the other, on a give-and-take principle'
was 'though the poorer, on a footing of social intimacy with the
Melburys'.[21] Certainly poorer than Winterborne, the aged and
somewhat demented John South is, like Winterborne, a life-
holder. The two families are related, and their lives are

intimately bound up with one another through legal, personal and working relations. On this vertical plane of contiguity even the workfolk—all of whom are distinguished by differences of character and personality—do not perceive themselves and are not perceived by other members of the community to be separated from their employers by any unbridgeable gulf. As each member of this community of labour knows the woods in which he or she works, so they know one another, and just as they can tell whether the greatest oak in the forest is sound or whether tainted by incipient decay, so they know that although Melbury is the chief man of business in the community he, like the great oak, is tainted.

Melbury stands at the frontier which divides Wessex from the encroaching world which surrounds it. In appearance and speech he is of Hintock. Physically a part of Wessex he is the *embodiment* of past labour:

> That stiffness about the arm, hip, and knee-joint, which was apparent when he walked, was the net product of the divers sprains and over-exertions that had been required of him in handling trees and timber when a young man, for he was of the sort called self-made, and had worked hard. He knew the origin of every one of these cramps; that in his left shoulder had come from carrying a pollard, unassisted, from Tutcombe Bottom home; that in one leg was caused by the crash of an elm against it when they were felling; that in the other was from lifting a bole.[22]

But a separation has taken place for Melbury has changed from being a small producer to being a small capitalist and the product of this new relation to his environment is the educated and cultured Grace who, in being turned into a 'lady', has been separated from the community of labour. To Melbury his daughter is, like the product of Marty South's labour, a marketable commodity. When Grace inadvertently sees some cheques which had been drawn to defray the costs of her education she says to her father; 'I, too, cost a good deal, like the horses and wagons and corn!' and Melbury replies, 'But if you do cost as much as they, never mind. You'll yield a better return.'[23] The individual woodlander has been 'fetishized' into an object. Transformed into an investment, Grace is the living embodiment of the radical separation where the direct social relations between the individuals of the community of labour are transformed into material relations between them and social relations between the marketable commodities they produce.

When barber Percomb goes to Little Hintock to persuade Marty South to part with her beautiful chestnut hair in order to make a wig for Mrs Charmond, he finds her busily working making thatching spars, the going rate for which was eighteen pence a thousand. In a day and half the night Marty could make fifteen hundred—two shillings and threepence worth (11p). In reduced circumstances, worried about her father's illness, working feverishly and in secret to fulfil his contractual commitments to Melbury, preoccupied with her love for Giles Winterborne, harried by Percomb to part with her crowning glory in order to satisfy the passing whim of the local landowner, Marty nevertheless produces work of such fine quality that Winterborne exclaims admiringly, 'Your father with his forty years of practice never made a spar better than that. They are too good for the thatching of houses; they are good enough for furniture.'[24] The fact that Hardy selects that particular product is significant. It is one of the simplest products of the woodland community—a sharpened timber peg for holding thatch in place. But it is not the thing which is important but the nature of its making. When Giles admires the spars he asks in amazement; 'But how could you learn to do it? 'Tis a trade!' Uttered by Giles that is an accolade. In the mouth of Mrs Charmond or Fitzpiers it would be a contemptuous dismissal.

In Wessex the distinction between 'tradesman' and 'gentleman' is more than a difference of class. Embodied in those simple artifacts is the 'true' value of labour, not its exchange value of 11p, but the value of a whole way of life, the value of a form of activity which expresses the life of the producer. The money value here is merely the 'apparent' value which conceals the 'real' value of the labour embodied in the product and which is hidden from the sight of 'gentlemen' as surely as the trees obscure the real nature of the Hintock woods from the sight of the lady Grace. In the world of work which Wessex here signifies the skilled individual is, or is potentially, an artist. In that community, individuals express themselves through their labour and in their products the social values of the community are realised. Although Marty works long and hard she is not like the urban worker. Like John Smith in *A Pair of Blue Eyes* she is free from the beach-pebble attrition with her kind which metamorphoses the unit Self into a fraction of the unit Class, and like him she is skilled in many crafts. This is necessary because in Wessex labour is not formal, abstract labour as was, progressively, the labour of specialization, but the vital mediation between the individual and his or her world. Those simple spars, the product of that labour, signify a mode of production in which the individual not only expresses him or herself but also a definite mode of life of the community as a whole. Once that product has been subsumed under the capitalist mode of production, produced as a commodity for the realization of surplus value, once that irreversible separation has taken place, that relationship is terminated.

But in Wessex it is still otherwise. Here the specificity of labour expresses an intimacy and connection, a knowledge and understanding of the world which is not a product of 'consciousness', not the knowledge of education, but the experiential knowledge 'of intelligent intercourse with Nature':

> The casual glimpses which the ordinary population bestowed upon that wondrous world of sap and leaves called Hintock woods had been with these two, Giles and Marty, a clear gaze. They had been possessed of its finer mysteries as of a commonplace knowledge; had been able to read its hieroglyphs as ordinary writing; to them the sights and sounds of night, winter, wind, storm, amid those dense boughs, which had to Grace a touch of the uncanny, and even of the supernatural, were simple occurances whose origin, continuance, and laws they foreknew. They had planted together, and together they had felled; together they had, with the turn of the years, mentally collected those remoter signs and symbols which seen in few were of runic obscurity, but altogether made an alphabet. From the light lashing of the twigs upon their faces when brushing through them in the dark either could pronounce upon the species of the tree whence they stretched; from the quality of the wind's murmur through a bough either could in like manner name its sort afar off. They knew at a glance at a trunk if its heart were sound, or tainted with incipient decay; and by the state of its upper twigs the

stratum that had been reached by its roots. The artifices of the seasons were seen by them from the conjuror's own point of view, and not from that of the spectator.[25]

Seen from the point of view of these two native inhabitants of Wessex who have spent their lives *working* in the forest, Nature is neither romantic mystery nor Darwinian struggle. Such views are those of uninvolved outsiders, to whom the experiential knowledge of the woodlanders is a matter of 'runic obscurity'. Thus the woodlands and orchards about Hintock do not represent Nature in the abstract, they are that part of Wessex where Giles and Marty live and work and that is how and why they understand it. The wood's mystery to them is *commonplace* knowledge, its signs and symbols an alphabet which they can read as ordinary writing. This knowledge is not symbolic; Marty and Giles are not 'wood spirits'.[26] Theirs is the experiential knowledge which comes of observation and practice, of skill and experience. It is the artisan's knowledge of his material, an empirical, sensuous knowledge. Their living labour is embodied in the wood—'they had planted together, and together they had felled'; they contributed to its life and it to theirs. Their intimacy with, and their knowledge of their community arises from their necessary labour in it. From that knowledge, that connection, that intimacy, that love, Grace Melbury is excluded by her forcible separation from the community of labour.

To the lady of the manor, the landowner Mrs Charmond, (for whom the land is merely a source of profit, a source of revenue to fund her endless search for pleasure) and even to Grace, after her return to Hintock, the 'true reality' of the woods is hidden. Separated from the community of labour, from 'the mass of hard prosaic reality'[27] the woods are a place of mystery and even terror; they seem to hold the threat of an unknown life. In chapter thirty-three Grace and Mrs Charmond lose their way in the woods and become tormented by suspicions and vague fears. But the most significant feature of this chapter is that the entire colloquy between these two isolated ladies who pathetically huddle together for warmth and comfort is about love and sexual passion. More than anything else this is indicative of their separation from the community of the woodlanders. For both these ladies 'love'—that idealized, evanescent and self-regarding passion—is the relationship to which they are condemned by virtue of their idleness. They may never experience the *camaraderie* (to use Hardy's term) of shared labour, that association of shared life, work and experience out of which, in Hardy's imaginary world, may grow 'the only love which is strong as death—that love which many waters cannot quench, nor the floods drown, beside which the passion usually called by that name is evanescent as steam'.[28]

It is that world of shared labour and the social relations which it signifies which is interred with the corpse of Giles Winterborne over whose grave Marty speaks the final words of the novel:

> 'Whenever I plant the young larches I'll think that none can plant as you planted; and whenever I split a gad, and whenever I turn a cider wring, I'll say none could do it like you. If ever I forget your name let me forget home and heaven! ... But no, no, my love, I never can forget 'ee; for you was a good man, and did good things!'[29]

This is surely a most poignant and moving funeral oration for the death of a mode of production and a way of life in which the relations between people were not those of squalid exploitation, not the internecine struggles of 'naked individuals', but the *camaraderie* of men and women who associated not competed in their labours.

It would not, however, be true to say that Wessex simply reflects the real historical transformations which affected the artisanal mode of production of the class of small producers in Dorset in the nineteenth century. This is not a fictive image of the real but the production of a reality, the elaboration of a specific form of perception. Labour in Wessex (as opposed to Dorset) denotes more than a number of specific activities; it has an ideal, essential value over and above its productive value, a value which is realized in association. In Wessex it is only that mode of production which the better informed class represents which allows the spontaneous, harmonious and voluntary association of individuals to take place, only here is the 'real' relationship possible. In Wessex the productive relations of the small producer in which a specific mode of labour is realized are apotheosized. What is so evidently present in this final perception of reality is the centrality of working people and the work they do as the sustaining foundations upon which the world of

Wessex is built. What is absent from this perception (an absence which is ideologically not subjectively determined) is the historical reality of the transformative role of the working *class*.

5

The Sovereignty of the Subject and the World of the Workfolk

One of the major means of production for Hardy's writing was what I have called (adopting his own phrase) the ideology of the thinking world, that is, those harmonizing discourses woven about the reality of class exploitation and domination which spoke of the general interest and the common good, of freedom and progress, culture and civilization. The function of these ideological discourses was to efface the contradictions between wage labour and capital by universalizing and 'naturalizing' the world of the bourgeoisie, equating the development of its economic organization, its legal, political and cultural forms with the inevitable progress of civilization in general.

In Hardy's novels these harmonizing and universalizing discourses are put into contradiction by the presence of the workfolk. By bringing into collision the 'thinking world' with the world inhabited by the workfolk the writing reveals the colonizing nature of bourgeois ideological forms showing them to be anything but natural and certainly not universal. However, while it was clearly Hardy's intention to show how 'civilization' was rapidly destroying local traditions, the writing produces a 'view' of ideology which is not dependent on that intention. In other words, what Hardy wants the reader to see is not necessarily identical with the view of the ideological which is produced by the writing. There are times when owing to the insistent demands of the aesthetic intention a *scenario* of the ideological is produced which is quite independent of the idealist project of the revelation of 'the true realities of life'. To show how this works I want to look at the presence of the workfolk in Hardy's writing first in terms of certain traditional cultural forms associated particularly with festival and secondly in terms of the articulation of distinctive 'non-literary' linguistic forms.

With regard to the first I should like to relate a particular aspect of the aesthetic project of Hardy's writing to Mikail Bakhtin's concept of grotesque realism. I refer here to Hardy's concept of artistic distortion (his own term), a technique intended to contribute to the revelation of reality. To further this end Hardy introduced an intentional 'coarseness' into his writing which constituted a conscious attack on sophistication, 'the artificial forms of living'[1], which were taken to be part of the structure of appearances which hid the true realities of life. As it was the function of art to reveal the true then, as Reuben Dewy observed in *Under the Greenwood Tree*, 'my sonnies, all true stories have a coarse touch'.[2] In his book on Rabelais, Bakhtin uses the term grotesque realism to describe the images of the 'material bodily principle' of the age old culture of folk humour associated with carnival. These images of grotesque exaggeration relate not to the private world of consciousness inhabited by 'economic man' but to the collectivity of the community, and Bakhtin suggests that the essential principle of grotesque realism is 'degradation, that is, the lowering of all that is high, spiritual, ideal, abstract'.[3] It is in this sense that the workfolk constitute the contradictory antithesis to the ideology of the thinking world, to their idealism and their preoccupation with consciousness.

Chapter three of *The Return of the Native* is a brilliant evocation of the reassertion of the repressed culture of the workfolk, of its precarious survival in the face of the onslaughts of 'civilization'. The conflict between these opposing forces is rendered in the vivid imagery of the antagonism between consciousness and community, perceived by the onlooker, the silent watcher of the heath at that 'transitional hour' when Egdon appears to be waiting for the final overthrow. In that moment of transition when time seems to hold its breath, Diggory Venn sees Eustacia, a figure of absolute isolation:

> There the form stood, motionless as the hill beneath. Above the plain rose the hill, above the hill rose the barrow, and above the barrow rose the figure. Above the figure was nothing that could be mapped elsewhere than on a celestial globe....
> The scene was strangely homogeneous.... The form was so

much like an organic part of the entire motionless structure.... Immobility being the chief characteristic of that
whole which the person formed portion of, the discontinuance
of immobility in any quarter suggested confusion.
    Yet that is what happened.[4]

In that dramatic image of ascent—'the vale, the upland, the
barrow, and the figure above it'—in that homogeneous unity in
which the single figure appears as the head and pinnacle, the
point of consciousness in which all natural and human history
appears to culminate, we have an image of the discourse of the
continuous which makes human consciousness the subject of all
historical development and action. Everything around the
figure of Eustacia appears to derive its validation from her
presence.

    Into this *motionless* structure in which immobility is the chief
characteristic, into the isolation of Eustacia's private, idealizing
world, the workfolk intrude, and the queen of the solitude is
displaced, the kingdom of the mind overthrown, put to flight by
a 'skybacked pantomime of silhouettes' with which she 'had no
relation'. These figures 'intrude' upon the perceiving consciousness to interrupt, disturb and subvert the smooth flow of
empathy between the perceiving subjects, those silent onlookers
who cling 'by preference to that vanished, solitary figure, as to
something more interesting, more important, more likely to
have a history worth knowing than these newcomers'.[5] It was as if
the bonfire-makers 'had suddenly dived into past ages, and
fetched therefrom an hour and deed which had before been
familiar with the spot'. Here is a continuity of another order.
The workfolk's bonfire—a 'lineal descendent from jumbled
Druidical rites and Saxon ceremonies', 'festival fires to Thor and
Woden'—does not celebrate the triumph of the spirit, of
consciousness, but the triumph of the flesh. Here 'all was
unstable; quivering as leaves, evanescent as lightening', everything is in motion:

    Shadowy eye-sockets, deep as those of a death's head,
    suddenly turned into pits of lustre; a lantern-jaw was cavern-
    ous, then it was shining; wrinkles were emphasised to ravines,
    or obliterated entirely by a changed ray. Nostrils were dark
    wells; sinews in old necks were gilt mouldings; eyeballs glowed

like little lanterns. Those whom Nature had depicted as merely quaint became grotesque, the grotesque became pre-ternatural; for all was in extremity.[6]

In those bodily images which the leaping flames exaggerate to Gargantuan proportions is that 'degradation' which is the essential principle of grotesque realism, the lowering of all that is high, spiritual, abstract and ideal. This transference continues in the image of the wild dance within the dying embers of the fire where 'all that could be seen on Rainbarrow was a whirling of dark shapes amid a boiling confusion of sparks, which leapt around the dancers as high as their waists'.[7]

Here the workfolk represent the popular opposition to the 'civilizing' culture of the thinking world. The combination of festival, song, dance and anecdote evokes the 'unconscious' ideological formations of the communal life of the people of Egdon which are profoundly anti-spiritual and unintellectual as Clym is to find. They still posess the joyful gaiety which those who have taken thought have lost. Standing against the 'coarse' world of the commonalty, and opposed to it, is the isolated figure of Eustacia. Briefly, the workfolk displace and eclipse this solitary figure and the idealizing consciousness she represents. Here the conflict is between the private, individual conscious-ness with whom the perceiving subjects (both the characters in the novel and the readers of the novel) identify, and the communal life of the workfolk which refuses that identification. Throughout Hardy's writing the lives and actions of the work-folk signify that celebration of the flesh which both reveals and subverts the ideology of the thinking world.

One of the most striking aspects of *The Mayor of Casterbridge,* for example, is the role of festival and the characters' perceptions of, and reactions to, the festive. The novel opens with Henchard, his wife and baby daughter arriving at Weydon-Priors fair. It is a scene of festive holiday in which 'the frivolous contingent of visitors' snatch a respite from labour after the business of the fair has been concluded. Here Henchard gets drunk and vents his bitterness and frustration at being unemployed on his marriage. Henchard negates the festive and celebratory nature of the fair by his egotism. What the people perceive as a joke permissable under the rules of topsy-turvy, the licence of the temporary release from the world of work, Henchard means seriously and in that act which refuses the spirit of festival he places himself in a position of antagonism to the workfolk, an antagonism which grows with time. From this opening the motif of festival shadows the story and mimes the 'tragic' history of this solitary individual culminating in the ancient custom of the skimmington ride. This motif forms a counterpoint to the dominant theme of work and the novel develops on the basis of a conflict between various images of the isolated, individualistic, egotistical and private forms of 'economic man' (Bakhtin's term) and the collectivity of the workfolk. The many images of festivity—the washout of Henchard's official celebration of a national event, Farfrae's 'opposition randy', the *fête carillonnée* which Casterbridge mounts to receive the Royal Personage, the public dinner presided over by Henchard where the town worthies drank and ate 'searching for titbits, and sniffing and grunting over their plates like sows nuzzling for acorns',[8] the scenes of revelry in the Three Mariners and Peter's Finger —culminate in 'the great jocular plot' of the skimmington. This 'uncanny revel', which like a 'Daemonic Sabbath' was accompanied by 'the din of cleavers, tongs, tambourines, kits, crouds, humstrums, serpents, rams'-horns, and other historical kinds of music' is completely hidden from 'official' Casterbridge for when the magistrates roust out the trembling constables, nothing is found: 'Effigies, donkey, lanterns, band, all had disappeared like the crew of *Comus*'.[9] It is the last we hear of the workfolk's mocking laughter for ironically the very success of this resurgence of carnival prepares the way for its suppression.

Elizabeth-Jane's marriage to Farfrae signifies the triumph of the serious, the organized, the moral, the rational, the final triumph of spirit over the disorganized, the passionate, the festive, the flesh. The essence of Elizabeth-Jane's character is restraint and, like Farfrae's, her actions are characterized by their 'reasonableness' and her perception of the world is consistently 'tragical'. In the closing passages of the novel she reflects that joy is no longer an integral part of life but an interlude in a general drama of pain, a sentiment which signals the victory of Christian morality over passion, the final triumph of the morality of the pale Galilean. That certainly is Hardy's intention, but in the very ambiguity of that victory the limitations of the ideology of the thinking world are revealed precisely through the 'colonial' status of the people over whom the new ideological forms now rule. Those ideological discourses which speak of unity and harmony and universality are put into contradiction by images of suppression, domination, conflict, not by virtue of the images *per se* but because they enable us to see the 'outside' of a discourse which, claiming to be universal, has no bounds.

In their periodic outbursts of 'pagan' celebration the workfolk throw off the impositions of sobriety and respectability in a spontaneous rebellion against social order in which anyone who partakes becomes involved. In that 'thumping state of uproar' of the wild dance in *Under the Greenwood Tree* even the fastidious, thoughtful, refined and respectable Fancy Day is transformed into a 'romping girl' who does not mind being held and kissed by her partner.[10] This is the first instance in Hardy's writing of the metamorphosis of festival. Tess also witnesses such a scene of 'mad metamorphosis' when the Trantridge workfolk appear as 'a multiplicity of Pans whirling a multiplicity of Syrinxes', 'satyrs clasping nymphs'[11] and in *The Return of the Native* Eustacia gets caught up in such an atmosphere of 'paganism' losing herself in its 'maze of motion' within which she experiences a sensual liberation, surprised by the 'enchantment of the dance' which had come 'like an irresistible attack upon whatever sense of social order there was in their minds, to drive them back into old paths'.[12]

Drink, its preparation, appreciation and consumption, plays an important part in the lives of the workfolk. But in Wessex there is none of the moral condemnation which was the almost invariable concomitant of the depiction, in nineteenth-century writing, of the consumption of alcohol by the working class. Here there is no sense of the 'evils' of drink, or the 'problem' of drunkenness. With the workfolk drinking is not a fatal prediliction which leads to ruin and death. Sometimes it is an act of personal revolt, as is the case with Henchard or Jude, but much more often it is an intimate part of the communal life of the workfolk mediating between the world of work (its production) and the festive (its consumption) and like working, drinking is always an occasion for talk and 'tuneful stories'. When Joseph Poorgrass, hauling Fanny Robin's coffin back to Weatherbury, stops for a quick one at the Buck's Head he meets Jan Coggan and Mark Clark and they fall to ruminating on drink and changing times. Clark observes that while the Lord had mercifully bestowed a signal talent for drinking upon them, 'what with the parsons and clerks and school-people and serious tea-parties, the merry old ways of good life have gone to the dogs'.[13] When they are well and truly tight Gabriel Oak bursts in on them and bawls them out crying, ' "Upon my soul, I'm ashamed of you; 'tis disgraceful, Joseph, disgraceful ... I wish you'd show yourself a man of spirit" ', to which Joseph replies, ' "Let me take the name of drunkard humbly—let me be a man of contrite knees—let it be! ... But not a man of spirit? Have I ever allowed the toe of pride to be lifted against my hinder parts without groaning manfully that I question the right to do so?" '[14] To designate such a passage as comic relief is to neutralize its effectivity.

In this typical example of Hardy's 'coarseness' we can see what Bakhtin means by laughter degrading and materializing, and also why that laughter is inherently subversive, for its object is all that is implied by *consciousness*. It is with Oak that the reader identifies, Oak who here represents the voice of respectability, duty, the work ethic. He is the *responsible subject*, the centre of initiatives, author of and responsible for, his actions, who works by himself and wishes that Joseph would also show himself 'a man of spirit'. But the laughter generated by the workfolk refuses this ideological interpellation and subverts the ideological identification effect produced by writing by degrading and materializing the spiritual, making it a question of Joseph's reaction to a kick in the backside. Similarly with the drinkers' shared feelings about Fanny's death; their attitude is certainly 'quite coarse to a person o' decent taste'[15] and shocking to those who live in the ideology of 'respectability'. There is a similar instance in *The Mayor of Casterbridge* concerning Susan Henchard's death. The four ounce pennies which had been used as weights for the dead woman's eyes were buried in the garden after the laying out. The whole ritual of respectable death which demands that the living obey the commands of the dead, thereby ensuring the continuity of those practices in which the subjects inscribe their 'belief' in the ideology of duty, is subverted by Christopher Coney who reasons that 'money is scarce, and throats get dry. Why *should* death rob life o' fourpence?' To the workfolk the material needs of the quick come before the spiritual needs of the dead. Coney's action signifies not dis-respect for Mrs Henchard, for she is dead and gone, but a denial of the 'respectable' which always seeks to repress the flesh in the name of the spirit.

There is a passage in *A Pair of Blue Eyes* where Stephen Smith enters the Luxellian family vault and finds his father and sundry workmen making preparations for the reception of Lady Luxel-lian's coffin. They are eating bread and cheese and drinking beer. As do all such respites from labour this becomes an occasion for talk. The high seriousness of the ritual of death, of official mourning and grandiose entombment, by means of which the ruling classes publicly display their solidarity, wealth and moral and spiritual superiority, is 'degraded' by the ban-quet in the vault.[16] Again, this cannot be taken as a scene of comic relief nor is it an expression of the sententious sentiment contained in the line which prefaces the chapter—'To that last nothing under earth'. As the workfolk eat and drink, gossip and exchange anecdotes about their lives, surrounded by a dead aristocracy, we hear an echo of the laughter which degrades the spiritual in the name of the flesh. The 'coarseness' of the lives, sentiments and language depicted in Hardy's text 'degrades' the spiritual life which is celebrated in that other text to which Hardy's alludes. It is through that allusion that this passage achieves it parodic intention. Here proximity to death produces a response in the workfolk which is the very antithesis to that of the individual's in Tennyson's 'The Two Voices', where the poet privately suffers his long dark night of the soul. Counselled to self-destruction by crazy sorrow, the poet nevertheless emerges from his ordeal on a Sunday morning to watch the faithful going to church, and proclaims his desire not for death but life to the accompaniment of a 'heavenly-toned' voice which whispers to him of 'a hidden hope'. The workfolk consistently refuse such visions of *Man's* spiritual salvation and subvert the thinking world's evolutionary *telos* of universal consciousness. Again this is not simply a matter of representation of 'scenes', but is inherent in the workfolk's 'living' discourse itself. The reality which the utterances of the educated thinking world dis-closes is an ideological reality which relates to all those *written* discourses—philosophical, religious, mythical, historical and poetic—all those discourses which constitute the means of production for Hardy's writing and by which it is always accompanied and to which it ceaselessly alludes. The reality to which the utterances of the workfolk relates is, on the other hand, customary, non-literary, unwritten, anecdotal. This is an experiential, non-intellectual, verbal mode which is based on telling. It is a popular mode comprised of the shared experiential knowledge of the community of labour which takes the form of talk, gossip, jokes, tales, 'tuneful stories' and the recounting of happenings past and present, where the saying is more important than what is said, for more often than not the community of listeners already knows what is to be said, so long have they known each other, so often have they heard the tale. It is language as ritual and part of growing up in the community is to be initiated into the ritualistic forms of telling, to learn the store of anecdotes and over the years contribute to it. It is a mode of discourse completely different from that of the 'alien' mode of the thinking world, the language of intellection of the idealizing consciousness. The language of the workfolk is non-conceptual and experiential; it is a kind of linguistic cement which binds people together in their communal activities like the copse-work in *The Woodlanders* which is always accompanied by 'tales, chronicles, and ramifications of family history'.[17] This is typical of the many scenes of association in Hardy's novels where the combination of doing and saying is expressive of the material unity of the speakers' world. In *Desperate Remedies*, for example, the communal activity of cider pressing generates talk between Springrove and his men. The form of these colloquies is always the same; it is like a stone dropped into a pool. From a specific point of immediate interest the talk ripples out in ever widening circles of association until it reaches a certain point where it becomes the re-telling of the speakers' anecdotal history. Both what is told and the manner of its telling are familiar. When Richard Crickett pauses in his tale his listeners 'waited for the continuation of the speech, as if they knew from experience the exact distance off it lay in the future'.[18]

Vološinov has suggested that the understanding of any utterance depends on the relationship between the said and the unsaid, between the verbally articulated and the assumed and that to understand the whole sense of any utterance the listeners must share the same ideological purview as the speakers. The 'behavioural utterances' of every-day life connect those involved in a situation as co-participants who know, understand and evaluate that situation in the same way, and such utterances thus depend on a shared common material existence. Far from being primarily individual and subjective behavioural utterances consist of 'the material unity of world that enters the speakers' purview ... and of the unity of the real conditions of life that generate a community of value judgments'.[19] The material conditions of a specific social group thus enters directly into speech as the unsaid, those assumed value judgments. The unsaid which constitutes a necessary part of all discourse—those 'sentiments, illusions, modes of thought and views of life that the individual derives through tradition and upbringing'[20] which are taken for granted and not subject to discussion—is precisely that 'unconscious' ideological reality in which the workfolk live. Vološinov also stresses the importance of intonation which lies at the border of the said and the unsaid establishing a connection between verbal discourse and the extra-verbal context. Intonation can only be fully understood when the listener is in touch with the assumed value judgments of the given social group and like gesture it requires the 'choral support' of the surrounding people.

There is a paradigmatic scene in *A Pair of Blue Eyes* which centres around the weighing and cutting up of John Smith's pig. It is a festive occasion, a gathering of neighbours, for the pig has been slaughtered in honour of Stephen's return and a feast is being prepared. The neighbours work and drink and talk; the supper is cooked, the pig cut up, the beer drunk and the stories told, and as the evening progresses the talk ripples out from the present occasion to tales of past experience.[21] The combination of labour, laughter and language which forms a unity of continuous association evokes the material unity of the community of labour. The 'behavioural utterance' of the workfolk connects all those involved in a situation as co-participants who know, understand and evaluate that situation in the same way. Time and again some communal activity sparks off such a chain of anecdotes. So, for example, on the day the butter will not churn, dairyman Crick declares that he will have to visit

Conjuror Trendle's son in Egdon if things do not improve. The ensuing conversation evokes the aged traditions of rural super-stition, and this evolves naturally into the humourous, slightly bawdy and often-heard tale of the way Jack Dollop was forced to make an honest woman of a girl he had seduced while working as a milker on the farm.[22] The broaching of the cider cask in preparation for the Christmas party leads Reuben Dewy to tell the tale of its purchase from Sam Lawson; Michael Mail and Joseph Bowman become drawn into the anecdotal history of buying and selling.[23] Enlarging the Luxellian tomb, the con-versation naturally turns into tales of the workfolk's past employers, the gentry and their peculiar histories.[24] And of course 'tales and toss-potting'[25] go hand in hand. It is in the tone of these tales (their very 'coarseness') that the unarticulated social evaluations of the community of labour is evoked. Thus the significance of the language of the workfolk lies not in the import of what is said but in the intonation of this language and in its relation to all those other discourses by which it is surrounded.

As the laughter of the workfolk degrades and materializes the ideal, the abstract, the spiritual, so their language 'degrades' literary language in a series of parodic confrontations. Take for example that memorable afternoon when Jude, returning to Marygreen deeply absorbed in his idealistic dream and speaking aloud of his educational attainments, is overheard by the girls washing pigs' intestines. Their response is mocking and derisive laughter. Perhaps more than any other single incident in Hardy's writing, the throwing of the pig's penis at Jude's head captures the sense of what Bakhtin means by folk laughter degrading and materializing the abstract and the ideal. To make the import of the throwing of that 'piece of flesh' completely effective a confrontation takes place between the language of the workfolk spoken by the girls and the language 'of the humaner letters'. When Jude confronts Arabella—that 'complete and substantial female animal'—he is 'almost certain that to her was attributable the enterprise of attracting his atten-tion from dreams of the humaner letters to what was simmering in the minds around him'. The moment of recognition of their sexual attraction is rendered in unmistakably 'literary' language:

somehow or other the eyes of the brown girl rested on his own when he had said the words, and there was a momentary flash of intelligence, a dumb announcement of affinity *in posse*, between herself and him, which, so far as Jude Fawley was concerned, had no sort of premeditation in it. She saw that he had singled her out from the three, as a woman is singled out in such cases, for no reasoned purpose of further acquaintance, but in commonplace obedience to conjunctive orders from headquarters, unconsciously received by unfortunate men when the last intention of their lives is to be occupied with the feminine.[26]

This is the language of consciousness into which Jude has been displaced and the measure of the separation wrought by this displacement is revealed in the later scene of the pig killing evoked by the speakers' conflicting intonations. Although Jude and Arabella perform the act together it is not a communal act. To Jude the slaughter is a private act of barbarism, to Arabella an act of material necessity: 'Poor folks must live'.[27] Their colloquy does not signify a community of value judgments. On the contrary, Jude expresses his individual emotions while Arabella expresses those of the world of the workfolk's common necessity. The value judgment expressed in the intonation of Jude's 'Thank God ... He's dead!' is parodied and degraded by that expressed in the intonation of Arabella's 'Od damn it all! ... You've over-stuck un!'

Arabella's speech signifies that 'internal' relationship to Wessex expressive of the material unity of world in which the workfolk and the better informed class live. But while the language they speak is common to them it is not a 'common language'; it is particular to them, a distinctive language which expresses both a community of values and the distinctive life of individual speakers and it thus expresses both unity and difference. But opposed to this language of the community are the alien linguistic practices of a 'common language' in which certain individuals are educated. Through this educational process they, like Jude, become displaced, 'educated into something quite different'.[28] It is not so much a question of what those who have been schooled in these new practices know (it is not their knowledge which separates them from the community of labour), but how they speak, the language they use. It is a taught language and in one form or another the majority of Hardy's female characters, daughters of the workfolk and the better informed class, undergo this important transformative educational process. Tess, for example, 'who had passed the Sixth Standard in the National school under a London-trained mistress, spoke two languages; the dialect at home ... ordinary English abroad and to persons of quality'.[29] Clearly there are differences between the education Tess receives and that received by, say, Cytherea Graye, who 'had been carefully educated';[30] or Fancy Day who 'went to a training-school, and ... stood first among the Queen's scholars of her year';[31] or Tabitha Lark who had received her education in London and had 'joined the phalanx of Wonderful Women who had resolved to eclipse masculine genius altogether, and humiliate the brutal sex to the dust';[32] or Grace Melbury, who went to a 'fashionable school' where she was 'mentally trained and tilled into foreignness of view'.[33] Whatever the differences in the form of education (which relates to the internal coherence of each individual novel), the result of the educational process is always the same; the acquired ability to 'spaik real language'[34] signifies an alienation from the communal world and also a suppression and domination.

The imposed uniformity of a common language was one of the ways by which the dominant class sought to establish its hegemony. By establishing a system of education which suppressed the dialects of the working people which were expressive of their different existential conditions, it sought to give its own ideology a 'classless', eternal and universal character. This ideological domination appears in Hardy's writing as the repressing of the distinctive and the particular, a transformation in which the Self literally becomes hidden beneath the 'veneer of ... education'.[35] 'As a nation gets older', he wrote in *A Pair of Blue Eyes*, 'individuality fades, and education spreads.'[36] In Hardy's last published novel, the Isle of Slingers 'home of a curious and well-nigh distinct people, cherishing strange beliefs and singular customs, now for the most part obsolescent'[37] is the remaining outpost of beleaguered Wessex making its last ditch stand against the invading 'civilisation'. 'Here', wrote Hardy, 'in this last local stronghold of the Pagan divinities, where Pagan customs lingered yet, Christianity had established itself precariously at best'.[38] The alien culture which advanced relentlessly upon Wessex had gained a foothold even here. Avice Caro has been educated, mentally trained and tilled. In her the customary culture of Wessex and the anecdotal language of the workfolk has already been suppressed. Avice could 'not only recite poetry at intellectual gatherings, but play the piano fairly, and sing to her own accompaniment':

> Every aim of those who had brought her up had been to get her away mentally as far as possible from her natural and individual life as an inhabitant of a peculiar island: to make her an exact copy of tens of thousands of other people, in whose circumstances there was nothing special, distinctive or picturesque; to teach her to forget all the experiences of her ancestors; to drown the local ballads by songs purchased at the Budmouth fashionable music-sellers', and the local vocabulary by a governess-tongue of no country at all.[39]

Wessex is the site of this linguistic conflict and this is one of its many significations. In Hardy's writing we see the ways in which the natural and individual lives of the workfolk and the better informed class are repressed and dominated by the imposition of an alien culture. In the cultural colonization of Wessex education is used not to liberate but to repress the dominated classes through the imposition of a linguistic uniformity. But while Hardy's writing is certainly situated in relation to a definable historical process it is not rooted directly in historical reality. Another reality mediates the relation between history and writing, the reality of ideology. For this reason the workfolk are not simply *representative*, they do not represent or reflect an external reality. They are rather the product of the labour of writing, constituting an important element in the production of a 'world' which represents a final form of (ideological) perception of that historical reality.

PART TWO

The
Structure of
Perceptions

6

The Structure of Perceptions

What I have designated as the ideology of the thinking world was, broadly speaking, the idealized expression of the conditions of existence of the late Victorian liberal bourgeoisie who, to paraphrase Marx, did not simply want to impose an egotistic class interest on society, but believed that the particular conditions of their own existence were the general conditions in the framework of which society could progress harmoniously avoiding the 'anarchy' of class struggle.[1] This was manifested in the active altruism of working for the common good, in the belief in the progressive identity of being and consciousness and in the desire for a natural process of gradual social harmonization. The various cultural, religious, philosophical, aesthetic, ideological currents stress harmonization through the expansion and development of consciousness. Indeed, progress itself was conceived as a progressive becoming conscious; as the Russian political economist Alexander Bogdanov wrote, 'Both where people agree in their judgments of progress and where they disagree, the basic meaning of the idea of progress is the same, namely, increasing completeness and harmony of conscious life.'[2] While Hardy identified himself philosophically with such a harmonizing world-view, there is in his writing a conflict between that general, teleological process and an individual, ego-centric process of 'taking thought'. This conflict is a product of the contradiction between his philosophical beliefs, which were themselves a reflex of the ideology of the thinking world, and the ideological view of 'civilization' which was determined by his class of origin. Out of this contradiction are produced those consistent images of separation, a product of Hardy's association of 'taking thought' with the colonizing civilization which progressively destroyed the world of the artisan and the small producer.

Hardy conceived this individual process in terms of the development of a 'false' idealism which he believed to be amongst the most disruptive and damaging tendencies in modern life, the result of the move away from the cohesive community towards the individuation, isolation, separation and self-interest of class society, a separation which takes the form in his writing of a disunity between flesh and spirit. Conceived as a disease of the flesh, taking thought has the effect of paralysing life, rendering the individual incapable of acting consistently or, most importantly, seeing correctly. Walter Pater expressed a similar view when he wrote that modern man had passed beyond the communal ideal of unity with himself, his physical nature and the world to strive for an individual perfection 'that makes the blood turbid, and frets the flesh, and discredits the actual world about us'.[3] Pater goes on to evoke a deeply pessimistic picture of the separateness of individual existence writing that:

> experience, already reduced to a swarm of impressions, is ringed round for each one of us by that thick wall of personality through which no real voice has ever pierced on its way to us, or from us to that which we can only conjecture to be without. Every one of those impressions is the impression of the individual in his isolation, each mind keeping as a solitary prisoner its own dream of the world.[4]

Hardy saw the egoistic phantoms of those isolated dreams as the spectres which haunted society. In his writings the conflict between the subjective world of the idealizing subject who exists 'in a strange state of isolation' and who, with 'the godlike conceit that we may do what we will' lives through the projections of his or her idealism, and the 'commonwealth ... of hearts and hands' in which individuals express themselves in the 'homely zest for doing',[5] appears in the motif of conflicting opposites. Each of the novels develops on the basis of the struggles developing out of this binary opposition: flesh and spirit, Self and class, altruism and self-interest, community and individualism, custom and education, being for others and selfishness, Paganism and Christianity, doing and contemplation, *cameraderie* and idealizing love, work and idleness, to name but some of the most prominent.

Thus we have in Wessex an image of the ground of an orginal unity, but not a final unity. In the myth of origin and the myth of consummation we see the nostalgia for a past unity (represented by the customary life of Hardy's class of origin) and the hope for a future unity of consciousness and being (the social utopia of the liberal intellectuals). But between the beginning and the end, and throwing them into conflict, the 'squalid reality'[6] of the present intervenes in the historical form of the radical separation which interrupts, disturbs and may possibly even terminate the developmental process of becoming conscious.

It would be a mistake, however, to think of Hardy's writing in terms of the elaboration of a philosophy, the expression or representation of his philosophical beliefs, for that would be tantamount to saying that the novels were simply a reflection of Thomas Hardy's consciousness. Rather we should think that one of the determining elements of the ideological structure of Hardy's writing is philosophical idealism which holds that, in Hardy's own words, 'The material is not the real—only the visible ... [but] because we are in a somnambulistic hallucination ... we think the real to be what we see as real.'[7] When applied to the field of aesthetics this ideological formation privileges art as a 'true' mode of perception in which the 'imaginative reason' strips away the veil of appearance so that even if the hidden essence cannot be finally known at least its effect can be perceived. Thus 'pure literature' is itself a way of understanding reality. Scattered throughout *The Life* is a number of observations on art and writing which show that Hardy's own aesthetic project was very much in tune with the idealist aesthetic theories of the time. 'Seeing into the *heart of a thing*', he wrote, 'is realism ... reached by what Matthew Arnold calls "the imaginative reason"' and he defined his own art as the attempt to 'intensify the expression of things ... so that the heart and inner meaning is made vividly visible'. He also wrote of 'abstract realisms' and of the 'true realities of life, hitherto called abstractions' and of wanting to 'see the deeper reality underlying the scenic, the expression of what are sometimes called abstract imaginings'. This was to be achieved in art by 'a changing of the actual proportions of things', and indeed this is what actually defined true art for Hardy, this distortion or 'disproportioning' of apparent reality in order 'to show more clearly the features that matter' *in* reality.'[8]

It is important to understand that the following observations on what I have called the structure of perceptions does not constitute a discovery of Hardy's 'real' meaning. The fact that I have given names to different 'modes of perception' does not mean that they are to be 'found' in Hardy's writing and certainly not that they are to be imposed upon it. These modes of perception are simply conceptual formulations to help us to understand the relation between writing and ideology. The purpose of the concept is not in any way to alter Hardy's writing but on the contrary to leave it intact, not to excavate the novels for their value (by separating the good from the bad) or to complete them (by the addition of their meaning), but to produce an understanding of their conditions of production. The three conflicting modes of perception which form the basis of the structure of perceptions of Hardy's writing I call: (1) the distracted gaze, (2) the idealizing vision, (3) the intuitive insight.

(1) The distracted gaze signifies that 'faulty' vision which takes the apparent (what we see) to be the real (essential reality). This is a form of 'blindness' in which things *are* what they *seem*, and knowledge is merely the awareness of the effect of the myriad, flickering, inconsistent impressions of the world on the individual consciousness and it is most frequently, although not exclusively, attributed to women in Hardy's writing. Christopher Julian expresses this form of seeing most succinctly when he says, 'that's the nature of women—they take the form for the essence'.[9]

(2) The idealizing vision signifies that mode of perception which is a form of self-reflexion, a process of the subjective consciousness whereby the subject projects 'against any suitable object in the line of [his] vision ... something in [his] head',[10] so that the subject lives his or her own dream of the world. This mode of perception is most characteristic of the intellectual male characters, although again not exclusively so. Goethe summed up this self-reflexive vision when he wrote in *Elective Affinities* that 'Man is a true Narcissus; he makes the whole world his mirror.' In this mirror structure the world is perceived as a psychological phenomenon, and the subject only sees in the real object of contemplation a reflection of his own subjectivity. Here knowledge is merely a confirmation of the self's own existence, the purest form of solipsism.

(3) The intuitive insight signifies that way of seeing which is determined by the common material existence of the working community of Wessex, a perception which is not based upon the individual and the subjective but the social. Grounded in the material unity of the world that enters the seer's purview the intuitive insight is non-developmental and knowledge is the 'unconscious' experiential knowledge of the community of labour.

As the structure of perceptions is a theoretical concept which is the product of materialist criticism not Hardy's writing, it is essential to make a distinction between the perceptions produced by the writing's aesthetic project and the knowledge produced by the critical discourse. What I am going to say *about* Hardy's writing cannot be located *in* Hardy's writing. There is, in other words, no *identity* between writing and the knowledge of writing produced by materialist criticism.

Each of Hardy's novels develops on the basis of a conflict between the sights and oversights of the characters who inhabit Wessex, an elaborate network of points of view such as the way Oak sees Bathsheba, what Jude fails to see about Arabella, Mrs Yeobright's insight into Eustacia's character, Pierston's idealization of Avice Caro, Angel's vision of Tess and so on. The aesthetic project guarantees that all these views display a significant failure of sight. It was Hardy's intention that these failures and the imaginary struggles they produce (with which the readers become involved through exercising their own viewpoints) should reveal the possibility of and the real necessity for a mode of perception which is different from those involved in the struggles. But as this necessity is itself ideologically determined, there are certain things which are excluded from the 'sight' of the imaginary solution the writing produces. The most glaring of these determinate absences is the possibility of working-class solidarity and of a viable working-class 'view'. This possibility is excluded from the writing's field of visibility while at the same time it displays innumerable examples of class prejudice, bigotry, injustice and exploitation.

In the following examples I want to show how the concept of the structure of perceptions enables a distinction to be made between Hardy's aesthetic intention which constructs the reader as seer, the ideological problematic upon which that intention is based and the knowledge of Hardy's writing which is not the 'discovery' of materialist criticism but its product. To show, in other words, how a theoretical concept can be used to say something about Hardy's writing which is not simply a repetition of what the writing itself is saying. The first example concerns the aesthetic intention of Hardy's writing.

In *Desperate Remedies* when Cytherea Graye refuses Manston's offer of marriage the rejected suitor retires to contemplate his position. Feeling deeply hurt in his pride and vanity, angry at the effect this refusal would have on his social standing and undecided as to what course of action he should take, he stops to gaze into a rainwater-butt:

> Hundreds of thousands of minute living creatures sported and tumbled in its depth with every contortion that gaiety could suggest; perfectly happy ... and all doomed to die within the twenty-four hours, 'Damn my position! Why shouldn't I be happy through my little day too? Let the parish sneer at my repulses, let it. I'll get her, if I move heaven and earth to do it!'[11]

Manston sees in the teeming, microscopic life of the water-butt a confirmation of the 'naturalness' of his vain and selfish desire for sexual gratification. The intricate mesh of sightings in which both characters and readers have become entangled is resolved in the decision to possess Cytherea at all costs. But from the multiplicity of modes of perception out of which the novel is constructed the reader is offered the possibility of discovering the true perception in so far as the text reveals the conflicting perceptions of the characters to be, each in their different ways, false. From this knowledge Manston is excluded by virtue of his 'blindness' which guarantees that at whatever he looks he will see only the reflection of his desire. In this sense he is a prisoner of his own dream of the world, that projection of his subjective consciousness. But what the blind Manston does not see, the clear sighted reader *may*. Thus conceived reading is a form of *gnosis*, literally a way of seeing, and 'pure literature'—as the 'spirit of all knowledge'—is an expressive discourse through which the reader can discover the presence of the true. In fact Hardy became progressively more bitter about the readers' inability to see the truth in his writing, commenting in a letter to Alfred Noyes in 1920, 'What a fool one must have been to write for such a public!'[12]

But if it is part of the aesthetic intention that the conflict of perceptions should operate in such a way that the reader may see Manston's idealizing vision as a form of blindness, the ideological problematic on which that intention is based itself produces certain absences in the writing. These are ideologically determined and are not the product of Hardy's subjective point of view. Thus it is that 'class vision' always has the status in Hardy's writing of a form of blindness. When Ethelberta Chickerel's 'radical' brother Sol accuses her of being a deserter to her class by marrying a viscount, he shows her his misshapen hand and says: 'If I were drowned or buried, dressed or undressed, in fustian or in broadcloth, folk would look at my hand and say, "that man's a carpenter"'.[13] Alive or dead, thus 'branded with work', Sol is seen by the collective view of society not for what he is 'really' but simply as a working man. Here the unit Self has been metamorphosed, in sight, into a fraction of the unit class. As with the perception of Tess as a 'peasant' this form of vision is a manifestation of the distracted gaze which sees no further than the inessential appearance, taking things to be what they seem, never able to perceive that (in Tess's case) she is 'only a peasant by position, not by nature'.[14] Similarly with old Swancourt's view of Stephen Smith. Swancourt sees Stephen as one man when he believes him to be a member of the aristocratic Fitzmaurice Smiths, but as a totally different man when he finds that he is the son 'of one of my village peasants'. In vain does his daughter plead that he is 'the same man ... the same in every particular'.[15]

If this perception of the 'lower classes' by the 'upper classes' conceals the individual's essential nature, the opposite is equally true. In this reciprocal class vision neither sees the other as they really are. Thus Melbury, with his 'touching faith in members of long-established families as such, irrespective of their personal condition and character',[16] is as blind to Fitzpiers' real nature as Swancourt is to Stephen Smith's. Neither, of course, is the radical worker Sol Chickerel's vision any truer than the rest, blinded as he is by his 'republican passions'.[17] Perhaps the most forceful image of this form of blindness is in *Jude*:

Every day, every hour, as he went in search of labour, he saw them going and coming also, rubbed shoulders with them, heard their voices, marked their movements. The conversation of some of the more thoughtful among them seemed oftentimes, owing to his long and persistent preparation for this place, to be particularly akin to his own thoughts. Yet he was as far from them as if he had been at the antipodes. Of course he was. He was a young workman in a white blouse, and with stone-dust in the creases of his clothes; and in passing him they did not even see him, or hear him, rather saw through him as through a pane of glass at their familiars beyond. Whatever they were to him, he to them was not on the spot at all.[18]

The Christminster students do not 'see' the individual Jude, only the reflection of a fraction of the unit class. This is an 'oversight' which is familiar to black people in predominantly white societies who, as Ralph Ellison's invisible man says, are invisible 'because people refuse to see me.... When they approach me they see only my surroundings, themselves, or figments of their imagination—indeed, everything and anything except me.'[19] Class vision has just this quality of blindness in Hardy's writing.

But what the writing itself 'fails to see', what constitutes the absence of this structure of perceptions, is not something which is left out or ignored, but something which is precisely present in the writing but excluded from the field of visibility by the ideological problematic by which that field is determined. In the last analysis, what Hardy's writing 'cannot see' is its own place and function in the class structure it is at such pains to reveal. While ceaselessly producing images of class conflict it denies the necessity of class struggle by 'revealing' it to be the concealing inessential form which must be stripped away in order that essential reality—the true realities of life—can be revealed and *take its place*. I say what Hardy's writing cannot see rather than what Hardy cannot see because this is not a matter of the writer's conscious intention but rather of the determinations operated by the writing's ideological means of production, especially those 'harmonizing' discourses which attempted to resolve the material contradictions of class society by 'doing away' with classes.[20]

Finally, I want to use the concept of the structure of perceptions to produce an understanding of Hardy's writing which is not simply a reflection of the writing's understanding of itself; to produce a form of statement which is not a reproduction of the writing but the production of its knowledge. What follows will of necessity be limited by the fact of having to take an example out of a body of writing and treat it in isolation. But bearing in mind that it should be reintegrated into the structure of the novel, I have selected a 'scene' on the basis of its relative coherence when standing on its own. It comes from *Under the Greenwood Tree* and prefaces two chapters which are almost entirely composed of a conversation between the members of the Mellstock Quire, the topic of which is the new parson and his plans to replace the Quire members and their musical instruments with a new church organ to be played by Fancy Day. The 'literary' language in which the scene is described stands in marked contrast to the anecdotal language of the musicians. To get the whole sense the passage will have to be quoted in its entirety:

It was the evening of a fine spring day. The descending sun appeared as a nebulous blaze of amber light, its outline being lost in cloudy masses hanging round it like wild locks of hair.

The chief members of Mellstock parish choir were standing in a group in front of Mr Penny's workshop in the lower village. They were all brightly illuminated, and each was backed up by a shadow as long as a steeple; the lowness of the source of light rendering the brims of their hats of no use at all as a protection to the eyes.

Mr Penny's was the last house in that part of the parish, and stood in a hollow by the roadside; so that cart-wheels and horses' legs were about level with the sill of his shop-window. This was low and wide, and was open from morning till evening, Mr Penny himself was invariably seen working inside like a framed portrait of a shoemaker by some modern Moroni. He sat facing the road, with a boot on his knees and the awl in his hand, only looking up for a moment as he stretched out his arms and bent forward at the pull, when his spectacles flashed in the passer's face with a shine of flat whiteness, and then returned again to the boot as usual. Rows of lasts, small and large, stout and slender, covered the wall which formed the background, in the extreme shadow of which a kind of dummy was seen sitting, in the shape of an apprentice with a string tied round his hair (probably to keep it out of his eyes). He smiled at remarks that floated in from without, but was never known to answer them in Mr Penny's presence. Outside the window the upper-leather of a Wellington-boot was usually hung, pegged to a board as if to dry. No sign was over his door; in fact—as with old banks and mercantile houses—advertising in any shape was scorned, and it would have been felt as beneath his dignity to paint up, for the benefit of strangers, the name of an establishment whose trade came solely by connection based on personal respect.

His visitors now came and stood on the outside of his window, sometimes leaning against the sill, sometimes moving a pace or two backwards and forwards in front of it. They talked with deliberate gesticulations to Mr Penny, enthroned in the shadow of the interior.[21]

This 'scene' is paradigmatic containing many of those 'painterly' and 'cinematic' techniques which critics point to as one of the most characteristic aspects of Hardy's style. However, the description of Mr Penny working inside his shop 'like a framed portrait of a shoemaker by some modern Moroni' does not really make us 'see a painting' but rather sets up a mode of perception from which Mr Penny himself is excluded. If we think of this representative passage in terms of the production/consumption process it is clear that the writing both determines a specific mode of consumption, a determinate way of reading, and constructs the reader as a perceiving subject. As an outside observer the reader is placed in a determinate relation to the 'seen' scene, his or her gaze transforming it into an object. In this sight Mr Penny and his shop (and indeed all the workfolk) become objects for consumption.

In terms of the structure of perceptions the presence in the text of a reference to Moroni is not an artistic 'fault', a lapse, a pedantic excrescence on a line of fine writing,[22] it is constitutive. For this reason there is no point in speaking of a failure in Hardy's art when he refers to painting in his portrayal of characters. It is not important to know whether or not Hardy was unable to describe his characters adequately and therefore had to fall back on references to art to help him out, or if he had a cultural 'inferiority complex' and was trying to show off his knowledge of painting in order to impress his readers. What is important is that such references set up a particular relation between perceiver and perceived which has more to do with the problematic of perception than the object or character depicted. In the present case the tension between inside and outside evokes a conflict between two antithetical modes of perception. The complex reality which the writing evokes goes far beyond the simple notion of 'historical change' which is 'symbolized' by Fancy Day's replacing the choir. The relation between the subject and the object of contemplation which the allusion to the relation between the observer and a painting suggests is quite different from the relations between the various members of the choir and their world. The painting-observer relation suggests a subjective mode of perception based on individual consciousness and in so doing the writing produces an image of an ideological mode of appropriating reality. It is the relation between such ideological modes of appropriating reality and writing that materialist criticism is concerned to explore.

In order to break with the concept which aesthetic ideology has imposed on writing, namely that the artistic work is a totality, the creation of its author's consciousness, what follows is intentionally 'fragmented'. This means that while exploring the relations between the aesthetic project of Hardy's writing and its ideological determinants using the concept of the structure of perceptions, I have given no consideration to the historical development of the writing itself. Bearing this is mind, chapter seven is intended both as an exploration of certain 'Moments of Vision' in *A Pair of Blue Eyes, Tess, The Woodlanders, Jude* and *Two on a Tower* and as an exploration of method, of the problems of theoretical criticism itself. Chapter eight continues this exploration but dealing with a single novel namely, *The Return of the Native*. Chapters nine and ten are 'thematic' in that while still working within the concept of the structure of perceptions they do not deal with individual novels in detail but with themes which run throughout Hardy's writing. The first has to do with the perception of women and the second with the 'love' relationship.

I should like, finally, to stress again that the following

chapters are not interpretive. Hardy's writing is treated neither as a container of meaning nor as a puzzle to be solved, but as the production of a *scenario* of the ideological process in which class and gender conflicts appear as conflicts of perception. The contradiction which materialist criticism focuses upon is that between the writing's aesthetic project and its productive capacity, that is, the way in which the writing actually produces an image of the ideological which is quite independent of authorial intention. Were Hardy's writing not determined by a specific aesthetic ideology, namely that the discourses of the imaginative reason could discover, uncover or reveal the true realities of life, then without a doubt, the final form of perception which the writing produces would be different. But the productive capacity of writing is not dependent on the writer's will. There is no identity between what Hardy wanted the reader to 'see' and the image of the ideological produced by Hardy's writing. The function of materialist criticism is not to discover Hardy's meaning but to enable us to read Hardy's writing as the sign of that production. It should be pointed out, however, that this is not the same thing as saying that meaning is produced by the reader. I cannot emphasize too strongly that the concept of production I am using here is not predicated on the idea that either the producer or the consumer of writing is the conscious 'author' of meaning. Whereas the discourses of aesthetic ideology treat writing as a coded message to be deciphered, materialist criticism treats it as an object of knowledge and seeks to elaborate the conditions of its production.

Moments of Vision

In *Tess of the d'Urbervilles* the structure of perceptions is deployed in the construction of two major *scenarios*. The first and more general is that of the repression and displacement of the customary and experiential relationships in which the inhabitants of Wessex stand to their world; the second and more specific is that of the contrasting ways in which Tess herself is exploited and subjected by the distracted gaze and the idealizing vision.

In chapter two Hardy *places* Tess in her natural environment, that 'engirdled and secluded region', the Vale of Blackmoor. Here we first see her engaged in celebrating the 'local Cerealia ... a gay survival from Old Style days, when cheerfulness and May-time were synonymous—days before the habit of taking long views had reduced emotions to a monotonous average'. Among the onlookers of this Pagan festival were the Clare brothers, 'the regulation curate', the 'normal undergraduate', and the 'desultory tentative student of something and everything'. Unlike his brothers who think it beneath their dignity to be seen dancing in public with a troop of country hoydens, Angel takes a partner. Significantly he does not dance with Tess because he fails to see her, and he senses afterwards 'that she was hurt by his oversight'. It is a significant oversight because throughout the novel Hardy makes a point of emphasising Tess's profoundly physical presence. He writes of her 'exceptional physical nature',[1] her 'luxuriance of aspect', her 'fulness of growth',[2] and her 'bouncing handsome womanliness'[3]. Indeed, despite the constraints of Victorian censorship, Hardy conveys a powerful sense of Tess's sexuality as well as her sexual attractiveness. But what Angel's idealizing vision fails to see is immediately apparent to the distracted gaze of Alec d'Urberville.

From the outset Tess's spontaneous relationship to her world takes a non-Christian form of expression. She reacts with horror to the biblical texts which the itinerant painter daubs on the walls and stile-boards about the village of Marlott. This 'hideous defacement—the last grotesque phase of a creed which had served mankind well in its time', she finds 'horrible ... crushing! killing!'[4] After her 'fall' she becomes terrified by the 'cloud of moral hobgoblins' which these accusatory texts create in her imagination. But Hardy stresses that it was they that were 'out of harmony with the actual world, not she.... She had been made to break an accepted social law, but no law known to the environment in which she fancied herself such an anomaly'. Accredited dogma forces an 'unnatural' perception upon Tess in which she 'looked upon herself as a figure of Guilt intruding into haunts of Innocence'.[5] This stands in stark contrast to the 'natural', spontaneous and harmonious relationship which is evoked when this 'daughter of Nature' comes to the Valley of the Great Dairies 'in which milk and butter grew to rankness'.[6] Here Tess manifests that 'invincible instinct towards self-delight',[7] the 'irresistible, universal, automatic tendency to find sweet pleasure somewhere, which pervades all life'.[8] Angel has a fleeting glimpse of this when he looks at Tess and seems 'to discern in her something that was familiar, something which carried him back into a joyous and unforseeing past, before the necessity of taking thought had made the heavens gray'.[9] This moment of vision reawakens in him memories which have long been repressed. Tess's spontaneous relation to her world is associated with the pagan, the flesh, with the customary and experiential forms of the native inhabitants of Wessex and 'the old-fashioned revelling in the general situation'.[10] On the other hand, confronting that relationship, stands the Wilhelm Meister intellectual. Here the associations are with the disease of flesh, with the spirit, Christianity, the ache of modernism, the modern vice of unrest, and with consciousness. Like all Hardy's intellectuals Angel floats about uneasily, restlessly, peculiarly unattached, seeking some ideological structure in which to live. It is not, of course, that the intellectuals live 'outside' ideology but that in abandoning that 'creed which had served mankind well in its time', they are deprived of a potent and effective ideological structure in which to inscribe their fundamentally religious 'ideas'. These ideas are manifested in a variety of idealizing visions. Thus when thinking about those 'feelings which might almost have been called those of the age—the ache of modernism', Angel reflects that what are called 'advanced ideas are really in great part but the latest fashion in definition ... of sensations which men and women have vaguely grasped for centuries'.[11] Whatever the apparent form of the individual subject's idealism, we notice that whenever the conflicts in which the intellecutals are involved reach a crisis and they must *act* according to their ideas, those actions are almost invariably determined by the religious ideology upon which, in the end, their ideas depend.

When Tess is drawn into the wild and overgrown garden by the sound of Angel's harp-playing[12] we have a sense of her profoundly physical intimacy with the natural environment. I have already mentioned the way Hardy suggests Tess's sexual presence, a presence which had to be fudged for the sake of the censor, hence the misty ambiguities about the incident in the Chase and the incongruity of the protestations of this country girl who did not know about Alec's intentions because she had not read novels! Nevertheless, as far as Tess (and Hardy) is concerned the only thing wrong with her relationship with Alec is that she does not love him. Tess, Hardy writes, was 'temporarily blinded by his ardent manners, had been stirred to confused surrender awhile: had suddenly despised and disliked him, and had run away. That was all.'[13] Tess's sexual relationship (but not the manner of its commencement) was, in this sense, 'natural'. The harm comes from the ideological equation of sexuality with ownership. The idea of a women 'belonging' to the man who first 'possesses' her—which is the way Angel sees it—depends upon the ambiguity of the word possession. Tess 'belongs' to Alec because he 'took' her in the Chase and 'made her his' (we can see here how the language of romantic love reproduces the possessive individualism of male sexist ideology); thus Tess is bound to him by powerful ideological fetters as later Sue is to Phillotson. In this sense Tess really has nothing to lose but her chains and her slaughter of Alec could be read as a throwing off of shackles little short of revolutionary. But the repression of Tess exercised by Alec's view of her as a sexual object is different from that exercised over her by Angel.

From the moment of the meeting in the garden the harmonious relations between Tess and her world begin to be repressed and displaced by certain abstractions mediated by Angel's idealizing vision. She is transformed in Angel's sight: 'She was no longer the milkmaid, but a visionary essence of woman—a whole sex condensed into one typical form.' He calls her Artemis, Demeter and 'other fanciful names'.[14] Angel's idealization has a profound effect upon Tess for she is treated according to how she is perceived and she is subjected by Angel's idealizing vision in a way which is totally different from the way she is expoited by Alec's distracted gaze. Perceived by Alec as a sexual object she is treated accordingly, but her seduction and subsequent pregnancy is represented as merely a 'passing corporeal blight' from which she emerges intact. In this part of her story (that of the pretty maid seduced by the squire, retold in ballad and popular song and here in the novel which alludes to those popular and superseded forms) we see the ideological reflex of those 'feudal' social relations where individuals enter into relation with one another as individuals imprisoned within a certain definition (landlord and 'peasant', squire and milk-maid) which appears as a personal restriction of one individual by another.[15] The relationship between Tess and Angel is different because whereas Alec appeared quite definitely as a man to Tess, Angel appears as an intelligence.[16] The material, physical relationship is replaced by a spiritual, idealized relationship. Here Tess is no longer subjected by the relations of personal dependence but rather by certain abstractions, that is not by the new conditions of existence themselves, but by the ideological reflex of new material conditions, by the 'reign of ideas' which was the peculiarity of this new age. But these abstractions are nothing more than the ideological expression of 'the material relations which are their lord and master', the belief in the permanence of which is 'consolidated, nourished and inculcated by the ruling classes by all means available'.[17] This transforma-tion is not directly reflected in Hardy's writing, rather it evokes the contradictions of the history of the radical separation through the conflicting ways Tess is perceived and consequently treated, ways which reflect different modes of ideological sub-jection.

It is àt Talbothays that the transition take place. In the

dairy farm we have an image of the relations of contradiction between two modes of production. In the working and social relations of the farm we have an image of the productive relations of the patriarchal industries of the yeoman or small producer, and at the same time those of the small capitalist farmer who produces commodities for sale in the large urban centres.Until this point the productive relations of Tess and her family were entirely those of the independent small producer in which the different kinds of their labour were direct social functions, functions of the Durbeyfield family. After Tess leaves Talbothays those relations are transformed. Thereafter the Durbeyfields have the status of propertyless wage labourers with nothing to sell but their labour power. By the time Tess reaches Flintcomb-Ash the radical separation has occurred. It is, however, Talbothays which is the site of that transformation, it is there that the radical break takes place.

Writing of this separation from a certain position, Hardy gives us an image of these superseded relations as 'idyllic'. To stress that this world was as yet unsullied by an alien and false idealism Hardy emphasizes the 'physical' nature of these relations in the 'oozing fatness and warm ferments of the Froom Vale'.[18] The associations here are with the communal, the customary, with physical labour, natural instinct, sexuality and with the essential paganism which lay concealed beneath this apparently Christian community where Sunday is a 'Sun's-day, when flesh went forth to coquet with flesh while hypocritically affecting business with spiritual things'.[19] All this is put in jeopardy by the 'spiritual' abstractions of 'the smear of "civilization"'.[20]

In so far as the aesthetic project of Hardy's writing is to enable the reader to perceive the real, *Tess* is structured upon a series of contradictory perceptions in the conflict between which those abstractions are revealed as inauthentic. The idealizing vision here represents the operation of a 'false' idealism which in Hardy's view had to be replaced by a 'true' idealism, true because it is understood not as a subjective projection but as a mode of perception which sees into the heart and inner meaning of things. Hardy believed that it was in the power of imaginative writing to effect that transformation because it allowed the reader to see, perhaps only catch a glimpse of, the possibility of the existence of that inner truth, that deeper reality. The idealist basis of the aesthetic project is revealed in the desired conjunction of perceptions in which the consciousness of the writer and that of the reader are fused into a single idealist point of view, a uniquely revelationary moment of vision.

Hardy's belief in the possibility of that 'true' perception and his prolonged attack on the 'false' idealism of the idealizing vision resulted in some of the most powerful 'visual' passages in his writing. One such occurs in chapter twenty-two of *A Pair of Blue Eyes* where the unfortunate Henry Knight is accidentally trapped on the slippery surface of the Cliff with no Name and hangs, suspended by his arms, six hundred feet above the sea. Clinging to the cliff face he sees embedded in the rock before his eyes a fossil:

> It was a creature with eyes. The eyes, dead and turned to stone, were even now regarding him. It was one of the early crustaceans called Trilobites. Separated by millions of years in their lives, Knight and this underling seemed to have met in their place of death. It was the single instance within reach of his vision of anything that had ever been alive and had had a body to save, as he himself had now.... His mind found time to take in, by a momentary sweep, the varied scenes that had had their day between this creature's epoch and his own.... Time closed up like a fan before him. He saw himself at one extremity of the years, face to face with the beginning and all the intermediate centuries simultaneously.

Suspended between life and death, Knight comes face to face with Nature. The two extremities of the evolutionary scale between which all natural and human history intervenes gaze into each other's eyes. In a backward rush images of cavemen, 'huge elephantine forms', dinosaurs and 'fishy beings of lower development' pass 'before Knight's inner eye'. The writing produces an image of Nature as a discourse which can be read and as a middle class intellectual who 'knew that his intellect was above the average', 'a pioneer of the thoughts of men', Knight instinctively reads Nature in the evolutionary terms that the 'thinking world had gradually come to adopt'.[21] But this is not to imply that the text which is alluded to here constitutes the meaning of the writing. This is not a reflection, representation or reproduction of the scientific text which enables us simply to read in the novel what we could elsewhere. The reality of *A Pair of Blue Eyes* does not reside in *On the Origin of Species*. Those precise 'scientific' words—trilobite, zoophyte, megatherium, myledon, and so on—do not have the same status in the novel as they would in a scientific discourse. Here they do not appear as concepts or even empirical descriptions but as images 'like the phantoms before the doomed Macbeth', images which indicate a certain determinate relationship between the seer and the seen. For if Knight can read Nature as a discourse, he is also the object of that discourse.

As the culmination of the evolutionary process, seeing himself 'at one extremity of the years, face to face with the beginning and all the intermediate centuries simultaneously', Knight, spreadeagled on the cliff in a sort of bizarre crucifixion, appears as the *observed spectator* 'in his ambiguous position as an object of knowledge and as a subject that knows'.[22] By showing the contemplation of those images of ascent from staring trilobite through all the intermediary stages culminating in contemporary man as a vision which relates the entire field of the visible to one corporeal gaze, the writing produces an image of the sovereignty of the subject and of the ideological reading of history which makes human consciousness the subject of all human development and action.

But this allusive passage is one of the terms of a relationship of contradiction which is immediately followed by a completely different perceptual reading of Nature. To the workfolk, Hardy writes:

> ... Nature seems to have moods in other than a poetical sense: predilections for certain deeds at certain times, without any apparent law to govern or season to account for them. She is read as a person with a curious temper; as one who does not scatter kindness and cruelties alternately, impartially, and in order, but heartless severities or overwhelming generosities in lawless caprice....
>
> Such a way of thinking had been absurd to Knight, but he began to adopt it now.

The rational terms of science are replaced here by images of torture. Knight is 'spitted' on the rock. 'New tortures followed', persecuting him with an 'exceptional persistency'. The rain sticks into his flesh 'like cold needles', shafts which pierce him with a 'torturing effect'. It is a vision of Nature as force personified; it is like the absolute and capriciously exercised power of the fuedal aristocrat or the Wessex Landowner such as Mrs Charmond or Alec d'Urberville. Now in one of her rages she puts her hapless victim to the torment. Here is no reason and no law, simply the exercise of repressive power. This is not the intellectual perception of the thinking world, but the experiential perception of the toiling world. Knight is literally forced to feel Nature as an 'agency, active, lashing', not merely to think about it, and the ensuing perception is determined not by consciousness but experience. And when Knight experiences Nature, even for those few brief moments, in the way that the workfolk are forced to throughout their lives (we are reminded here of the farm workers' experiences at Flintcomb-Ash in chapter forty-three of *Tess*), he begins to see with their eyes and adopts that collective way of seeing which had seemed absurd to him in the sheltered isolation of his middle-class existence. But this is not the end of the matter, for Knight is to have one further vision.

As the rational/intellectual perception had been succeeded by the feeling/sensational, so that in its turn is succeeded by the subjective/emotional. The blue sea appears 'distinctly black to his vision', the foam 'a white border to a black sea—his funeral pall and its edging', and the sun 'a red face looking on with a drunken leer'. So, writes Hardy, 'we colour according to our moods the objects we survey'. In this passage Hardy utilises the pathetic fallacy, he does not fall into it. Essentially the pathetic fallacy is a relationship of sight determined by individual subjectivity and is conceived as a 'falseness' in the individual's perception of the real. It is in effect the antithesis of the insight of the imaginative reason which sees into the heart of a thing because it *imposes* upon the structure of the real an obscuring veil. Through the process of projection the real is 'covered up', hidden still further by the distorting gaze of the idealizing vision. Thus in Knight's successive visions of Nature the three modes of perception are brought into conflict. The irreconcilable historical contradictions of the radical separation are transposed in the writing and appear as a conflictual structure of perceptions.

The contradictions between the moments of vision, however, can be resolved by the writing in so far as the aesthetic project is to produce a 'view' of the truth. In this sense the writing itself functions as a compromise formation.

In the internal development of the book this incident advances the conflict in the love relationships between the three main characters, that complex of sights and oversights in which they are enmeshed. This highly charged scene of near death and sudden rescue provides an outlet for the hitherto repressed feelings Knight and Elfride have for one another. They now dare to see each other in a completely new way:

> At sight of him she leapt to her feet with almost a shriek of joy. Knight's eyes met hers, and with supreme eloquence the glance of each told a long-concealed tale of emotion in that short half-moment.Moved by an impulse neither could resist they ran together and into each other's arms.
>
> At the moment of embracing, Elfride's eyes involuntarily flashed towards the *Puffin* steamboat. It had doubled the point, and was no longer to be seen.

The whole scene produces a realignment of vision, for the tacit declaration of love in that eloquent glance excludes Stephen Smith, Elfride's first love, to whom Knight is friend and mentor. Ironically Stephen is both present at the scene of rescue and absent from it, in sight of the cliff but on board the steamboat in the bay. He is the silent onlooker (as we are the silent witnesses) watching the pair through his telescope as previously they had watched him through theirs. At the moment of embrace Stephen passes from Elfride's sight replaced in her vision by the man she has just rescued. But what the aesthetic project intends the reader to see is first, the hopeless incompatability of the lovers' perceptions of one another based as they are on Elfride's distracted gaze and Knight's idealizing vision, and second the *blindness* of his passionate glance. The aesthetic intention is to reveal the operation of that false idealism which precludes the revelation of the true. Ultimately what this intellectual knight sought was the grail of the ideological guarantee—self recognition, for as he later tells Elfride 'a religion was building itself upon you in my heart. I looked into your eyes, and thought I saw there truth and innocence as pure and perfect as ever embodied by God in the flesh of woman.'[23] In this act of seeing (and it is an *act* and not simply the passive reception of a sensation) we have an image of the ideological process about which Feuerbach wrote:

> Man—this is the mystery of religion—projects his being into objectivity, and then again makes himself an object to this projected image of himself thus converted into a subject; he thinks of himself, is an object to himself, but as the object of an object, of another being than himself.[24]

This false idealism is 'exposed' by the imaginative reason and it is that true moment of vision which the writing is intended to produce. But the writing is not simply the bearer of its aesthetic intention. It is actually productive, not so much of meaning as of images of the ideological. The aesthetic project of this powerful and emotive 'moment of vision' is plain to see. It is a progressive stripping away of the concealing veils which obscure the perception of the truth. From the rational perception of Nature in the description of which 'scientific' images prevail, through the sensational perception dominated by images of pain, to the subjective perception rendered in terms of that 'mental cloud of many-coloured idealities'[25] which prepares the way for the reception of the vision of Elfride, the writing's aesthetic intention is to lay bare for the clear sighted reader the perception that the subjective mode of vision is simply a form of self-reflection, a manifestation of the idealizing vision in which the subject sees in the real only a reflection of his own subjectivity.

But in the conflicts of these contradictory visions the writing produces a powerful image of ideological displacement, a displacement which has its roots not in the consciousness of the writer (and certainly not in that of the reader), but in the historical process of radical separation and in the different ways the relations of that historical process were ideologically 'fought out'. There are, of course, many other instances of such complex structures of conflicting perceptions in Hardy's writing. One which has received much critical attention occurs in *The Woodlanders*.

In this passage Grace Melbury, her father and Giles Winterborne are walking through the woods towards a timber auction.[26] As they traverse the natural scene it unfolds before them and the reader as a series of differences. The image of Nature is here overdetermined by a multiplicity of significations in so far as the 'scene' is composed of a complex of contradictory meanings. Some of these meanings are external to the novel—those which spring from the allusion to other discourses—and some internal—those which relate to the specific imaginary situation of this particular story. Again, the writing produces both a reality effect and a mythopoeic effect, emphasising them alternately, and develops on the basis of this duality. We are able to identify with the characters on the basis of the reality effect in so far as they are like 'real' individuals in a 'real' situation. But we can never lose sight of the fact that this is an imaginary situation because of the complex of significations which this imaginary discourse evokes.

The 'moment' is structured as a multiplicity of perceptions, the first of which is of contradiction and synthesis. The antitheses of the natural cycle, winter and summer, are held for an instant in peculiar coexistence:

> Although the time of bare boughs had now set in there were sheltered hollows amid the Hintock plantations and copses in which a more tardy leave-taking than on windy summits was the rule with the foliage. This caused here and there an apparent mixture of the seasons; so that in some of the dells they passed by holly-berries in full red growing beside oak and hazel whose leaves were as yet not far removed from green, and brambles whose verdure was rich and deep as in the month of August.

To Grace these peculiarities 'were as an old painting restored'; it is to her the revelation of a temporarily lost familiarity, a return to a former mode of perception which has been repressed by her removal from her 'natural' environment.

The second perception operates in the same way as the 'Moroni painting' passage in *Under the Greenwood Tree*, constructing the reader as seer. It is a very 'visual' image of change, of nature's cyclical retrogression from summer's curvaceous baroque to winter's angular primitivism:

> Now could be beheld that change from the handsome to the curious which the features of a wood undergo at the ingress of the winter months. Angles were taking the place of curves,

and reticulations of surfaces—a change constituting a sudden lapse from the ornate to the primitive on Nature's canvas, and comparable to a retrogressive step from the art of an advanced school of painting to that of the Pacific Islander.

This in turn is followed by the simplicity and charm of the pastoral in the image of the harmonious coexistence of the wood-landers and the woodland creatures:

> ... as they threaded their way through these sylvan masses ... it seemed as if the squirrels and birds knew him. One of the former would occasionally run from the path to hide behind the arm of some tree, which the little animal carefully edged round *pari passu* with Melbury and his daughter's movement onward, assuming a mock manner as though he were saying, 'Ho, Ho! you are only a timber-merchant, and carry no gun!'

And a little later on at the auction itself:

> A few flakes of snow descended, at the sight of which a robin, alarmed at these signs of imminent winter, and seeing that no offence was meant by the human invasion, came and perched on the tip of the faggots that were being sold, and looked into the auctioneer's face whilst waiting for some chance crumb from the breadbasket.

As they walk further into the wood there is a sense of fairytale:

> They went noiselessly over mats of starry moss, rustled through interspersed tracts of leaves, skirted trunks with spreading roots whose mossed rinds made them like hands wearing green gloves; elbowed old elms and ashes with great forks, in which stood pools of water that overflowed on rainy days and ran down their stems in green cascades. On older trees still than these huge lobes of fungi grew like lungs.

These are the mysterious woods of Hansel and Gretel, of Snow White, the woods of legend and the imagination of children. This is immediately followed by the famous 'Darwinian' perception:

> Here, as everywhere, the Unfulfilled Intention, which makes life what it is, was as obvious as it could be among the depraved crowds of a city slum. The leaf was deformed, the

curve was crippled, the taper was interrupted; the lichen ate the vigour of the stalk, and the ivy slowly strangled to death the promising sapling.

This in its turn is followed by the mythical:

They dived among beeches under which nothing grew, the younger boughs still retaining their hectic leaves, that rustled in the breeze with a sound almost metallic, like the sheet-iron foliage of the fabled Jarnvid wood.

And finally by the perception of the woods as the inhabitants' natural work-ground, an image of nature as the source of the woodlanders' physical existence:

The character of the woodland now changed. The bases of the smaller trees were nibbled bare by rabbits, and at diverse points heaps of fresh-made chips, and the newly cut stool of a tree, stared white through the undergrowth. There had been a large fall of timber this year, which explained the meaning of some sounds that soon reached him.

Involved also are the perceptions, the sights and oversights, of the subjects. First the characters themselves: Grace's re-seeing of nature from which she had been detached by her father's ambition; then Melbury's non-seeing as he walks 'lost in thought', concentrating on his inner vision; and Winterborne's observation of father and daughter whom he 'followed [keeping] his eye upon the two figures'. Winterborne, like Oak and Venn, is the concerned onlooker, the embodiment of that 'watchful loving-kindness', 'that patient attention' which is not repressive. Significantly, Giles loses sight of Grace and follows on alone. Finally, there are the observing eyes of writer and reader.

There is nothing unique about this passage for there are many such moments throughout Hardy's writing which constitute similar structures of perceptions. What is quite clear about this and similar passages, however, is that they are founded upon a multiplicity of meanings and that there is no informing centre. To designate the perception of the 'Unfulfilled Intention' as the central meaning, as many critics have, is to quite arbitrarily circumscribe the passage in order to reveal its 'totality', its centredness in the name of its *essential* meaning.

Materialist criticism cannot impose on writing such a false unity of meaning. Shadowed by the allusive presence of those other discourses—mythical, pastoral, fabular, philosophical, poetic and scientific—against which the writing is elaborated, its reality is produced from the incompatibility of these readings of Nature, not one or the other of them, but their *difference*. It is in the possibility of that interplay that the writing achieves its reality as a social form, not in its 'reflection' of a reality external to it. But while this passage certainly constitutes a complex of conflictual perceptions of Nature, it occurs in a specific novel which is itself structured upon a number of conflicting perceptions of the specific environment which the perceiving subjects inhabit and of the entire mode of production which that environment supports. By means of these contradictory perceptions the writing evokes the historical contradictions involved in the presence of that mode of production which exists as a survival, and the relationship between it and a mode of production by which it is being superseded. But, in the conflicts between the various modes of perception which the novel elaborates—the distracted gaze, the idealizing vision and the intuitive insight —the writing realizes its aesthetic project by revealing those modes of vision as misperceptions which fail to see the true reality. It is the writing itself which is intended to act as the agent of purification so that the heart and inner meaning of things is made vividly visible to the attentive gaze of the perceiving subject. But the interpellation of the reader as seer also has an ideological effect which, as we shall see later, aesthetic ideology consistently guarantees through the endless succession of subject-centred points of view which are elaborated in the discourses of literary criticism. Hardy's last attempt to remove the scales from the eyes of his readers is in *Jude*. In this novel he tried to force his readers to see by using some of the most violent 'disproportioning' techniques he ever deployed and his failure to achieve his end led him to despair of its possibility.

Jude the Obscure develops on the basis of a conflict between Jude's search for the unity of being and consciousness and those ideological structures which deprive him of that possibility. Through this process of deprivation the novel traces Jude's reduction to the 'naked individual'. Thus his quest for knowledge is reduced to his membership of the Aldbrickham

Artisans' Mutual Improvement Society, one of those self-help institutions set up by the bourgeoisie to incorporate the working class, where working men could 'meet for conversation, business and mental improvement, with the means of recreation and refreshment, free from intoxicating drinks'.[27] So too his passionate yearning for a relationship of loving-kindness, of comradeship, is reduced to the drunken mock marriage with Arabella which kills the spirit of sympathy, friendship and benevolence but reasserts the letter of the law of respectability.

But this image of deprivation is not simply the expression of an inevitable humanism, the revelation of the impossibility of genuine human relationships through the depiction of the accidents, mistakes, fears and errors of a (natural) relationship which is twisted and contorted by 'society', and of which Little Jude is 'the nodal point ... focus, [and] expression in a single term'.[28] Through the structure of perceptions the novel establishes itself in relation to that inevitable humanism, it does not simply reflect it.

Jude's visionary quest is realised not only in the image of the search for the unity of flesh and spirit but also, crucially, in the exploration of language. The novel is strewn with textual references, allusions, quotations, words in dialect, in Latin and Greek, even in Gothic script. There are references to mythology, the classics, philosophy, philology, to history, poetry, the Bible; there are lists of texts and authors. The whole novel is a labyrinth of discourses, a web of languages living and dead, and Jude's self-education takes the form of the progressive mastery of reading in order that he may be equipped to go to Christminster and read there the texts which contain the knowledge he seeks. In Jude's idealizing vision Christminster appears as a place where the 'tree of knowledge grows ... a castle, manned by scholarship and religion'.[29] Significantly the only first-hand account Jude receives of the city is from one of the workfolk who likens it to the Tower of Babel. And when Jude eventually arrives in the city of his dreams it really does appear to him to be full of language. He imagines he hears the various discourses—of the critic, the politician, the historian, the poet, the essayist, the Christian divine—issuing from the porticos, oriels and doorways of the city's venerable buildings. And yet there is something radically wrong. The material substance, the structure in which all these discourses are housed, is crumbling. The colleges appear 'wounded, broken, sloughing off their outer shape' and Jude is impressed by the 'rottenness of these historical documents'.[30] They have an 'extinct air'; 'It seemed impossible that modern thought could house itself in such decrepit and superseded chambers.'[31] The place appears not so much peopled by living speakers as haunted by the ghosts of dead words. The writing evokes a powerful sense of disembodiment. It is as though those discourses themselves have become displaced, have lost their material existence and, having no point of anchorage, haunt this superseded structure which was their erstwhile home.

If we see Jude's quest, as the aesthetic project intends we should, as the search for the harmonious conjunction of being and consciousness, then we are obliged to see that what stands in the way of that realization are the ghosts of those superseded forms which refuse to *recognize* him. Wherever Jude turns he finds himself 'left out', literally unseen. In this blindness we are intended to see the absence of an effective and viable ideological apparatus which would not only recognize Jude, but in which the alliance between religion and complete rationality could take place, and which could provide Jude with the potent myth of unity he seeks. Christminster is the image of that failure. But it is not only this for it has a variety of significations around which the novel weaves a complex structure of contradictory meanings.

In the 'eyes of the world' Christminster is the University, a place of learning and culture. But beneath that 'apparent' reality it is a bastion of privilege where real talent is 'elbowed off the pavement by the millionaires' sons'[32] and where honorary degrees are conferred 'on the Duke of Hamptonshire and a lot more illustrious gents of that sort'.[33] It is the very symbol of the corrupt exclusiveness of a visionless ruling class, a manifestation of the distracted gaze in its collective rather than its individual form. As such the University can only express 'polite surprise ... at the efforts of such as [Jude]'[34] to gain admission. Its doors are closed to the 'very men [it] was intended for', men 'with a passion for learning, but no money, or opportunities, or friends'.[35] But there exists another Christminster, the working town, a place of trades where an artisan, an all-round man like

Jude may still find work. Here the division of labour had not reached the stage of specialization where Jude would have been forced to become a moulding mason, a foliage-sculptor or a statuary. We find in the antagonism between town and gown and the disunity between flesh and spirit it suggests an image of radical separation, and when Jude surveys the university buildings from the cupola of the theatre he sees 'that his destiny lay not with these, but among the manual toilers in the shabby purlieu which he himself occupied, unrecognized as part of the city at all by its visitors and panegyrists, yet without whose denizens the hard readers could not read nor the high thinkers live'.[36] And then, descending to the town, he stands 'in the middle of the city', gazing at its teeming life:

> It had more history than the oldest college in the city. It was literally teeming, stratified, with the shades of human groups, who had met there for tragedy, comedy, farce; real enactments of the intensest kind. At Fourways, men had stood and talked of Napoleon, the loss of America, the execution of King Charles, the burning of the Martyrs, the Crusades, the Norman Conquest, possibly the arrival of Caesar. Here the two sexes had met for loving, hating, coupling, parting; had waited, had suffered, for each other; had triumphed over each other; cursed each other in jealousy, blessed each other in forgiveness.
>
> He began to see that the town life was a book of humanity infinitely more palpitating, varied, and compendious than the gown life. These struggling men and women before him were the reality of Christminster, though they knew little of Christ or Minster. That was one of the humours of things. The floating population of students and teachers, who did know both in a way, were not Christminster in a local sense at all.[37]

In this vision Christminster has the same status as Overcombe Mill and the Great Barn at Weatherby. For an instant Jude sees the *real* Christminster, the unwritten book of humanity which the written discourses embodied in the other Christminster conceal. In those moments of vision Jude sees beyond the inessential appearance and perceives the fleeting presence of the essential reality of Christminster, but it is a perception continually repressed by the false idealism of the idealizing vision.

When Jude, the aspiring servant of God, enters Christminster, he finds in that once inhabited place not the essence but the crumbling and decayed form, the empty shell, the mediaeval husk; the Absolute Spirit is no longer in residence there. But it is just these 'delusive precincts'[38] which Jude's labour and that of all those of the town maintains yet from which they themselves are completely separated. When Sue says that the 'mediaevalism of Christminster must go, be sloughed off, or Christminster itself will have to go'[39] she is referring to the ideological structure which maintains 'the old transcendental ideals ... tricked out and made to masquerade as belief'[40] and which now stand in the way of the evolution of consciousness. What defeats Hardy's characters time and again is their inability to find a suitable ideological structure to replace that from which they have become detached. But it would be a mistake, however, to see this in terms of the 'death of God'. We cannot see the sitution of the questing Hardian character as that of the lonely and isolated individual who, confronted by an 'indifferent' universe and abandoned to the despair of his realization of his God-forsakenness, looks to some Other to fill the void as the central meaning of Hardy's writing. The pursuit of the well-beloved, the projection, the dream, the idealization is an image of an inherent fault in the sight of the perceiving subject, not an index of the absence of God. It is the manifestation of a 'false' idealism which must, in Hardy's view, be replaced by a 'true' idealism if the development towards the harmonious unity of being and consciousness is to proceed.

But the novel cannot be reduced to the *expression* of an ideology, the *reproduction* of an ideal reality; it produces its own object. Through the conflict of the various perceptions of Christminster which the structure of perceptions sets up, and the characters' contradictory relations to it as a place—of work, of ruling-class privilege, of learning; as a symbol of superseded mediaevalism; in the construction of the image of the freezing negative, the letter which killeth, the writing declares the absolute necessity of what it does not say, the ideological hope for the religious triumph of the Idealism of Fancy. The novel reveals this necessity through the very 'pessimism' of its conclusion. But if Jude is beaten, he does not refuse. His last words are those of Job in that story of the ultimate test of the ideological

specular relationship between Subject and subject which concludes with the affirmation:

> I will demand of thee, and declare thou unto me.
> I have heard of thee by the hearing of the ear:
>   but now mine eye seeth thee.[41]

Of that sight Jude himself is deprived. The 'grind of stern reality'
spoils the dream for Jude, but the spirit of his dream will
continue to haunt the place he loved. But 'Art is the secret of
how to *produce* by a false thing the *effect* of a true';[42] Jude's tragic
history reveals, to those who have eyes to see, the presence of the
spirit which inhabits the letter. The clear sighted reader is
meant to see beyond Jude's idealizing vision of the 'gorgeous
city—the fancied place he had likened to the New Jerusalem'[43]
the vision of the hoped-for 'alliance between religion, which
must be retained unless the world is to perish, and complete
rationality, which must come, unless also the world is to
perish'[44]—the truth of the utopian dream of the conjunction of
being and consciousness.

It is, perhaps, not surprising that the single most vivid image
in Hardy's writing of that desired conjunction takes an
architectural form. It is not mere hyperbole to suggest that from
the imaginary top of the structure which plays such a prominent
part in Hardy's ninth published novel, *Two on a Tower*, it is
possible to see the ideological problematic by which the
aesthetic project of Hardy's writing is determined. In the complex relations between the antagonistic points of view which this
novel sustains the writing produces an image of the ideology of
the thinking world as a compromise formation, the 'agnostic
compromise'[45] between materialism and idealism.

The opening of the novel is a classic example of the Hardian
scenario where the writing structures and directs a complex of
sightings to produce the setting of the seen. Author, characters
and reader gaze at the central overdetermined image of the
tower which is both the image of a 'real' object and the sign of a
relationship between a multiplicity of conflicting meanings
which are evoked not only by the image of the tower itself, but
also by the conflicting perceptions of the gazers, in so far as what
is seen is determined by who is seeing. The lady and her servant
drive up to the crest of a hill in Wessex and look out across the
country:

The central feature of the middle distance, as they beheld it, was a circular hill, of not great elevation, which placed itself in strong chromatic contrast with a wide acreage of surrounding arable by being covered with fir trees. The trees were all of one size and age, so that their tips assumed the precise curve of the hill they grew upon. This pine-clad protuberance was yet further marked out from the general landscape by having on its summit a tower in the form of a classical column, which, though partly immersed in the plantation, rose above the tree-tops to a considerable height. Upon this object the eyes of lady and servant were bent.[46]

Close to, the column 'showed itself a much more important erection than it had appeared from the road'. Built 'in the Tuscan order of classic architecture' that 'robust and unadorned' style, 'the simplest and rudest of the five classical orders', the 'pillar rose into the sky a bright and cheerful thing, unimpeded, clean and flushed with the sunlight' an 'aspiring piece of masonry, erected as the most conspicuous and yet ineffaceable reminder of a man that could be thought of'. That the column is intended as a sexual sign is quite clear from the fact that the lonely, idle, bored and unhappily married lady is drawn to the tower in a mood which would have welcomed 'even a misfortune', a phrase which clearly indicates her having accepted the possibility of, even if not the conscious desire for, a sexual encounter. Standing at its base and 'finding that the door was not fastened she pushed it open with her foot and entered'. She climbs to the top and there beholds 'the beautiful youth', Swithin St Cleeve. Swithin, aloft in the tower existing 'in a primitive Eden of unconsciousness'[47], is strongly reminiscent of that other aerial innocent, the welkin-eyed Billy Budd who appeared in the top sails 'as Adam presumably might have been ere the urbane Serpent wriggled himself into his company'.[48] It is, of course, a meeting of opposites. The lady, Viviette Constantine, was 'herself of a totally opposite type. Her hair was black as midnight, her eyes had no less deep a shade, and her complexion showed the richness demanded as a support to these decided features'. There is no need to pursue the implications of this meeting between 'the dark lady' and the fair-haired, sun-worshipping 'simple boy' whose 'sublime innocence of any thought concerning his own

material aspect or that of others' bespeaks his pre-sexual innocence.

This moment of vision· is the first of that multiplicity of
'oppositions' about which the novel is constructed: between the
poor man and the lady—the dependent and the employer, the
page and the *châtelaine*—between the 'impersonal monsters,
namely, immensities' of the universe and the 'human insignifi-
cance' of individual lives;[49] between 'astronomical stupendous-
ness' and 'such ephemeral trivialities as human tragedy'; between the rational and the emotional, the spirit and the flesh;
between Swithin's 'vast romantic endeavours'[50] and Viviette's
sentimentalism; between labour and idleness, the domestic and
the universal; between the 'cruelty of the natural laws' and 'that
charity which "seeketh not her own"' ;[51] between 'loving kindness' and 'lover's love';[52] between will and destiny, isolation and
community; between 'the celestial' and 'the lamentably
human';[53] between the pagan and the Christian, earth and
heaven, personal inclination and duty, selfishness and selfless-
ness.

But it is the tower itself in which the poor man and the lady
meet which signifies the *relationship* of antagonistic interdependence. This column, 'which rose like a shadowy finger pointing to
the upper constellations',[54] is grounded in ancient history, in the
primitive, dark, uncultured earth of Wessex. Grounded in the
material, in the soil of Wessex the tower reaches up to the realm
of the ideal, those 'voids and waste places of the sky ... deep wells
for the human mind to let itself down into'.[55] Body and mind,
flesh and spirit, being and consciousness; the tower brings these
two realms into relationship, it is the sign of their conflictual
connection. But that phallic column is more than the sign of a
relationship for it is itself a point of view, both materially and
ideally. It is a vantage point from the summit of which the
observer's gaze may be directed both downwards to the
minutiae of Wessex life and upwards to the black immensities of
inter-stellar space where 'minds who exert their imaginative
powers ... bury themselves in the depths of that universe'.[56]

The observers are situated by the tower, situated as
perceiving subjects in the field of the visible. In this constitutive
siting of the subjects, the relationship which the tower signifies is
revealed as a relationship of vision, a relationship, furthermore,

which is operative in this novel in three separate but related areas: the universal, the personal and the social, occupied by the themes of Swithin's astronomical endeavours, the love relationship between Viviette and Swithin and the class conflicts inherent in the poor man and the lady theme. But as the philosophical motif of the novel is that of discovery, which takes the form of a search for knowledge, the encounter between the subject's gaze and the field of the visible is decisive. The whole of Swithin's endeavour is determined by the hope of discovering—literally seeing—what is there beyond the immediately visible and in his scanning of the hemisphere the writing constructs an image of that process which takes place between a given subject and a given object, that is, the relationship of sight which underlies the empiricist/idealist concept of knowledge. In this sense it is representative of the problematic which underlies all the sightings in the structure of perceptions in Hardy's writing. Significantly Swithin goes to South Africa to pursue his observations in the southern hemisphere. In this the image of the field of the visible (and thus also of knowledge) as a circle, a closed space, is complete. However, this relationship appears in this novel neither in its purely empirical nor is its purely idealist form, but in the terms of the agnostic compromise between subject and object, entity and existence, thinking and being, the material and the ideal. This contradiction is reflected in those conflicts on the basis of which the novel develops.

Feuerbach's description of Kant's philosophy as 'idealism based on empiricism'[57] can be taken as an exact description of Swithin's 'vast and romantic endeavours'. What Swithin really sees, the objects of his perception, are not the real stars (the things-in-themselves), but merely their appearance, the entity which lies 'behind' that appearance being always beyond his knowledge. But in accepting the appearance the existence of the thing-in-itself is admitted; yet the objects of the senses—what Swithin sees—are, for the mind, only appearances and not the truth. Although the aesthetic project of Hardy's writing is determined precisely by an ideological problematic the function of which is to harmonize conflicting extremes and of which the agnostic compromise is the philosophical form, it ceaselessly produces images of the limitations of that formation. Nowhere is this more apparent than in the 'vacillation' of the intellectuals.

However, the writing is not merely the 'container' of a philosophy. In the novel the philosophical attempt to find a compromise between materialism and idealism appears as a significant image of contradiction, an overdetermined image which activates the ideological. Hardy's writing does not, in consequence, simply reflect pre-existent meanings, it is itself *productive* of meaning. It achieves this through the confrontation of conflicting points of view which involve not only those of the characters, but also those of the writer and the readers. In the ceaseless flow of oppositions and in the revelation of the endless ambiguity of the multiple perceptions of the material and the ideal, the writing produces a coherent imaginary world which is analagous to the real world but does not reflect it. Furthermore, by means of contradictory images the writing evokes the contradictions inherent in the ideological readings of the history of the radical separation which attempt to 'harmonize' the antagonistic relations upon which it is based. Most importantly, by establishing a distance between itself and the ideology from which it emerges and to which it alludes, the writing produces a space in which ideology is established as a visible object. In the revelation of the ambiguity of the agnostic compromise Hardy's own ambiguous and contradictory relation to the history of his time is clearly evident. This ambiguity is determined by the contradiction between the customary and experiential ideological forms of Hardy's class of origin and the ideology of the thinking world, an ambiguity which finally determined the production of that specific, unique and privileged view of history which his writing elaborates.

The Radical Separation and the Conflict of Perceptions

In conceptualizing *The Return of the Native* as a structure of perceptions I suggest that the members of the better informed class (Mrs Yeobright, Thomasin Yeobright, Diggory Venn) and the workfolk in general are representative of the intuitive insight, Damon Wildeve of the distracted gaze and Eustacia Vye of the idealizing vision, and that the novel brings these modes of perception into conflict, a conflict which leads to the deaths of the three major representatives of these disparate 'ways of seeing'. The structure of the novel can be understood as a complex of sights and oversights in which Clym Yeobright plays the role of mediator who attempts a *reconciliation* between the intuitive insight which signifies the 'unconscious', communal, experiential and customary perception of the world which is determined by the material conditions of life of the Egdon community, and the idealizing vision which signifies the conscious, individual, spiritual and idealist perception determined by the 'alien' relations of the encroaching 'civilization'. Although the communal perception is tentatively reasserted at the end in the marriage between Diggory and Thomasin, the main thrust of the novel lies in the destructive conflict between the idealizing vision and the intuitive insight. The 'site' of this conflict is a particular moment in history. What we are confronted by as we gaze into Egdon's grim and solitary old face is the history of the life and labour of the workfolk and the better informed class. Egdon signifies the material unity of their world at its moment of transition. At that historical moment Egdon awaits not change but overthrow:

> ... precisely at this transitional point ... the place became full of watchful intentness.... Every night its Titanic form seemed to await something; but it had waited thus, unmoved, during

so many centuries, through the crises of so many things, that it could only be imagined to await one last crisis—the final over-throw.[1]'

The very ambiguity of Hardy's description of Egdon, the rich suggestiveness of the image, already brings into play a host of possible points of view.

Because the intuitive insight represents the natural, spontan-eous and customary ways the native inhabitants of Wessex per-ceive their world, it is 'taken for granted'; it is implicit in all their actions, habits and modes of thought, although it does allow differences of viewpoint. There is one characteristic of the intuitive insight, however, which is particularly emphasized and that is the altruism of the community of labour—the commonwealth of hearts and hands—suggested by Diggory Venn's selfless regard of the heath and the heathfolk.

In one of his aspects Venn appears to be the heath's eyes, the living embodiment of Egdon's 'watchful intentness'. All Venn's actions, even his occupation of reddleman, are motivated by his love for Thomasin, a love which takes the form (like Gabriel Oak's) of 'watching over'[2] the interests of his loved one and those close to her. Engaged in this constant surveillance, it is his eye, 'which glared so strangely through his stain ... keen as that of a bird of prey',[3] that sees the secrets of the heath. Indeed, at one point he literally becomes the eye of Egdon. Concealing himself beneath the turves that lay strewn about the heath, appearing 'as though he burrowed underground',[4] he becomes invisible to watch the secret meeting between Eustacia and Wildeve. But Venn is associated with the heath not only materially but also mythically. He 'represents' the world of Egdon in a dual form. Hidden beneath the lurid red dye which permeates him, he appears first in the form of an historically superseded survival:

... one of a class rapidly becoming extinct in Wessex, filling at present in the rural world the place which, during the last century, the dodo occupied in the world of animals ... a curious, interesting, and nearly perished link between obsolete forms of life and those which generally prevail.[5]

Secondly, he appears as a kind of mythical demon, a 'Mephis-tophelian visitant' whose ghostly presence was a 'sublimation of all the horrid dreams which had afflicted the juvenile spirit since imagination began'.[6] In this role he attempts to counteract Eustacia's malign influence. This duality is paradigmatic of the way that the 'material' relations between the main protagonists in the novel are mimed by an allusive shadow play of mythical significations. The contending forces appear both on the level of the production of a 'reality effect' and a 'fabular effect'. Characters appear both as 'real persons' with whom we can identify, and imaginary or fabular beings. So Clym appears as the 'Spirit of Egdon', Eustacia as the 'Witch of Egdon', Damon Wildeve as her 'demon lover', and Diggory Venn as a benign and protective genie who watches over the heath's inhabitants. The novel emphasises first one and then another of these dual roles, developing on the basis of this allegorical diversity.

Venn's watch over Thomasin is quite unlike Wildeve's avid vision of Eustacia. Wildeve's perception of Eustacia as a sexual object is a typical manifestation of the distracted gaze, and while Venn can see that Eustacia's 'comeliness is a law with Mr Wildeve',[7] he cannot perceive the true nature of that 'law'. He really cannot see Eustacia as Wildeve sees her: 'There was a certain obscurity in Eustacia's beauty, and Venn's eye was not trained'.[8] This is because the intuitive insight cannot see love as passion. Venn is blind both to the perceptions of the distracted gaze and the idealizing vision. He cannot see that Wildeve, dominated by 'the curse of inflamability', sees Eustacia as the compelling object of his sexuality, or that Eustacia sees Wildeve as 'the single object within her horizon on which dreams might crystallize'.[9] This is not to suggest that the intuitive insight is determined by a lack of imagination or a spurious morality, but rather that it is dependent on that community in which men and women associate in their labours and where love is never the whole but only a part of (and here we might legitimately use Raymond Williams' term) the structure of feelings, and grows up 'in the interstices of a mass of hard prosaic reality'.[10]

If Venn can be regarded as the eyes of the heath intently watching over the various relationships of its inhabitants, a mode of perception which signifies the relationship of intimacy with, and experiential knowledge of the community of labour, Eustacia has the status of an 'onlooker'. She is not part of that world, but detached from it; she regards it from a distance.

Silhouetted against the sky, she gazes at the heath through the captain's telescope. When the object of her 'spying' finally appears she lets 'her joyous eyes rest upon him without speaking, as upon some wondrous thing she had created out of chaos'.[11] She tells Wildeve that she wanted to get a little excitement 'by calling you up and triumphing over you as the Witch of Endor called up Samuel. I determined you should come! I have shown my power'.[12] Thus the Queen of the Night, with her 'pagan eyes, full of nocturnal mysteries',[13] calls up her demon lover to revive the embers of Wildeve's passion. Eustacia appears both as a mythical witch/succubus and, through her longing for 'the abstraction called passionate love more than any particular lover', as the embodiment of philosophical idealism. This idle lady fills up her existence by 'idealizing Wildeve for want of a better object'. We should read 'idealizing' in the strict Berkeleyan sense of Wildeve's existing in Eustacia's sight. Thus not only does Eustacia *haunt* the heath, she also *perceives* it, that is, 'creates' her world through her idealizing vision. As she roams over Egdon, she bears with her the twin symbols of the Kantian subjective *Anschauung,* space and time, 'her grandfather's telescope and her grandmother's hour glass'. But Eustacia is also the 'raw material of a divinity' with the 'passions and instincts which made a model goddess' who could 'look like a Sphinx'. The mythical associations pile up—Athena, Artemis, Hera; Egdon was her Hades, and a 'true Tartarian dignity sat upon her brow'. Then again, she is a figure from romantic literature who had 'mentally walked round love, told the towers thereof, considered its palaces' and who yearned and prayed to be sent a great love 'else I shall die'. Biblical temptress, classical divinity, mythical witch, romantic heroine, perceiving subject. Constituted against those other texts through the allusion to myth, history, philosophy, literature, the Bible, Eustacia's reality is generated out of these contradictory meanings, out of the differences between the various discourses to which Hardy's writing is allusively connected.

But if Eustacia's vision is a projective dream of the world, Clym's vision is an introspective dream. As Eustacia is both queen of the night, a divinity who wilfully creates the objects of her world,[14] and the prisoner of Egdon,[15] so Clym, who feels free on the Egdon he loves, is the enslaved sovereign of the kingdom of his mind. The conflict between these two antithetical modes of perception is inevitable from the outset; both fail to see the other at the commencement of the relationship. Eustacia sees in Clym the lover she had prayed to be sent, he sees in her his help-mate in the fulfilment of his idealist dreams of educating the workfolk. Clym instinctively thinks of a relationship with Eustacia as a *working* relationship, but from such an idea she instantly recoils, fearing precisely that possibility. It is, however, in their perceptions of Egdon, the world in which they live, that their views are most at odds. The relationship between the two develops on the basis of their perceptions and misperceptions of each other and of the world of Wessex. Clym cannot see that Eustacia hates her fellow creatures because she hates what Edgon represents and he, more than anyone, is its product. There is a fatal incompatibility between the 'voluptuous and idle woman' whose desire was 'to be loved to madness' and the spiritual Clym whose love for Eustacia 'was as chaste as that of Petrarch for his Laura'.[16] Yet Clym does not marry Eustacia blindly: 'As his sight grew accustomed to the first blinding halo kindled about him by love and beauty' he perceives that Eustacia 'loved him rather as a visitant from a gay world to which she rightly belonged than as a man with a purpose opposed to that recent past of his which so interested her'. Clym does not idealize Eustacia as Angel does Tess: 'Eustacia was no longer the goddess but the woman to him, a being to fight for, support, help, be maligned for'. Whatever misgivings or fore-bodings he has about his hasty marriage, he knows that he must make a choice, and having chosen he feels himself 'embarked': 'the card was laid, and he determined to abide by the game'.[17] If Clym's marriage to Eustacia appears to be undertaken on the basis of a wager this is not because, as Mrs Yeobright suggests, he is blinded by Eustacia, but because he stakes everything on being able to change Eustacia's perception of the world. But it is a gamble which Clym loses.

Within two months of their marriage Eustacia's vision of Clym is changed utterly. While to the now purblind Clym, Eustacia is the wife of an unambitious man who has not lost the homely zest for doing, to her he is a fallen idol; far from being the Promethean lover her idealizing vision had made of him, he is 'merely' a workman, and seeing him as such she feels degraded.

To escape this degradation she flees Egdon and has her final vision of what she believes to be its malign nature, a vision which is suitably constructed from the discourses of history, myth and religion, a vision of disaster and chaos.[18] Those who live and labour on Egdon perceive it quite differently. When Thomasin goes out into the same raging storm, her perception is totally unlike Eustacia's:

> To her there were not, as to Eustacia, demons in the air, and malice in every bush and bough. The drops which lashed her face were not scorpions, but prosy rain; Egdon in the mass was no monster whatever, but impersonal open ground. Her fears of the place were rational, her dislikes of its worst moods reasonable. At this time it was in her view a windy, wet place, in which a person might experience much discomfort, lose the path without care, and possibly catch cold.[19]

It is this perception which is finally reasserted. Unlike Eustacia, Thomasin does not get lost on the heath because of 'her general knowledge of the contours, which was scarcely surpassed by Clym's or by that of the heath-croppers themselves'. It is that experiential knowledge of their material world which is manifested in the intuitive insight that the natives of the heath embody. Unlike Eustacia they see Egdon as a work place. As they bend to their work what they see in Egdon's grim old face is something which is 'neither ghastly, hateful, nor ugly; neither commonplace, unmeaning nor tame', but like themselves, 'slighted and enduring'.[20]

The idealizing vision condemns Eustacia to living in her own dream of the world. To her Egdon is a prison because she sees in it nothing but the reflection of her own subjectivity. Even her desperate search for love is nothing but the self-reflexive quest for the conformation of her own being. She is blind to the realities of the world in which she lives because no matter upon what object her gaze falls, she sees only the reflection of herself, or nothing at all, an incomprehensible blankness. Eustacia believed that by escaping from Egdon she would be free. She cannot see what the clear sighted reader may—that it is not the place which imprisons her, but her vision of it. It is not in the object of contemplation that the fault lies, but in the sight of the perceiving subject. If the writing achieves this perception in the reader then the aesthetic project is realized.

When Clym returns to Edgon his perception has been radically transformed. He now 'lives' in another 'world', and yet his one desire is to return to the world of his origin and take up his existence there. But these two 'worlds' are not just incompatible: there exists a deadly animosity between them like that between Egdon and 'civilization'.

One of the better informed class, Clym, the bright yeoman, was seen as something of a prodigy by the people of Egdon. Much had been expected of him and the heathfolk saw it as only right and proper that he should 'get on' in the world. But on his return from Paris with his head full of vague, messianic, Saint-Simonian ideas based on the antagonism between workers and idlers, he fails to see what is as plain as a pikestaff to the workfolk; to dream of educating them in the 'humaner letters' before solving the problem of their poverty was absurd. Clym loves Egdon and he loves its people; it is just that he no longer sees them, but gazes past them, beyond them to that utopian vision of a conflict-free altruistic world of universal consciousness. Clym becomes the focus of conflict between these two worlds, a conflict which is developed through a complex structure of contradictions.

There is that between the intellectual work Clym wished to do and the physical work he is forced to do; between his sweeping intellectual vision and his myopic physical sight in which 'his whole world [is] limited to a circuit of a few feet from his person'.[21] Starting out determined to teach ennoblement, he ends by preaching repentance; while physically identified with the heath—that 'obscure, obsolete, superseded country'[22]—he is 'mentally ... in a provincial future'[23]. While on the one hand 'indulging in a barbarous satisfaction'[24] at the heath's resistance to cultivation, Clym returns to 'cultivate' its people, attempts to change the heath intellectually as the farmers had done physically. Wanting, on his return, to raise the class at the expense of the individual by educating the workfolk, he then decides to establish a good school for farmers' sons and although longing for a world free from ambition, he dreams of becoming 'the head of one of the best schools in the country';[25] determined on keeping alive the 'three antagonistic growths ... his mother's trust in him, his plan for becoming a teacher, and Eustacia's happiness',[26] he succeeds only in destroying all three. The conflicting demands of Clym's love for his mother, his love for his kind and his love for Eustacia force him to act in progressively more contradictory ways.

These contradictions are inherent in the various relationships between the heath and its observers, for Egdon is not only the 'place' where the workfolk and the better informed class live and work, it is also an object of contemplation in which the observing subjects see themselves reflected. Egdon thus signifies both the material and ideological world of the characters who inhabit it, and the novel proceeds on the basis of a number of conflicting 'readings' of that world. However, the conflicts and contradictions of that world are 'embodied' in Clym. The real contradictions in the history of the radical separation are transformed in Hardy's writing into the imaginary conflicts between unity and disharmony in the life of Clym Yeobright himself. In this sense Clym is representative of the world he inhabits both materially and ideologically, for not only is he its 'spirit' but also its 'product'. The material relation is one of almost complete identity for 'Clym had been so inwoven with the heath in his boyhood that hardly anybody could look upon it without thinking of him'; Egdon 'permeates' Clym 'with its scenes, with its substance, and with its odours. He might be said to be its product.'[27] This identity between the man and his world signifies the unity and harmony of the working and customary relations of the community of labour. But this original unity is disrupted on Clym's return.

In the fifth chapter of the second book titled 'The Two Stand Face to Face', Hardy deploys another of those painting analogies which structures the relationship between subject and object as a relationship of sight. Clym is leaning against the dark wood of a settle against which his face shines out in Rembrandt-like chiaroscuro so that the 'observer's eye was only aware of his face'.[28] In the ensuing description of Clym's face the reader is 'constructed' as seer. The aesthetic intention, however, is not that the reader sees a 'picture', but the very act in which he or she is engaged—reading the text—as an act of sight and to see/read in the transparency of that well-shaped face 'the typical countenance of the future'.[29] In Sir Edward Dyer's line, 'My Mind to me a Kingdom is', with which Hardy prefaces the passage describing Clym's intellectual physiognomy, we have a poetic image of the self-centredness of rationalistic thought which finds its most cogent expression in the Cartesian *cogito*: *I* think, therefore *I* am. The emphasis on self and mind evokes the profound subjectivism of the 'false' idealism of taking thought which is in direct contradiction both to the social and communal mode of life of the community of labour and to the altruistic ideals inherent in the concept of the general process of becoming conscious. This is why the legible meaning by which Clym's countenance is overlaid bespeaks a disharmony, a conflict:

> The face was well shaped, even excellently. But the mind within was beginning to use it as a mere waste tablet whereon to trace its idiosyncrasies as they developed themselves. The beauty here visible would in no long time be ruthlessly overrun by its parasite, thought ... an inner strenuousness was preying on an outer symmetry.... Hence people who began by beholding him ended by perusing him. His countenance was overlaid with legible meanings.... He already showed that thought is a disease of flesh, and indirectly bore evidence [of] the mutually destructive interdependence of spirit and flesh.[30]

The conflict inscribed in this sighting is that between beauty and thought, flesh and spirit. What it had once been possible to see in the expressive totality of Beauty, namely the pagan or (in Pater's words) 'Hellenic ideal in which man [was] at unity with himself, with his physical nature, with the outward world', the 'old-fashioned revelling in the general situation',[31] is here no longer visible. What we see on that face are the marks or symbols of a radical separation. The readers of this discourse are meant to see in Clym an image of the end of a specific history, a finality which becomes fully visible in the face of this man who is the spirit and product of Egdon which he, as the last of the yeomen, embodies in his tangible existence. The text obliges us to see not only the final overthrow of that structure of unity which Hardy believed his class represented but also, in the futurity which Clym's face foreshadows, the disharmony of taking thought, that disease of civilization which disrupts the unity of the commonwealth of hearts and hands and subverts the future unity of being and consciousness. As Wessex is the 'site' of this conflict, so in this specific case Clym is its 'embodiment'.

Certain historical, geographical and ideological realities were all contributory elements in the production of *The Return of the Native* but the writing is not a fictive image of these realities. The novel is not a reflection of the history or a representation of an ideology. It is produced out of conflicting ideological perceptions and itself produces a *scenario* of the way people become conscious of the conflicts between the forces and relations of production and fight them out. But, determined as it is by an idealist aesthetic, the conflicts appear not as conflicting relations between individuals, but as conflicts between individual subjects' conflicting perceptions, those contradictory acts of sight. What materialist criticism enables us to see is that point of view, is the idealized expression in its aesthetic form of the ideology of the thinking world.

The Appearance of Women and the Construction of Woman

There is no other writing in English which elaborates a more profound contemplation of women than Hardy's. In every novel women are minutely observed and their actions, appearance, motives, views, desires, hopes and fears are ceaselessly reflected on by the author, an onlooking character, the woman herself, or by another text, usually literary or biblical, and always by the reader, in a complex structure of perceptions. Through these innumerable observations Hardy's writing puts the ideological construction of 'Woman' into contradiction by showing that the perception of women's 'essential nature' is always conditional upon who is doing the seeing. Again this is not a matter of the writer's conscious intention. In the structure of perceptions produced by the writing the writer's own views have no primacy. It is not important to know what Hardy's views on women 'really' were by attempting to deduce them from the evidence of his comments in the novels. At times he writes with great sympathy about the subjection of women, at others his comments appear to us now to display the typical male attitudes of his time which would certainly be called sex blind and perhaps sexist. In this respect his writing reflects the contradictions of its moment of production. What constitutes the absence of the structure of perceptions here is the construction of Woman as a mystery. Whereas male characters, blind, vain, selfish, class-biased, foolish though they may be are seen as individual men, female characters, whatever their situation, contemplated as *women*, are mysterious beings, unfathomable, contradictory, illogical and finally unknowable Others. However, the revelation of the essential Woman in discrete individual women always takes place in the context of specific imaginary conflicts in which the ideological is *activated* so that between the subject's action and the perception of that action a relation of contradiction is revealed.

For example, in the structure of perceptions it is taken for granted that women's sight is determined in the main by the distracted gaze, their tendency to take the appearance for the essence expressed by Christopher Julian in relation to Ethelberta—'That's the nature of women—they take the form for the essence.' This perception appears in *The Mayor of Casterbridge* as an authorial observation when Lucetta Templeman refuses to notice the impoverished Henchard because he appeared 'far from attractive to a woman's eye, ruled as that is so largely by the superfices of things'.[1] Similarly when Giles Winterborne meets Grace Melbury on her return from school she is perceived as manifesting the same 'weakness' and Giles wryly observes to himself that 'external phenomena' such as clothes or appearance 'may have great influence upon feminine opinion of a man's worth, so frequently founded on non-essentials'[2]. Through the observations of author and characters we are clearly given to understand that women perceive the real as the apparent through the operation of the distracted gaze so that a woman's knowledge of people or the world appears to be merely the awareness of the effects of the impressions made by the things she looks at.

But these observations are made in the context of women who have been, in one way or another, socially displaced and in different ways artificially transformed into 'ladies'. They are all in a sense acting a part and, most importantly, because of the role they have assumed—or been forced to assume—are perceived in different ways. The servant's daughter, Ethelberta Chickerel, is about to marry Lord Mountclere 'to benefit her brothers and and sisters';[3] the once poor Lucetta Templeman has just been elevated, as the attractive consort of Donald Farfrae, to the position of first lady of Casterbridge; Grace Melbury has just returned from finishing school where she has been transformed from wood merchant's daughter to a 'finished lady'. Clearly every female character is different and each performs a different role in the novel in which she appears and in which she achieves her reality as a 'living' character in the imaginary struggles in which she (and we) becomes involved. Thus the 'tragic' consequences of Grace Melbury becoming a 'lady' bear no resemblance to the 'comic' consequences of Ethelberta Chickerel becoming Lady Mountclere. Ethelberta 'gets her own back on men' at the end of *The Hand of Ethelberta* in the parodic reversal in which the butler's daughter rules the estate and the peer of the realm is relegated to the level of badgered servant. Yet this 'comedy in chapters' does not differ significantly in its visual structure from Hardy's other novels. In her guise of a lady Ethelberta is as subjected in the sight of her suitors as any other of Hardy's women who are subjected in the sight of men to the images those men have of them. Ideologically constituted as 'ladies' the roles they are expected to play are determined by forms of behaviour, attitudes and modes of perception which are not naturally their own. Deprived of real work, condemned to exist in the masculine gaze as the idle adornments of the male ego, they are confirmed in their roles of inferiority and superficiality. Subjected subjects, they all, as *individuals,* go into hiding, becoming like Grace Melbury the embodiment of the collective image men have of them:

> ... there never probably lived a person who was in herself more completely a *reductio ad absurdum* of attempts to appraise a woman, even externally, by items of face and figure ... there can be hardly anything less connected with a woman's personality than drapery which she has neither designed, manufactured, cut, sewed, nor even seen, except by a glance of approval when told that such and such a shape and colour must be had because it has been decided by others as imperative at that particular time.
>
> What people therefore saw of her in a cursory view was very little; in truth, mainly something that was not she. The woman herself was a conjectural creature who had little to do with the outlines presented to Sherton eyes; a shape in the gloom, whose true quality could only be approximated by putting together a movement now and a glance then, in that patient attention which nothing but watchful loving-kindness ever troubles to give.[4]

The structure of perceptions both establishes the alter-ideology of women as the *sexus sequior* as a visible relationship and puts it in contradiction. In showing how a woman's vision is conditioned by the way she is seen, by the way she exists in the masculine gaze, and how in conforming to that vision of herself she becomes obscured, a shape in the gloom, her 'essential weakness' is revealed as a structural condition of the way in which she is interpellated as a subject by the dominant sexist ideology. Appearing to the sight of others as 'something that was not she', she eventually comes to see what she is, what she does and everything she herself sees in terms of that appearance.

Another characteristic of essential Otherness is inconsistency, whim, capriciousness. Hardy structured an entire novel (*A Laodicean*) on this aspect of the 'essential feminine', but it is a perceived characteristic of nearly all his major female characters both as regards intellect—that 'illimitable caprice of a woman's mind'[5]—and as regards the emotions where, as with Bathsheba Everdene, 'feeling was always to some extent dependent upon whim, as is the case with so many other women'.[6] In so far as those 'narrow womanly humours on impulse' are 'necessary to give her sex'[7] and as a woman acts 'according to the rule of women's whims'[8], a determinate difference is postulated between men and women—men tend to act rationally, women irrationally and on impulse although they cannot help it (it being a condition of their natures) and the source of their irrationality is, *ipso facto*, not open to rational understanding. Indeed, it usually appears that a woman's actions take the form of *reactions* to external circumstances, so that 'Women are always carried about like corks upon the waves of masculine desires.'[9] Hardy elaborates this 'essential' difference in terms of a conflict between emotion and intellect, so that while women are not, of course, bereft of intellect, their 'understanding' is always being suppressed by their 'womanliness'.[10] Perceived as the intellect's Other, women pose a constant threat to the development of consciousness; the male stands helpless before the arouser of his 'passions'. Although there is no novel in which this is not articulated in one form or another the letter of advice Swithin St Cleeve's uncle sends the aspiring astronomer is paradigmatic:

> If your studies are to be worth anything, believe me, they must be carried on without the help of a woman. Avoid her, and every one of the sex.... An experienced woman waking a young man's passions just at the moment when he is endeavouring to shine intellectually, is doing little else than

committing a crime ... [for she] too frequently enervates his
purpose, till he abandons the most promising course ever conceived.[11]

Leaving aside the question of women's implicit culpability in
stimulating the man's sexuality and thus standing between him
and his 'well-formed schemes',[12] this passage is exemplary in its
revelation of the prevalent perception of women as men's
intellectual inferiors. As such they are seen as the passive
recipients of men's ideas. As Alec d'Urberville says to Tess,
'Whatever your dear husband believed you accept, and whatever he rejected you reject, without the least inquiry or reason-
ing on your own part. That's just like you women. Your mind is
enslaved to his.'[13]

This appears to be the case even with the most intellectual of
Hardy's women, Sue Bridehead, whose ideas are simply the
reflection of those of the undergraduate with whom she had a
platonic relationship and all the male authors she had read;
significantly she can only think her 'freedom' in J. S. Mill's
terms. Indeed, Sue is the most powerful image in Hardy's
writing of the way in which women are determined by the
masculine gaze, a determination which is manifested in the
strongly epicene quality of her character, appearance and 'presence'. This is particularly strong in chapter four of 'At Mel-
chester' which opens with Jude's landlady mistaking her for a
'young gentleman' and closes with her sleeping in the chair
looking 'boyish as a young Ganymede'. Sue's 'understanding' is
constantly being repressed by her 'womanliness' and in the
aftermath of Little Jude's terrible act it finally asserts itself in her
'irrationality'. Jude's question, 'Is woman a thinking unit at all,
or a fraction always wanting an integer?'[14] is left open as possibly
impossible of answer. What is even stranger is that women
cannot develop intellectually for there is a 'strange difference of
sex' which determines that 'time and circumstance, which en-
large the views of most men, narrow the views of women almost
invariably.'[15] Thus Sue's 'decline' is inevitable, mirroring that
of Mrs Somers in *The Well-Beloved* who

> once the intellectual, emancipated Mrs Pine-Avon—had now
> retrograded to the petty and timid mental position of her
> mothér and grandmother.... She was another illustration of

the rule that succeeding generations of women are seldom marked by cumulative progress, their advance as girls being lost in their recession as matrons; so that they move up and down the stream of intellectual development like flotsam in a tidal estuary. And this perhaps not by reason of their faults as individuals, but of their misfortune as child-bearers.[16]

In the elaboration of the conflict between 'womanliness' and 'understanding' we see how Hardy's writing is constituted in relation to the ideology of woman as the inferior sex, an inferiority which is ideologically validated as a 'natural' difference between the sexes. As von Hartmann put it, 'the teleological design of nature' determines 'that one sex is *instinctively active* and the other *instinctively passive*'.[17] But again I must stress that the writing does not simply express this ideology but puts it into contradiction because the perceptions of women's passivity is always accompanied by a 'shadow' image of their subjective captivity.

Women live their subjection in ideology through the roles which have been assigned to them as the Other. Captured by the masculine gaze, interpellated as subjects, subjected to the myth of being the weaker sex and recognizing themselves in that image, they behave accordingly. Sometimes they appear to behave, as though in expiation of their innate guilt of being women, 'perversely' and even masochistically, as they 'court their own discomfiture by love'[18] like Eustacia, or like Grace Melbury who took 'her scourgings to their exquisite extremity',[19] or Sue who acts 'for the odd and mournful luxury of practising long-suffering in her own person'.[20] It is, of course, Sue who takes this expiation to its most extraordinary extremes, yet this 'self-immolating' tendency exists already in Hardy's first heroine, Cytherea Graye, about whom the author comments:

> Perhaps the moral compensation for all a woman's petty cleverness under thriving conditions is the real nobility that lies in her extreme foolishness at these other times; her sheer inability to be simply just, her exercise of an illogical power entirely denied to men in general—the power not only of kissing, but of delighting to kiss the rod by a punctilious observance of the self-immolating doctrines in the Sermon on the Mount.[21]

Often the process of the internalization of the woman's subjection takes the form of the desire to be 'mastered' by a man as with Fancy Day,[22] or Elfride Swancourt who 'had her sex's love of sheer force in a man',[23] or Bathsheba who tells Oak 'I want somebody to tame me',[24] or Arabella who tells Phillotson that there is 'nothing like bondage and a stone-deaf taskmaster for taming us women' and who quotes Mosaic law to prove the point: 'Then shall the man be guiltless; but the woman shall bear her iniquity'.[25] Over and over again women appear to acquiesce in their own subjection. But as individuals are ideologically interpellated as subjects in order that they 'recognize' the existing state of affairs as right and proper and behave accordingly, we cannot wonder at this. When women experience their sexual domination and exploitation ideologically as the inevitable consequence of their naturally inferior position they are deprived of the ability to defend themselves. They become their own enemies because the enemy is not without but within in so far as in this ideological formation it is not men who dominate women but their own 'essential natures'.

Hardy's writing constantly displays the manner in which women 'naturally' live their ideological suppression. Often this takes the form of an 'unconscious' revelation on the woman's part of her essential vanity by a gesture, a passing observation, a look, a spontaneous action, such as that which Gabriel Oak catches sight of when Bathsheba takes out her mirror and looks at herself. Caught up in an intricate mesh of sightings, the author, the reader and the characters are constituted as onlookers in a complex of visual alliances to behold 'woman's prescriptive infirmity [stalking] into the sunlight'.[26] In *Desperate Remedies* there is a startling authorial observation on this aspect of women's essential nature and of the way a woman unconsciously presents herself for the masculine gaze. Cytherea is about to marry Manston whom she does not love. She is passively obedient to the demands of the men who have manoeuvred her into this hated position, deeply unhappy, going through the motions like an automaton and appearing to the congregation 'more like a statue than Cytherea Graye' yet:

> ... she was prettily and carefully dressed; a strange contradiction in a man's idea of things—a saddening, perplexing contradiction. Are there any points in which a difference of

sex amounts to a difference of nature? Then this is surely one. Not so much, as it is commonly put, in regard to the amount of consideration given, but in the conception of the thing considered. A man emasculated by coxcombry may spend more time upon the arrangement of his clothes than any woman, but even then there is no fetichism in his idea of them—they are still only a covering he uses for a time. But here was Cytherea, in the bottom of her heart almost indifferent to life, yet possessing an instinct with which her heart had nothing to do, the instinct to be particularly regardful of those sorry trifles, her robe, her flowers, her veil, and her gloves.[27]

This is a straightforward case of the presence in the writing of the ideological construction of woman as the Other. The writer posits an innate 'difference of nature' between the sexes which means that where a man's actions are bizarre or even perverse he remains consciously in control of them. Women on the other hand are not consciously in control of their actions because they are controlled by something even deeper than emotion, namely instinct. In the alter-ideology of masculine superiority men act rationally (even when their actions appear to be absurd), women act irrationally because they are creatures of instinct. The consequences of this are considerable in so far as it suggests an irreconcilable contradiction between those ideological discourses which spoke of progress as an increasing completeness and harmony of conscious life, and those which proclaimed that women were the 'unconscious' creatures of instinct. In Hardy's writing the thinking world's idealist teleology of universal consciousness is brought into head-on collision with the alter-ideology of women as the weaker sex. In ideological terms it is a fatal collision for each dramatically reveals the limits of the other: if women are unconscious creatures of instinct then universal consciousness is an impossibility, but if universal consciousness is indeed the goal of progress then women cannot be the inferior second sex. In the *scenario* of conflicting perceptions produced by Hardy's writing class and gender ideologies are thrown into contradiction. But this is not the only contradiction produced by the writing for we still have to consider those involved in the structure of perceptions, the conflicts between the writing's sights and oversights.

In so far as the aesthetic project is the writing of a discourse which will reveal the true, we are meant to see Cytherea's actions in a certain light. In effect the attentive reader should see that 'woman's prescriptive infirmity' which appears to the distracted gaze as vanity is in fact a condition of her existence which she cannot help or alter. What the writing 'cannot see' is that when Cytherea, or any other woman, 'fetichises' her appearance she acts not instinctively but ideologically, surveying in her appearance the image men have of her. As an ideological subject, Cytherea is subjected to and dominated by the masculine gaze, a subjection and domination which she experiences as guilt.

In *Under the Greenwood Tree* there is a conversation between Dick Dewy and Fancy Day about dress. The whole conversation is structured around the different ways in which men and women perceive their own and each other's appearance. Fancy's concern is always with how she will appear in the eyes of the world, to the collective sight of men, a concern which she *cannot help*.[28] All Fancy's actions appear as reactions to the acts of sight of the men who surround her, she 'exists' in their sight as the subject 'lives' in ideology. In this respect there are three chapters in this early novel of specific interest. These are chapters one and two of the third part, 'Summer', and chapter one of the fourth part, 'Autumn'. The short chapter 'Further Along the Road' constitutes one of those amazingly complex structures of perception in which, as so often in Hardy's writing, a woman becomes enmeshed in the masculine gaze. Throughout Hardy's writing this visual entrapment almost invariably has the result of a forced, and often disastrous, commitment on the part of the woman. This visual coercion takes the form of the woman being obliged to play the role into which she has been cast by being seen. This image of the ideological interpellation of a subject occurs repeatedly always emphasising the domination effect the woman experiences, like Bathsheba who felt 'that Gabriel's espial had made her an indecorous woman without her own connivance'.[29] So in the drive from Budmouth Fancy is seen not only by Dick but by Shiner and his handsome friend, by the farmer and his wife and man, by the carpenters and the landlord of the inn, and always and ceaselessly by the surveyor in herself. She is interpellated as a subject, called into being by those gazes to which she is subjected, as the handmaiden of the man by whose side she sits. John Berger has aptly summed up this visual relationship in the formulation '*men act* and *women appear*. Men look at women. Women watch themselves being looked at.'[30]

As objects of vision about which the conflicts of vision take place Hardy's women exist in a peculiar state of isolation like Eustacia Vye 'solitary and undefended except by the power of her own hope',[31] or Elizabeth-Jane 'lonely ... construed by not a contiguous being',[32] or Sue Bridehead who felt 'utterly friendless ... a woman tossed about, all alone, with aberrant passions and unaccountable antipathies'.[33] The 'mournful want of someone to confide in' which the 'absolutely alone' Grace Melbury experiences[34] haunts all Hardy's women, particularly in times of crisis, and finds its most complete form in Tess. In her too we have the most dramatic image of the way Hardy's women are harried, harrassed and in Tess's case hunted by the masculine gaze. As Anne Garland expresses it: 'How you all beset me.... It makes me feel very wicked in not obeying you.'[35] That is precisely the point. Confronted by the complex of contradictory visions of herself, each of Hardy's women becomes embroiled in a conflict of perceptions. She is constituted as the observed subject whose very existence is determined by her reactions to the conflicting acts of sight of the perceiving subjects by whom she is beset. Every man demands that she should be seen only by him and treats her according to his vision of her—sexual object, idealized virgin, dutiful daughter, passive wife, prized possession, willing helpmeet, respectable lady. Unable to reconcile these conflicting visions of herself, she experiences her subjection as guilt in expiation of which she must suffer the remorse of seeing the suffering of those who 'love' her, suffering of which she is held to be the cause.

These perceptions do not, however, exist in isolation but operate in the context of choosing a marriage partner. This has a double articulation—who shall the individual choose and how is the subject being chosen? In each of Hardy's novels, in one form or another, this problem is posed afresh and appears as the complex, conflictual pattern of sightings and oversights which constitutes the structure of perceptions, the conflicts between the distracted gaze, the idealizing vision and the intuitive insight.

10

Being and Consciousness:
The Imaginary Resolution

The perception of the Other as a sexual object is a function of the distracted gaze which confuses appearance with the real itself. The subject perceives—and in the case of 'the Passion'[1] the 'transitory instinct'[2] desires to possess—only the impression that the object of contemplation makes upon the senses. Thus a man who perceives a woman sexually is blind to her essential nature for he experiences the 'sensuous joy in her form only'.[3] For a brief period (and it is only a matter of months, weeks or even days) there appears to be an identity between the object perceived and the impression that the object makes. Once the sexual passion abates however, that identity breaks down and the erstwhile lovers, now man and wife as often as not, face each other with the mutually antagonistic antipathy of strangers trapped by 'circumstance' into a relationship which neither desired. There is no instance in Hardy's writing of a viable relationship based on sexual recognition but many examples of its disastrous consequences. The 'problem' of marriage in Hardy is nothing more than his perception of the absurdity and cruelty of the legal institutionalization of this transient perception. In the 1892 version of *The Well-Beloved*, Marcia Pierston expresses this most cogently when, musing bitterly on 'their ill-matched junction on the strength of a two or three days' passion' she says to her husband Jocelyn, 'Was there ever anything more absurd in history ... than that grey-headed legislators from time immemorial should have gravely based inflexible laws upon the ridiculous dream of young people that a transient mutual desire for each other was going to last for ever!'[4]

The idealizing version, on the other hand, is characterized by the inability to see the true nature of the object of perception because the perceiving subjects project their own subjectivity onto the Other and then see only these reflections. Thus Fitz-piers idealizes Grace Melbury, George Somerset idealizes Paula Power (with a passion 'so imaginative ... that he hardly knew a single feature of her countenance well enough to remember it in her absence'[5]) and the painter Ladywell idealizes Ethelberta Chickerel. So Dick Dewy idealizes Fancy Day; Boldwood, Bath-sheba Everdene; Henry Knight, Elfride Swancourt; Angel Clare, Tess. Jocelyn Pierston pursues his 'migratory, elusive idealization'[6] through three generations of the Caro family and Jude idealizes not only Sue but even that 'complete and substan-tial female animal' Arabella, 'his idea of her [being] the thing of most consequence, not Arabella herself'.[7] The complex web of idealizations operates in every one of Hardy's novels. Sometimes a character is purely the embodiment of the idealizing con-sciousness as are Ladywell, Knight, Fitzpiers, Pierston and Boldwood (and their class status should not be ignored), and these invariably see the world in the form of the projections of the idealizing vision. The separation of these characters from the community of labour is total whereas for those who, like Dick Dewy, Stephen Smith, George Somerset, Henchard, Clym, Jude, Gabriel Oak retain some connection with that com-munity, the idealizing vision is not a constant but an inter-mittent mode of perception.

Yet even these are in some measure tainted by taking thought which, in Pater's words, defies 'all that is outward, in an exaggerated idealism'. In fact the further they become separated from the community of labour the more they stand in danger of becoming imprisoned by their own subjectivity. Through the process of separation, differentiation and inter-nalization, the world is absorbed, drawn inward so that the space which each thinking subject inhabits becomes de-populated. Thus when Gabriel Oak spies on Bathsheba what he sees as he gazes down from his aerial position is 'a satisfactory form to fill an increasing void within him'[8]; his soul, writes Hardy, required a divinity. This separation of body and soul, flesh and spirit, being and consciousness finds its expression in the modern 'vice of unrest' which grips Hardy's male char-acters. That 'yearning of [the] heart to find something to anchor to, to cling to'[9] leads almost inevitably to an idealization of the Other. It is a characteristic motif which runs throughout

Hardy's writing and one which is suggested by the title of his first, but never published, novel 'The Poor Man and the Lady' with all the poetic, mythic, religious and class connotations that title signifies. Thus at various times characters do become 'divinities' for one another—Angel for Tess, Sue for Jude, Bathsheba for Gabriel, Eustacia for Clym and so on. The aesthetic intention is to reveal these visions as a false idealism, to show how that mode of perception, by making the Other a divinity, conceals the true from sight, represses essential reality. All these misperceptions get in the way of something, block something off, prevent something from taking place, but it something which tends to be overlooked. The reason for this is that the ideological identification effect produced by the writing comes into conflict with the aesthetic intention.

This effect works in such a way that the subjective empathy between reader and character so foregrounds the 'individual'—the plight of Tess or Jude or Clym—that the aesthetic intention is obscured if not altogether hidden. When so much meaning devolves upon the 'love' relationship then it can be said with justification that 'love' becomes overdetermined and the acts of sight involved in the process of 'falling in love' significant moments in the ideological interpellation of the subject. While, of course, it is a truism that every image in writing is overdetermined the meeting of lovers is without parallel.

In chapter twenty-eight, 'The Hollow Amid the Ferns', of *Far from the Madding Crowd* Bathsheba and Troy meet alone and in secret in that 'pit' of rank and luxuriant nature which is situated in the middle of uncultivated land. Undoubtedly if Freud had been available to Victorian publishers such passages as this would have been excised so rich are they in sexual imagery. As figures in a landscape the two are alone, isolated from the surrounding world and about to establish their love relationship on the basis of their mutual misperceptions of one another. But as imaginary characters in the discourse of writing they arrive on the scene accompanied by a host of poetic, mythical, biblical, balladic and romantic significations. Bathsheba has already been cast in the role of 'divinity' by Gabriel. She is Venus goddess of love and Ashtoreth the goddess of fertility.[10] Troy calls her the 'Queen of the Corn-market' and of course she is Bathsheba. But she is also the 'pretty maid' of the folk ballad, as Troy

is the dashing red-coated soldier. Born of the secret liaison between Mediterranean passion and aristocratic ardour an aura of
'romance attaches to him'.[11] His name has both martial and
mythical signification and where women were concerned he
'lied like a Cretan'.[12]

In that dazzling display of swordsmanship which Troy performs 'quicker than lightning, and as promiscuously', Bathsheba
is subdued. The sword which she sees at first as 'murderous and
bloodthirsty' she sees at the end as 'magic': 'She felt powerless to
withstand or deny him. He was altogether too much for her....
She felt like one who has sinned a great sin'.[13] But if 'he' draws
his sword of power, 'she' weaves her spell of illusion and seduction. Bathsheba is the temptress, 'the Wile-weaving daughter of
Zeus', the 'implacable Aphrodite herself'.[14] Troy would not have
married her he says, 'If Satan had not tempted me with that face
... and those cursed coquetries'.[15] The meeting in the hollow
constitutes one of those many moments of vision in which
Hardy's characters fall in love. This Eden-like moment of recognition works on the basis of a reality effect—two 'people' about
to embark on a recognizably 'real' relationship in the terms of
the realist novel—and a mythopoeic effect based on the
ideological, cultural and psychic associations connected with
this primal scene and the characters who enact it. And in both
cases it *is* a fall, that is both in the biblical sense of the word and
in terms of the structure of perceptions and the writing's
aesthetic intention. Marriage here signifies a post-lapsarian
reality and confronted by the prosaic necessity of having to live
and work together the realization dawns that what had seemed
to belong to the object of contemplation belonged in fact to the
perceiving subject and the couple are left in a state of mutual
antipathy. Trapped and isolated by those visions the relationship cannot *evolve*.

But this is simply the recognition of the obvious, merely a
description of those images and their significations. To go
beyond this simple description it is necessary to consider what
the writing itself produces, to think of the writing as a *scenario*
which enacts the ideological. By constructing the reader as seer,
Hardy's writing enables the reader to get a 'view' of the
ideological as it were from the 'outside'. While the writing's
aesthetic project and Hardy's ironic intentions are certainly ele-

ments in this production it cannot be said that they determine it. It is, perhaps, an oversimplification, but it approaches my meaning to say that the image of the ideological under consideration is not a product of Hardy's mind but of Hardy's writing.

In *A Pair of Blue Eyes* Hardy wrote that every woman who makes a permanent impression on a man 'is usually recalled to his mind's eye as she appeared in one particular scene, which seems ordained to be her special form of manifestation throughout the pages of his memory'.[16] Edward Springrove experiences such a moment of vision when he suddenly meets Cytherea in the street:

> He looked at her as a lover can;
> She looked at him as one who awakes—
> The past was a sleep, and her life began.[17]

Hardy goes on to elaborate this awakening as 'the only bliss in the course of love which can truly be called Eden-like ... before reflection has set in'.[18] The two lovers, alone for the first time, step into a boat and Edward rows out into the still calmness of the bay.

> Everything on earth seemed taking a contemplative rest, as if waiting to hear the avowal of something from his lips ... he kissed her. Then he kissed her again with a longer kiss. It was the supremely happy moment of their experience. The 'bloom' and the 'purple light' were strong on the lineaments of both. Their hearts could hardly believe the evidence of their lips.
>
> 'I love you, and you love me, Cytherea!' he whispered.[19]

What happens in that moment of vision, in that Eden-like primal instance? In the reflexive statement to which the whole scene, with mounting emotional tension, leads—'I love you, and you love me'—which Edward addresses to Cytherea, we see the interpellation of the individual as a subject by a subject who names him or her—my love. Thus in the images of falling in love which all the perceiving subjects, both characters and readers, recognize and with which they can identify, the mechanism of ideological interpellation is made visible. In the constant sighting of the individuals by one another, in the ceaseless reciprocal flicker of recognition of the self in the Other in Hardy's writing, the interpellation of the individual is revealed. Through the poetic evocations of those images of the Other the writing produces the ideological identification effect, the identification of a subject with another subject which is, in the final analysis, the Self. This process is possible because we recognize 'her' (we all do, both men and women) since 'she' is that 'delicate dream which ... is more or less common to all men and is by no means new to Platonic philosophers',[20] and to which the mythographer Carl Gustave Jung gave the name 'anima' and its counterpart in a woman 'animus' remarking that when such 'projections' meet 'the animus draws his sword of power and the anima ejects her poison of illusion and seduction'.[21] 'She' exists in the imaginary language of poetry, myth and fairytale and is 'a favourite subject for novelists, particularly West of the Rhine';[22] she is the princess, the queen, the fairy, the goddess, the nymph. Her forms are legion: Helen, Grace, Lamia, Circe, Aphrodite, Ashtoreth, Freyja.... No matter whether she appears as Cinderella or succubus, in her myriad manifestations this ideological construction of 'Woman' is familiar to us from our earliest youth. When we meet her in Hardy's writing she is no stranger to us for we always already know her.

But this mythopoeic figure is not simply present in Hardy's writing, it is ideologically activated in so far as the aesthetic project demands that the constitutive sighting of this form be recognized as only the beginning of an evolutionary process, not as an end in itself. The initial moment of vision must evolve into the recognition of the necessity for the sympathetic conjunction of the two, the longing to possess transformed into the longing to cherish:

> ... when the woman is shifted in a man's mind from the region of mere admiration to the region of warm fellowship. At this assumption of her nature, she changes to him in tone, hue, and expression. All about the loved one that said 'She' before, says 'We' now.[23]

It is that 'mere admiration' which Boldwood bestows on Bathsheba; his 'ideal passion'[24] could never become warm fellowship because although he tells her 'I will protect and cherish you with all my strength', it is a cherishing which deprives her of her material self-determination, a relationship based on the radical separation. 'You shall have no cares', he says, 'be worried by no household affairs, and live quite at ease.... The dairy super-intendence shall be done by a man.... You shall never have so much as to look out of doors at haymaking time, or think of the weather in the harvest.'[25] Both Boldwood and Troy attempt to separate, isolate and repress Bathsheba. By giving her every-thing, by turning her into a lady and surrounding her with the luxuries bought by the labour of others, Boldwood would separate her from the community of labour. Troy, on the other hand, by taking everything from her, would reduce her to a 'naked individual', an isolated wage labourer. Only with Gabriel, whose love undergoes the evolutionary process and who is not detached from the community of labour as are Bold-wood and Troy, can the unity of labour and love, being and consciousness, be achieved.

Bathsheba is constituted as a 'spiritual' object by Boldwood's idealizing vision and a sexual object by Troy's distracted gaze. Both of these are static perceptions. The resolution is in Gabriel's vision, in the evolution from the first constitutive sighting of Bathsheba as a divinity to the friendship, good-fellowship and *camaraderie* of their mutual regard, 'that love which many waters cannot quench, nor the floods drown, beside which the passion usually called by the name is evanescent as steam'.[26] Those 'affinities that alone render a life-long comrade-ship tolerable'[27] must grow, evolve out of the initial attraction. The writing's aesthetic project thus involves a redefinition of the word love. Love has a history which runs parallel to the evolu-tion of consciousness:

> Love between man and woman, which in Homer, Moses and other early exhibitors of life, is mere desire, had for centuries past so far broadened as to include sympathy and friendship; surely it should in this advanced stage of the world include benevolence also.[28]

Such sympathy, friendship and benevolence Grace Melbury perceives to be lacking after her own Fitzpiers' mutual idealiza-ti⌐⌐ had ended in marriage:

> In truth, her ante-nuptial regard for Fitzpiers had been rather of the quality of awe towards a superior being than of tender

solicitude for a lover. It had been based upon mystery and strangeness.... When this structure of ideals was demolished by the intimacy of common life, and she found him as merely human as the Hintock people themselves, a new foundation was in demand for an enduring and staunch affection—a sympathetic interdependence, wherein mutual weaknesses are made the grounds of a defensive alliance. Fitzpiers had furnished nothing of that single-minded confidence and truth out of which alone such a second union could spring....[29]

While the evolution of the second union out of the first is crucial to the development of the love relationship it is impossible for those separated individuals who remain trapped in their isolated dreams of the world. For these the harmonious unity of consciousness and being which the relationship of loving kindness signifies is an impossibility because their false idealism traps them into a self-reflexive egotism. As Fitzpiers confesses to Winterborne, 'I am in love with something in my own head, and no thing-in-itself outside it at all.'[30]

It is this 'idea which we project against any suitable object in the line of our vision'[31] which Jocelyn Pierston, that 'Wandering Jew of the love world'[32], relentlessly pursues. This idealizing artist is fully aware of the fact that 'the migratory, elusive idealization he called his Love who, ever since his boyhood, had flitted from shell to human shell an indefinite number of times'[33] is a projection which belongs to the perceiver and has nothing to do with the object of perception because he had 'quite disabused his mind of the assumption that the idol of his fancy was an integral part of the personality in which it had sojourned for a long or short while'.[34] But he is 'under a curious curse ... posed, puzzled and perplexed by the legerdemain of a creature—a divinity rather'[35] to which he has always been faithful and he is quite 'powerless in the grasp of the idealizing passion'.[36] It does not matter in which material form the projection takes up residence; the repressive effect is always the same, discrediting, in Pater's words, the actual world and imprisoning the idealist in his own dream:

How incomparably the immaterial dream dwarfed the grandest of substantial things, when here, between those three sublimities—the sky, the rock, and the ocean—the minute personality of this washer-girl filled his consciousness to its extremest boundary and the stupendous inanimate scene shrank to a corner therein.[37]

We see in Jocelyn's pursuit of the Well-Beloved the most developed image in Hardy's writing of that false idealism which represses the real and isolates the individual from his environment by substituting an illusory relation to the seen for a real one.

It is clear from the sharp, ironic ending of the serial version and even from the milder ending of the final version of *The Well-Beloved* that Hardy did not intend an identity between Pierston's art and his own. There is about this novel which was written between *Tess* and *Jude* a quality of irony which surpasses even them in bitterness. I think the reason for this is Hardy's increasing disillusionment with either the ability or willingness of his audience to 'see the truth' and even possibly also with the ability of writing to make them see it. Whatever the reason, in this novel which is obsessed by the problems of perception, Hardy gives us in Jocelyn Pierston's life and art a fiercely satirical view of the idealizing vision.

When the sculptor Pierston chips away at the marble block he creates the essential form of his idea out of the material on which he works. He does not, as Hardy believed a true artist should, chip away the concealing material in order to disengage, to abstract from that concealing 'inessential' materiality, the essential form of the real within. The difference between Pierston's art and Hardy's is, to pursue the sculptural metaphor, that between the art of Praxiteles and the art of Michelangelo. Unlike Hardy's, Pierston's art is *not* that of the imaginative reason but is the purest form of Platonic mimesis. His is not that 'disproportioning' which makes true reality vividly visible. What he pursues in that 'Shelleyan "one-shape-of-many-forms"'[38] is *his* idea, *his* vision of all that is desirable in life. He is, in other words, the embodiment of that ego-centred false idealism just as his pursuit of the Well-Beloved is the idealizing vision made manifest. That is why we cannot possibly confuse what Pierston spends his life doing—giving his idealizations, his 'dream-figures',[39] tangible form in marble—with the aesthetic project of Hardy's writing. The intention of Hardy's art is to expose the falsity of Pierston's. That the writing also actively produces an image of the process of ideological interpellation is no part of the aesthetic project nor is that production determined by the reader. And so we are brought back inevitably to the relations between the aesthetic project, the ideological problematic by which that project is determined, the productive capacity of the writing itself and the historical moment of its production.

Rooted in the long process of the radical separation of the producer from the means of production, Hardy's writing attempts to negotiate contradictory ideological positions at a particular moment of historical crisis in terms of certain discourses which were elaborated towards the end of the nineteenth century. Founded on an idealist problematic the aesthetic project of Hardy's writing is the production of a work of revelation. The 'moment of vision' which is the imaginative reason's aim is to be achieved by producing in the reader an apprehension of the deeper reality beneath appearance. That deeper reality is construed as an underlying natural unity which has been radically disturbed. Thus we find in Hardy's writing the myth of a past unity (signified by the commonwealth of hearts and hands of the community of labour) and the hope for a future unity of being and consciousness. But between these the present appears as an interregnum of disunity produced by the radical separation. This hiatus is signified in Hardy's writing by the structure of binary oppositions (materialism–idealism, flesh–spirit, custom–education and so on) on the basis of which each novel develops.

In this sense Hardy's writing poses a question: if the synthesis was possible in the past and if it will be possible at some future point then why does it appear not to be possible now? The question is posed on the basis of its answer namely that it *is* possible and necessary and even desired but it is not realized because people's *perceptions of reality* are faulty. It is, in effect, an always present necessity, but one which is literally overlooked. Hardy believed that it is the task of 'imaginative literature' to make this necessity visible. This aesthetic intention has the ideological effect of a radical depoliticization in so far as class and gender struggles are transformed into conflicts of perception. Hardy's writing thus produces the *scenario* of an ideological resolution to specific historical contradictions even where images of conflict and separation prevail such as in *Tess* and *Jude*. Where a synthesis actually appears it is always in terms of the marriage of sympathetic *camaraderie* such as in *Far from the Madding Crowd,* an image of the unity and harmony of the relations of production of the community of labour. But this is only an image of synthesis in the terms of the conflicts which the writing itself sets up, a resolution of the conflicting moments of perception, the sights and oversights, in the structure of perceptions. Thus the 'good' relationship based on the intuitive insight is an image of synthesis while the 'bad' one, the purely idealistic or sexual relationship based on the idealizing vision and the distracted gaze, is an image of the antagonistic extremes of the radical separation. In terms of the structure of perceptions the relationship itself, the sympathetic harmony, the unity, is primary, not the characters themselves for they are simply the bearers of the relationship, its agents.

But if the aesthetic project is to 'open the reader's eyes', to produce through all those images of disharmony and conflict a clear sighted understanding of the necessity for unity, the writing itself actually produces an image of the ideological which is quite independent of the aesthetic intention. What I hope to have shown is how a materialist criticism can deploy a theoretical concept such as the structure of perceptions to enable the reader to recognize that writing is not only a product but is itself productive and that its productive capacity is dependent neither on the consciousness of the writer nor on that of the reader. Indeed, I believe the most important contribution a materialist criticism can make to the understanding of imaginative writing is an understanding of its capacity to articulate the ideological, to give the amorphous sphere of the ideological a form, to produce it as a visible object, a production which is quite independent of intention.

Hardy's writing is not, however, a static object, something produced once and for all. It has itself become part of a complex process of consumption and reproduction (hereafter designated by the formulation (re)production) in which it is ideologically activated. It is this (re)productive process which constitutes the object of the final part of the present study.

PART THREE

Aesthetic Ideology and the Production of Thomas Hardy

11

Separation and Evaluation:
Thomas Hardy's
'Curiously Qualified Greatness'

In the discourse of aesthetic ideology 'Literature' appears not as
the product of criticism but as its pre-existent domain upon
which criticism operates in order to discover its immanent
value, truth, meaning or significance. The methodology of such
a critical enterprise is idealist in that it imposes its own ideality
upon writing, and empiricist in so far as it depends upon the
abstraction or extraction of 'Literature's' latent essence. The
techniques it employs are those of separation, evaluation and
revelation. In this sense, as Macherey has pointed out, all such
criticism 'can be summed up as a value judgment in the margin
of the book: "could do better"'.[1] Thus when F. R. Leavis says
that the critic must be quite clear about what he 'sees and
judges',[2] he points to the fundamental procedures of literary
criticism. What Leavis sees is 'the field of fiction belonging to
Literature'. When Leavis says that the novelists who belong to
the Great Tradition (which he defines as 'that tradition to which
what is great in English fiction belongs') are all 'very much concerned with "form"' and that 'perfection of form' is a product of
the novelist's 'vital capacity for experience, a kind of reverent
openness before life, and a marked moral intensity', he is making
a judgment on the basis of which the question 'what is Literature?' will be posed. When this critical gaze is focused on
Hardy, then:

> ... the appropriately sympathetic note is struck by Henry
> James: 'The good little Thomas Hardy has scored a great
> success with *Tess of the d'Urbervilles*, which is chock-full of
> faults and falsity, and yet has a singular charm'. This
> concedes by implication all that properly can be conceded....
> It is ... a little comic that Hardy should have been taken in the

early nineteen-twenties—the Chekhov period—as preeminently the representative of the 'modern consciousness' or the modern 'sense of the human situation'.[3]

As the function of the discourse of aesthetic ideology is to transform writing into 'Literature' through the process of separation, evaluation and revelation, Leavis's judgment on Hardy, although somewhat extreme, does not differ in its operation from criticism in general but it does emphasize the 'problem' which aesthetic ideology has imposed on Hardy's writing, namely that of its 'greatness', for the form of his writing has from the first reviews been conceived as the concealing dross in which the true gold of its value lies embedded. But because of this perceived 'impurity' aesthetic ideology reveals its methods most openly.

For over one hundred years criticism has construed Hardy's most calamitous 'fault' to be his use, or misuse and even abuse, of 'English'. Closely connected with this are three related 'faults': the infelicities of his style, the unevenness of his 'art' or 'craft' and the improbability of his plots. Of course, the construction of these failings also has the necessary function of validating criticism; in the face of such shoddy artistry the discourse of aesthetic ideology can exercise its authority over its domain and separate the 'true' from the 'false'.

The techniques of separation and evaluation have been used both to separate 'major' works from 'minor' works and to separate the good from the bad in each of those novels which are considered to have value. Crucially, the criterion against which these judgments are made is that of realism; the more 'unrealistic' Hardy's use of language, the more 'improbable' his plots, the more the novels diverge from a norm of realism, the further down the scale of 'major' they appear. This is fundamental to the ideological (re)production of writing as 'Literature'. Leavis accurately defined the function and object of criticism when he stated that 'some challenging discriminations are very much called for ... [in] the field of fiction belonging to Literature'.[4] Now, as Macherey has pointed out, to define 'Literature' as 'fiction' means confronting a fictional discourse with reality 'so that the text is a transposition, a reproduction, adequate or not and valued accordingly and in relation to standards of verisimilitude

and artistic licence'.[5] Writing is thus always being matched with
'reality'; but what 'reality'? Whose 'reality'? Are we to take
'reality' to mean, as Leavis does, 'sophisticated human consciousness', 'ideal civilized sensibility', 'humanity', 'complex
moral economy' all of which Henry James 'registers' with such
'astonishing' success and Hardy so signally fails to do?[6] Clearly
what is involved here is not an empirical reality but an
ideological 'reading' of reality. Realism is the refeleclion of that
ideological reading. That is the way the empiricist construction
of criticism makes it appear, that is, it presupposes a valued
reality—call it a sophisticated human consciousness—which the
great writer registers or reflects in his art; this registration is
realism.

We find that the techniques of realism appear as an articulated 'creative' process of perception-(re)creation in which
the writer/artist perceives essential reality and then (re)creates
that essence in the work of Literature/art. Inevitably this is,
even with the greatest writer/artists, an imperfect registration
and it is criticism's task to discriminate between the good, the
bad and the worthless. In this way criticism not only reveals the
value, truth, meaning and significance of 'Literature' but also
demonstrates and exercises its mastery over it. What is absent
from the discourse of aesthetic ideology's own construction of its
task and function is its own materiality, for in defining
'Literature' as 'fiction' or, which is the same thing, defining
realism as a fictive image of reality, it conceals its own role in the
production of that (ideological) reality which it 'reveals' 'Literature' to be reflecting. The production of aesthetic ideology' s
own reality is nowhere more apparent than in criticism's
construction of Hardy's writing as significant but profoundly
flawed. It should be borne in mind that in what follows the
sometimes explicit and sometimes implicit but always present
confrontation between Hardy's writing and a norm of reality is
used both to denounce his 'false notes' and announce his 'greatness'.

When Horace Moule observed in his review of *Under the Greenwood Tree* in 1872 that 'There is one definite fault in the
dialogues ...' the first step was taken on a critical path which
leads to the comment made a century later by the Warton
Professor of English Literature at Oxford that Jude and Sue talk

like an Ibsen translation.[7] That path is strewn with marginal inscriptions: 'could do better'. In 1873 one reviewer of *A Pair of Blue Eyes* wrote of 'a sprinkling of small oddities of style, and of minor errors of taste', while another of *Far from the Madding Crowd* complained of 'monstrous periphrases' and 'specimens of the worst "penny-a-liner's" language'. Yet another wrote that 'Mr Hardy disfigures his pages by bad writing, by clumsy and inelegant metaphors, and by mannerism and affection' and *The Return of the Native* was castigated for 'the clumsy way in which the meaning is expressed. People talk as no people talked before'. A decade later Coventry Patmore professed himself bewildered as to why 'such a master of language' should have, in *The Woodlanders*, 'repeatedly indulged in ... hateful modern slang ... and in the equally detestable lingo of the drawing-room "scientist"'. And while Henry James saw *Tess* as 'chock-full of faults and falsity', Sir William Watson criticised Hardy for his 'over-academic phraseology' and expressed 'nothing but regret for these nodosities upon the golden thread of an otherwise fine diction', and Edmund Gosse complained in a review of *Jude*: 'as to the conversations of his semi-educated characters, they are really terrible. Sue and Jude talk a sort of University Extension jargon that breaks the heart.... She could not have talked like that'. The basis of all these criticisms of Hardy's language is, of course, its 'unreality'. Hardy could avoid this when he stuck to what he 'knew'. As a realist chronicler of the passing away of English country life he was considered to be unsurpassed by J. M. Barrie who wrote in 1889 that 'among English novelists of today [Hardy] is the only realist to be considered, so far as life in country parts is considered'. But Barrie adds a rider that echoes down through the years: 'He is only on firm ground in the country, and not even then when he brings society figures into it.' Even that scourge of Hardy's last novels, Mrs Oliphant, bases her criticism on an accusation of their basic unreality.[8]

But it is in Lionel Johnson's *The Art of Thomas Hardy*, published in 1894, that we see the first comprehensive reading of Hardy as a great writer. Significantly at the height of the new imperialism the discourse of aesthetic ideology not only establishes this 'countryman' as a great English writer in the great tradition of English Literature which is itself represented as a Great World Literature, but it also establishes the major/minor canon. 'In Mr Hardy's work', writes Johnson, 'there is a manner of presentation which has about it something Elizabethan, something Shakespearean; or something of later date, Jacobean or Caroline.'[9] He writes of Hardy's 'affinity with the great makers of English Literature' and alludes not only to Evelyn, Bacon, Marvell, Pope, Milton, Fletcher, Shelley, Browning, but to Hawthorne, Pascal, Senacour, Virgil, Dante, and he writes of 'the power, the beauty, the fidelity, to his own visions of truth, which I reverence in this writer, as I reverence them in Lucretius'.[10] But there are, inevitably, the failings so that while Johnson confesses to having read *Tess* 'eight or ten times' from the first 'with that ravishment and enthusiasm, which great art, art great in spite of imperfection, must always cause', he also writes of 'a certain touch of unpleasantness, and taste of vulgarity ... something unkind, an uncanny sort of pleased and sly malevolence ... a somewhat mean unpleasantness'[11] which pervades novels such as *A Laodicean, The Hand of Ethelberta, Two on a Tower*. But while Johnson reveals the writer's 'failings', *The Art of Thomas Hardy* represent him as 'major', above all as a major English writer whose 'great achievements ... [which] will surely stand the test of time',[12] are to be found in what were later to be called the Novels of Character and Environment rather than in the Romances and Fantasies or the Novels of Ingenuity.[13]

Thus began the production of 'Thomas Hardy' as a great but deeply flawed writer and the long critical process of separating the nodosities from the golden thread in the coarsely but powerfully woven fabric of this 'peasant and woodlander's' craft. And in W. J. Dawson's comments in *The Makers of English Fiction* (1905) we begin to see how both Hardy's 'strengths' (truth, simplicity, strong feeling, heroism, dignity, sincerity) and his 'weaknesses' in the areas of plot, style, language, taste, are to be attributed to his being a countryman. Dawson writes that 'The secret of Hardy's unique power in rendering rural scenes, is that they are essential to himself. They are a part of his own blood and fibre. They belong to his heritage as peasant and woodlander, and are expressive of his temperament'.[14] But his bluntness of feeling sometimes betrayed him into errors of taste and 'in most of Hardy's writing there is also a certain laboured stiffness. He has no natural eloquence of language' and while his style is 'grave, masculine, and usually impressive in its sincerity' it lacks the 'finest literary discriminations'.[15] One particular aspect of the failure of realism in Hardy's art is regularly attributed to his 'peasant' origins and that is the unreality of his depictions of the 'upper classes'. This constant complaint is itself an interesting reflection on the class orientation of the discourse of aesthetic ideology; for well over half a century the production of 'Thomas Hardy' was in the hands of a distinctly definable group—the metropolitan bourgeois intelligentzia, although its members would deny both the term and that they constituted a group. This had a considerable effect on the construction of Hardy's 'failings'. The 'dialogue between educated persons is noticeably formal', wrote H. B. Grimsditch in 1925, 'removed from "the real language of men"…. The rustic talk is more convincing',[16] a view endorsed by Virginia Woolf who wrote that Hardy is unhappy when he 'leaves the yeoman or farmer to describe the class above theirs in the social scale'.[17] And while Woolf believed Hardy to be 'a profound and poetic genius'[18] she also found his novels full of inequalities, 'lumpish and dull and inexpressive'[19] claiming that no style in literature was more difficult to analyse than his because 'it is on the face of it so bad, and yet it achieves its aim so unmistakably'.[20] Bonamy Dobrée used the perceived inequalities to separate the Romances and Fantasies and the Novels of Ingenuity which 'are distinctly bad', 'wooden in language and creaking in movement' and where 'Hardy sometimes comes perilously near cheapness',[21] from the Novels of Character and Environment in which Hardy displays a tragic perception like that of Shakespeare and Aeschylus.[22]

Frank Chapman's 1934 *Scrutiny* essay 'Hardy the Novelist', firmly rooted in the concepts of realism, again separates the valued content from the worthless form of Hardy's fiction. 'In the style, if anywhere,' writes Chapman, 'we shall find an expression of Hardy's sensibility; and yet, if any analysis is attempted, the style seems almost wholly bad'. He points to Hardy's 'clumsy aiming at impressiveness' which has 'disastrous effects'; to his 'naive ideas of scholarship and education', to his use of 'heavy, ponderous words', his 'awkward, Victorian journalese' and his inability to write 'simply and straightforwardly', all of which evidences a basic lack of realism. When Hardy *is* successful it is because he manages to reflect accurately village life, 'the solid, intimately-known, habitual background of experience'. But, 'the further Hardy gets from this background, the less successful he is.... He has an intuition of the real value of the village life he describes and this, combined with his intimate knowledge of it, gives rise to many fine passages.'[23] While Chapman's final assessment is of 'a curiously qualified greatness', T. S. Eliot's essay of the same year attempted no such discrimination and, maintaining that Hardy was 'indifferent even to the prescripts of good writing', dismissed him as 'popular'.[24]

The last major assessment of Hardy's work to appear in the 1930s was William Rutland's *Thomas Hardy: A Study of his Writings and their Background*. The tone of this lengthy work is often an exasperated 'could do better' and it is exemplary in its use of the techniques of separation and valuation; Hardy's 'dominant ideas' are vigorously pursued and the 'minor' novels ruthlessly dealt with, the characters in *The Hand of Ethelberta*, for example, being described as a 'box of puppets' which are 'simply tiresome' and parts of the plot 'tenth rate'.[25] Thus while the Romances and Fantasies and the Novels of Ingenuity are firmly relegated to the 'minor' league, the 'major' novels are ruthlessly mined for their meaning which is separated from the spoil of their form. The main thrust of this criticism, however, is the accusation of deviance from the norms of realism. Thus characters in *The Woodlanders* are described as 'stilted dummies, cut out with scissors from a vulgar fashion plate'[26] while so improbably deviant from the norm of realism does Rutland find *Jude* that his assessment of this 'terribly wearisome book' is that 'as a work of art it is a complete failure. It is, indeed, not a work of art at all. It is a treatise on the misery of human existence', and he concludes that its 'greatest, fundamental, fault ... is that it is false to life'.[27] In fact, 'improbability' is Hardy's main fault; 'the excessive use of tragic coincidence until it becomes entirely unconvincing and the mind rebels against the artificial burden, is, as most of the critics have pointed out, the great weakness in Hardy's novels'.[28]

One of the reasons why the discourse of aesthetic ideology is such an effective ideological form is that in the practice of criticism the individual appears to be offered a complete freedom of (self) expression. In fact what we find in an analysis of critical discourses is that the exercise of this freedom produces an infinite variety of individual variations on certain clearly defined ideological themes. Thus while the well modulated tone of David Cecil taking Hardy to task in *Hardy the Novelist: An Essay in Criticism* (1943) is distinctly different from William Rutland's exasperated irritation at Hardy's 'failings', we nevertheless find in the magisterial reasonableness of this patrician intellectual the same underlying concepts and the same critical techniques deployed to produce Hardy as a faulted genius. The concept on which Cecil's judgment is based allows the separation and valuation to take place. He writes: 'The writer who is a genuine artist is distinguished from the writer who is not by the fact that his creations are imbued with a vitality that does not grow less with time.'[29] Furthermore, the great writer 'apprehends reality in such a way as to present us with a new vision of it' but 'only some aspects of his experience fertilize his imagination.... His achievement, therefore, is limited to that part of his work which deals with these aspects of his experience.'[30] We may break this down thus: the value of great art is its ability to reflect reality; this reality is conceived in the humanist terms of the human essence, a relationship which could be expressed by the formula—great realist art reflects life. Certain life experiences fertilize the great writer/artist's imagination allowing him or her to represent the human essence in new ways; in Hardy's case this crucial determination was his (limited) experience as a countryman; Hardy is, in consequence, a great, but limited, artist. Once this ideological structure has been set up all the critic needs to do is utilize the critical techniques in his or her own way thus stamping the production with his or her own mark of individuality. Cecil goes on, 'The so-called realist painstakingly describes the body emphasising its more unpleasing features. Hardy pierces beneath to reveal the soul.' Thus while Hardy's art is that of 'true' realism—the perception and representation of the human essence—he, the artist, is limited by the man, by his experience of life: 'Brought up in a peasant community, he can only successfully vitalize characters of a peasant-like simplicity. This cuts out the Knight-Angel type. To draw the self-conscious intellectual needs a deeper acquaintance with sophisticated human nature than Hardy possessed. Again, Hardy's range does not include great ladies.'[31] Needless to say, as an aristocrat and Oxford don Cecil felt himself well able to discriminate in these matters.

Inevitably the Romances and Fantasies and the Novels of Ingenuity are castigated for their lack of realism, Cecil commenting on Hardy's depiction of the 'higher ranks of society' in two of the 'minor' novels: 'This is fashionable life as imagined by Miss Daisy Ashford'[32] (Daisy Ashford was nine years old when she wrote the book to which Cecil refers), and on that in *The Hand of Ethelberta* as 'the rural person's simple dreams of rank and fashion',[33] and so on. Cecil's conclusion takes us back half a century to Lionel Johnson's construction of Hardy as a representative of essential Englishness (the yeomen-bowmen of Agincourt as depicted by Shakespeare Englishness) when he writes that 'The only tradition Hardy thoroughly assimilated was the ancient Shakespearean tradition, which is the heritage of all Englishmen.'[34] Inevitably the critical discourse, having cleared away the concealing dross, reveals ' the central significance of the truth about [Hardy's] genius, the key to his riddle, the figure in the carpet ... [he] is the last repesentative of the tradition and spirit of the Elizabethan drama',[35] in him 'we learn to see the old England as we have not seen it before'.[36] The ideological necessity of Cecil's concluding perception may well have been determined by its moment of production—the darkest days of the Second World War when the descendents of those Agincourt bowmen were defending this sceptered isle against the heathen Hun in the skies over the Garden of England—but it still stands as a paradigm of criticism's schizophrenic construction of 'Thomas Hardy'. For the fact is that Cecil cuts Hardy in half: the genius, the humanist, the great Englishman, the inheritor of the tradition of Shakespeare who could imbue the Novels of Character and Environment with life, is tragically shadowed by the unsophisticated peasant —'poor, simple, conscientious Hardy'[37] displaying 'the touching pedantry of the self-educated countryman, naively pleased with his hardly acquired learning'[38] in his execrable Fantasies and Romances. Were this merely an isolated or eccentric point of view displaced by succeeding generations of critics we could afford to ignore it, but it is an enduring critical construction and occurs over and over again in the following years.

So A. J. Guerard (1949) sets a 'rich and humane imagination' against a 'plodding and at times even commonplace intellect';[39]

Edwin Muir 'poetry' against 'absurdity';[40] Desmond Hawkins (1950) 'the greatest delineator in prose of rural England' against 'humdrum verbosity', weak dialogue and his 'besetting sin ... unmitigated solemnity';[41] Douglas Brown (1954) a tragic view of life against 'unserviceable, even shoddy' prose;[42] Frank O'Connor (1957) his 'genius' against his 'simplemindedness';[43] David Daiches (1960) 'genius' against 'clumsy, sometimes pretentious, generally rough-hewn and unequal' prose;[44] Frank Lodge (1966) his 'sublimity' against his 'bathos, false notes, confusions, and contradictions';[45] Irving Howe (1968) his registration of 'the essential unity of human life' against 'the pretentiousness of [his] style';[46] J. I. M. Stewart (1971) 'one of the greatest distillations of emotion into art that English literature can show' (*of Tess*) against his 'wierdly fluctuating command of English prose' and 'the obstinately primitive character of much of his craft';[47] N. Page (1977) the realism of his 'major' novels against the 'ponderous', 'cerebral' and 'mechanical' prose of his 'minor' novels.[48] Criticism consistently reveals the rare, the true, the beautiful, the *essential* moments of vision and separates them from the plodding, the commonplace, the humdrum, the shoddy, the clumsy, the rough-hewn, the primitive, the ponderous, the mechanical, the *false*.

But where criticism does register Hardy's value it continues to do so in terms of realism. Howe claimed that for writing to be 'Literature' its form must 'create an illusion of the rich formlessness of reality'.[49] That the perception of that reality differs does not matter. J. Hillis Miller, for example, writes that 'Hardy's form of realism combines subjectivity and objectivity in a contradictory balance which is the basis of his art' revealing a 'previously hidden design of life'.[50] While from a different perspective, Merryn Williams writes 'From *The Return of the Native* on, the recognition of simple humanity is extended and complicated by questions of education, mobility, and aspiration, beyond the customary rural ways.' This she calls 'the highest form of realism, and Hardy's permanent achievement as a realist'.[51] The important point is that the concept of realism always suggests a relation between two idealist categories, 'reality' and 'Literature', in which the second term has the status of a reflection of the first.

With its techniques of separation and evaluation, criticism

not only demonstrates its mastery over writing but it also produces 'Thomas Hardy'—in the image of a countryman—as a flawed genius. These are the terms of a contradiction in so far as both Hardy's 'sublimity' and his 'bathos' are attributed to his being a countryman. On the one hand Hardy is great when he realistically represents some essential quality of humanity or of Englishness associated with the country (which in the final analysis has a lot to do with 'humanity'). This expression of his 'natural' genius is located in the 'major' Novels of Character and Environment. On the other hand, it is precisely *because* he was a countryman that his genius was 'flawed', marked by the primitive, unsophisticated gaucheness of the 'peasant'. Hardy's attempts to leave his 'natural' environment resulted in inevitable disaster. The record of this disastrous failure is to be found in the 'minor' Novels of Ingenuity and the Romances and Fantasies and these criticism 'sets aside'. We should hardly be surprised to find that having established which of Hardy's novels are to be treated as 'Literature' it is upon these that the critical gaze is turned to reveal Hardy's essential meaning/significance. It is in this revelation that the writing is most openly ideologically activated by the discourse of criticism, the successive moments of consumption/reproduction producing a number of historically and ideologically determined readings.

12

Revelation: Chance, Change and the (Re)production of Thomas Hardy

Having evaluated Hardy's writing and separated the good from the bad, the next and most important function is to reveal the meaning of the valuable texts. In the discourse of aesthetic ideology this revelation is conceived as a knowledge and it is comprised of two separate but related methods of treating the critical domain. The first approaches it from the point of view of the archaeologist. Here the writing constitutes the field of exploration and all the facts pertaining to each individual literary work must be brought to light. As a technique of empirical description this constitutes an *explanation* of the literary text, a technique which is based on methods of literary research. Explanation plays an important role in education where a 'knowledge of the text' develops on a quantitative basis ranging from CSE examination questions and answers to the level of doctoral thesis. Every 'major' writer is accompanied by a great mass of empirical data concerning every aspect of his or her 'life and work' as are the texts themselves. Thus there is, for example, a greater number of explanatory notes in the New Wessex edition of Hardy's novels than pages of text.

The second method approaches the critical domain from the point of view of the prospector. Here something is actually to be found in the text, the text itself is mined, excavated, panned for its valued contents. The techniques of discovery are determined by the empiricist concept of knowledge which takes knowledge to be a process taking place between a given object and a given subject which Althusser has called abstraction. 'To know', he writes, 'is to abstract from the real object its essence, the possession of which by the subject is then called knowledge.'[1] Implicit in this concept of the knowledge operation is a theory of reading on which critical discourse is structured. When literary texts are subjected to the critical gaze what is perceived by the discerning eye of the critic is the truth they contain, their essence. Thus J. Hillis Miller writes in the introduction to his work on Hardy: 'Literary criticism is language about language, or, to put it another way, a recreating in the mind of the critic of the consciousness inscribed in the texts studied, generated there by the words ... the critic can do his job only while he remains caught within this web, [of meanings] following its filaments'.[2] This empiricist process of *interpretation* reproduces writing in a very specific way in so far as the writing is reconstructed, in Macherey's words, '*in the image* of its meaning, to make it denote directly what it had expressed obliquely'.[3] This reproduction has two important functions. First, it prepares the text for consumption; second, it abstracts certain (ideologically determined) meanings and emphasises them as 'central'. In these ways the writing is both aesthetically and ideologically reproduced and activated. It is on this aspect of the critical reproduction of Hardy's writing that I shall concentrate here.

Given the fact that interpretation is offered as a completely 'free' reading of the literary text, a consensus as to the essential meaning of a writer's 'major work' suggests and reinforces the idea that the prevalent perceptions really are that work's immanent central meaning or meanings, else why should so many experts readers, scholars and critics, come to the same conclusion? That, of course, is criticism's self-reading of its own techniques. In fact Hardy's central meaning(s) is not the discovery of the keen-eyed critic but the product of the discourse of aesthetic ideology, a product which is ideologically determined and, as we shall see, completely coherent.

In the discourse of aesthetic ideology Thomas Hardy appears as a 'philosophical' writer in that his writing is seen both to 'contain ideas' and to be the aesthetic elaboration of certain well defined 'philosophical themes'. Helen Garwood in her revealingly titled thesis 'Thomas Hardy: An Illustration of the Philosophy of Schopenhauer' (1911) regarded the expression of ideas in literature as a condition of its realism: 'Some politics, some economics, some religious unrest, some philosophy must be reflected in the literature of to-day.... An utterly unphilosophical literature ... would be as much of an anomaly as an untheological Milton.' She goes on to say that 'an unordered world of nature suggests its counterpart, an unordered world of man. This is Hardy's attitude toward history. It leads nowhere....' Furthermore, the idea 'that chance rules, that caprice is everywhere, that "the inherent will to enjoy" and the "circumstantial will against enjoyment" are ever in conflict lies at the bottom of Hardy's philosophy'. Hardy's perception of the purposelessness of existence determined his tragic view of life as well as his 'resignation', his acceptance of the inevitable and, like Shakespeare, he regarded the 'manifestation of a purpose-less world as tragedy of an insignificant, petty and hopeless nature'.[4]

How does this productive consumption (re)produce Hardy's writing? In the first place the title of the critical discourse suggests that 'the work of literature' contains a meaning (it is that meaning's expression) which criticism reveals. Hardy's writing is an expression (in this particular reading) of those ideas elaborated in the philosophy of Schopenhauer. Secondly, the writing is dehistoricized and universalized, history is set aside and 'man' is centred as universal protagonist. Thirdly, of the many conflicts and contradictions in Hardy's writing, one is selected as central and informing and it is around this that the writing's meaning is elaborated. Fourthly, this conflict is represented as 'enacting' the writing's essential meaning which criticism reveals as the universal condition in which man finds himself, namely the struggle between the individual and the 'blind' forces of existence—Fate, Chance, Circumstance, the Universal of Immanent Will. Finally, criticism attributes to writing a didactic intention by emphasizing the great writer's tragic view of life; his perception and recognition of things as they really are leads to his submission and resignation to, and acceptance of, the 'inevitable' human condition. His humanity is manifested in the stoicism with which he (and by implication, we) confront that recognition. Not only is this reading exemplary of the techniques of interpretation but it produces a construction of Hardy which is strikingly consistent over the next forty years.

Even those critics who have maintained that Hardy was 'not a philosopher' do not usually deny that he 'had a philosophy' and that he 'expressed his ideas' in his novels. What they find fault with is the quality of his mind and the 'inconsistency' of his ideas. In other words, they hold that while Hardy certainly inscribed his ideas in his writing he was not a very profound thinker. Thus Frank Chapman wrote that Hardy's was 'not a truly philosophical mind, and ... he was incapable of any real thinking', and that whenever his philosophy obtrudes on our attention 'it becomes tedious and unconvincing'[5] and A. P. Elliott, while agreeing with this view writing that 'the further one goes into the works of Thomas Hardy, the more he begins to doubt that the man was a philosopher at all', nevertheless reveals him to be both a fatalist and a determinist declaring that his 'fatalistic philosophy finds its supreme and final prose expression' in *Tess* and *Jude*.[6] More recently David Daiches, who sees Hardy's novels as a display of 'elemental figures whose passions were doomed to run the course that the human condition set for them', concludes that 'Hardy was neither a philosophical novelist nor a subtle psychologist; his view of man is neither wholly consistent nor in any degree profound.'[7] Perhaps Ian Gregor takes this tendency furthest when he claims to find Hardy's writing characterized by its absence of 'intellectual concerns' writing that if Hardy is 'predominantly a philosophical novelist, then it is remarkable how little gets into the fiction of such dominant nineteenth-century intellectual concerns as the clash between science and faith, the maintenance of ethics without religion. Matthew Arnold's doubts, for instance, are not aired in Wessex.'[8] Such views while maintaining that Hardy was not a 'philosophical' writer, or at least could have done better, nevertheless reveal the central informing idea of his writing, reproduce it in the image of its meaning. Thus Gregor can say that in the image of the web 'we have a ruling idea in Hardy's development as a novelist, an idea which at once determines the shape of the fiction and its structure'.[9]

The discourse of critism has produced Hardy's writing as either the aesthetic expression of a particular philosophy or, more generally, of his 'ideas' about the human condition. Here the techniques of explanation and interpretation are often used together the former being used to validate the latter. This is done through the process of tracing 'influences' and F. B. Pinion's *Thomas Hardy: Art and Thought* is exemplary in this respect. This critic, who maintains that Hardy was 'advanced in modern philosophy', selects Darwin as a crucial influence on Hardy's ideas writing that 'though Hardy's views were influenced by other scientists and philosophers, such as J. S. Mill, Spencer, Huxley, and Comte, they had changed very little fundamentally from 1865, a few years after he had read Darwin'. However, Pinion also reveals that 'Hardy's own philosophy was rooted in Comte's positivism' and that 'Shelley's influence on Hardy's thought and basic outlook was greater than that of any other writer'. Hardy was also 'much influenced' by Pater's essay on Winckelmann from which he took his ideas about the 'great web' as well as by J. A. Symonds' *Studies of the Greek Poets* 'on which Hardy made notes in 1876'. While this by no means exhausts the list of influences, suffice it to say that Pinion does not fail to present us with the key with which to unlock Hardy's essential meaning: 'Chance and Change', he writes, 'are the key to his work and philosophy'.[10] When we examine the history of Hardy criticism we find that it has produced a variety of descriptions of these two central meanings, reproducing the writing in their image and structuring that image upon a conflict between opposing forces.

The construction of this conflict as timeless and universal rather than historical began in the post-Edwardian era when Hardy was accorded the status of poet-seer crying in the wilderness of social disintegration. Hardy's writing began to be produced as a dramatization of the human tragedy, a great Book of the World in which could be read the story of the individual's stoical and heroic acceptance of man's fate. Thus Lascelles Abercrombie (1912), claiming for Hardy's novels the 'metaphysical power of art', wrote that Hardy perceived 'the general tragedy of existence' namely that 'temporal things [were] irresistably wielded by eternal things'. But while man could not escape his tragic destiny he could face it: 'The general, measureless process of existence, wherein all activity is included, cares nothing, in working itself out, for the deeds and desires of individual existence; the only relation between the two (but it is an utterly unavoidable relation) is that in the long run the individual must obey the general.' The 'prime antagonism' between individual and the forces of existence 'is a modern version of the oldest and most unshakable of all religious or philosophical doctrines, the doctrine of original sin, of the fatal antinomy between man's nature and the divine impulse of the world.'[11] It is hardly surprising that the theme of man's heroism in the face of his tragic destiny and the necessity for stoical acceptance is strongly foregrounded during the First World War, Child, for example, writing that:

> Philosophically, the novels, taken as a whole, are an expression of the belief that the world is governed by a force neither good nor evil, and indifferent to man's feelings. Artistically... they are the creation of a world so governed, a world in which human individuality and desire are always in conflict with the indifferent governing power, just as in much Greek tragedy human individuality and desire are in conflict with fate, or the gods, or custom.

Significantly he sees the novels producing a resolution to this universal conflict in terms of compassion for the human condition:

> In that opposition between the blind, unconscious operation of Circumstance and the passionate consciousness of man lies the secret of Hardy's tragic power and tragic intensity.... He is the poet of common humanity; and his creative fire, his artist's passion, is kindled by the sadness and the splendour of common humanity's condition in the real and daily world.[12]

'To have read Hardy', wrote H. C. Duffin in 1916, 'is to be prepared to meet the injustices of existence with a shrug of contemptuous and unsurprised acceptance; it is a better training than average life itself, for it is more concentrated.' From the novels, full with the 'undeniable indications of the endless miracle of existence' the reader obtains 'a knowledge of life'.[13]

Over a period of approximately four decades which saw two world wars, revolutions in Russia and China, the rise and fall of European fascism, world capitalist crisis, mass unemployment and the beginning of the break up of the British Empire, the discourse of aesthetic ideology consistently produced Hardy's writing as the expression of a remarkable quietism. Sometimes this is stated directly, more often implied by the designation of the writer's central theme as a universal conflict which people are powerless to change but could only suffer. This central theme appears as 'a struggle between will and destiny' (1921),[14] 'the eternal clash of human aspirations and passions, one with

another and all with fate' (1925),[15] 'man's own consciousness of
futility', the 'fatal web in which ... man [is] entangled' (1929),[16]
a universal conflict, 'a drama which knows no end or consummation, set in motion by the Immanent Will' (1929),[17] 'Man as
the victim of Fate and Circumstance' (1931),[18] 'the inevitable
clash between ... "the inherent will to enjoy and the circumstantial will against enjoyment"', between individual human
wills and the Immanent Will (1935),[19] as the conflict between
'"Shapes that bleed, mere mannikins or no" and the Immanent
Will' (1938).[20] Rutland, in fact, identified the two dominant
ideas by which Hardy's writing is determined as firstly that 'the
Primal Cause was Immanent in the Universe, not transcendent
to it, and secondly, that the individual being was of very small
significance in the scheme of things; all the critics are agreed that
these two conceptions are those which dominate all Hardy's
work'.[21] And in the middle of the Second World War Cecil reinforced that view, writing that Hardy's subject 'is not men but
man. His theme is mankind's predicament in the universe', and
consequently the conflict which lies at the heart of Hardy's
writing is 'a struggle between man on the one hand and, on the
other, an omnipotent and indifferent Fate—that is Hardy's
interpretation of the human situation'. But Cecil takes the de-
historisization a stage further, makes it explicit, writing that,
'seen in the terrific perspective in which Hardy surveys the
human being, man's struggles as a political and social character
seem too insignificant to fire his creative spark. Compared with
his relation to the nature of the universe, his relation to government and social systems dwindles to such infinitesimal proportions as to be invisible.'[22] In the humanist themes of man's
enduring humanity in the face of such overwhelming odds H. C.
Webster wrote in 1947 'most of us can find, if not a common
faith, at least a common hope'.[23]

While the perception of the informing centre of Hardy's
writing as the universal conflict between the individual and
Chance continued to be reproduced in such views as those of
David Daiches who wrote of Hardy's characters being 'elemental figures whose passions were doomed to run the course
that the human condition set for them, figures who, contemplated against a background of immemorial and indifferent
nature, of the recurring procession of the seasons, and of sugges-

tive and mysterious relics of the human past ... acted out their generally tragic dramas with a dignity imposed on them by the simple fact of their having to endure the human lot',[24] we may take 1948 to be the date around which a shift of emphasis took place. In 1948 Thomas Hardy, who is 'offered to us among the great novelists ... supposed to be philosophically profound about life', is emphatically dismissed from Leavis's Great Tradition of the English novel. Ironically, what now began to replace the universal readings are much more in tune with Leavis's own position in *Culture and Environment* and *For Continuity*. In 'Mass Civilization and Minority Culture' Hardy is included in a tradition—'Dante, Shakespeare, Donne, Baudelaire, Hardy (to take major instances)'—to recognize and appreciate which was to be one of the select minority who 'constitute the consciousness of the race'.[25] It is, however, in what Leavis and Thompson write, not about Hardy directly, but about the 'organic community' and its passing that we find the general sense of criticism's construction of Hardy's central meaning after the Second World War.

Relying heavily on George Sturt's *The Wheelwright's Shop* Leavis and Thompson construct the organic community around Sturt's idealized reminiscences of the mode of production of the rural small producer. Commenting on a passage in *The Wheelwright's Shop* where Sturt writes of farm-waggons having been adapted 'through ages, so very closely to their own environment that, to understanding eyes, they really looked almost like living organisms', Leavis and Thompson write: 'It is plain that the waggon seemed to Sturt an organism because it reflected something that is still more fitly described as one. What was really organic was a relation of men to one another and to the environment.... Men in such a relation to the environment and one another constitute an organic community.' It was an ideal text for Leavis's purpose, enabling him—with considerable effect—to link his own position to those anti-mechanistic ideological discourses of the nineteenth century, a 'tradition' going back over a hundred years, creating a continuity from Carlyle's *Signs of the Times* (1829) —'Men are grown mechanical in head and in heart, as well as in hand.... There is no end to machinery ... on every hand, the living artisan is driven from his workshop to make room for a speedier, inanimate one'; through

Arnold's *Culture and Anarchy* (1869)—'Faith in machinery is ...
our besetting danger.... Our modern world ... is ... mechanical
and external and tends constantly to become more so.... Now,
then, is the moment for culture to be of service ... the formation
of the spirit and character must be our real concern'; to *Culture
and Environment: The Training of Critical Awareness* (1933)—'What
we have lost is the organic community with the living culture it
embodied.... In a world of this kind—and a world that changes
so rapidly—it is on literary tradition that the office of maintaining continuity must rest.' But what Sturt mourned, Leavis
and Thompson ideologically activated: the passing of the
organic community bears a politically reactionary message in
Culture and Environment:

> Sturt speaks of 'the death of Old England and of the
> replacement of the more primitive nation by an "organized"
> modern state'. The Old England was the England of the
> organic community, and in what sense it was more primitive
> than the England that has replaced it needs pondering. But
> ... the organic community has gone.... Its destruction (in the
> West) is the most important fact of recent history.... How did
> this momentous change—this vast and terrifying disintegra-
> tion—take place in so short a time? The process of the change
> is that which is commonly described as Progress.[26]

I indicate this passage not to suggest any direct connection
between Leavis and post-war Hardy criticism but rather to
point to a certain construction of history, explicit in this passage
and throughout Leavis's cultural discourses, implicit in
criticism's reading of Hardy. History is not eclipsed here but
written as the discourse of the continuous. Here the 'most
important fact of recent history' is not to be found in the discontinuities of revolution, slump, fascism or war, but in the idea
of 'change'. The notion of historical change is a crucially
important ideological reading of history in so far as it makes the
radical separation appear as a moment in a consciousness-
centred continuity which preserves 'against all decentrings', in
Foucault's words, 'the sovereignty of the subject, and the twin
figures of anthropology and humanism'.[27] Just as we were to see
in Chance the workings of a universal fate, so we are to see in
change the workings of an historical destiny. The workings of

the Free Market, however, are no less mysterious than those of the Immanent Will and man appears just as powerless before inevitable change as he did before capricious Chance. The later construction also allows an equallly free play of points of view. Thus the theme of change appears as: the passing of the stable rural life, deracination, a rural equilibrium threatened by urban complexity, stability by invaders from the outside world (1949),[28] the break up of the English peasant community depicted by 'the greatest delineator in prose of rural England' (1950),[29] the invasion of the stable agricultural world by 'men and women from outside the rural world, better educated, superior in status, yet inferior in human worth' (1954),[30] 'the passing of the old rhythmic order of rural England' (1960).[31] Howe (1968) writes that 'organic culture', which Hardy experienced as a powerful reality, 'was a culture notably at a distance from—through not of course untouched by—the great crises and passions of nineteenth-century history', and that the Wessex novels 'form a prolonged celebration ... of the English Country-side' which embodies 'the accumulated richness ... of an old and stable culture' the loss of which Hardy regrets but believes un-avoidable, and despite social change and personal displacement 'Hardy favours a harmonious submission to the natural order' believing in 'the virtues of passivity'.[32] 'The characteristic scene of the Wessex novels', writes Ian Gregor (1968), 'is that of the human figure seen in silhouette. Where there is conflict, it is con-flict with a way of life, a social attitude, a cast of mind',[33] or a conflict between 'the old order and "modern unrest"', the 'dissolution of an ordered community in the face of modern disturbance' (1972),[34] of change from *Gemeinschaft* to *Gesellschaft*, from the organic community to differentiated bourgeois society (1975),[35] of the history of Wessex life 'its past, its present and how its changes came about' (1977).[36]

Accompanying the idea of historical/social change is that of intellectual change and here Hardy's writing is frequently read as the pessimistic expression of the spirit of an age of transition. H. C. Webster described Hardy's own intellectual development as a faithful reflection of the change in the nineteenth-century from belief to doubt, writing that Hardy started out as 'an ortho-dox believer, an optimist with a Shelleyan tendency to expect more of the world than he reasonably could' but that his reading, especially of *Essays and Reviews* and *On the Origin of Species*, made him feel 'that life was cruel and not much worth living'. Webster concludes that 'the increasingly deterministic and pessimistic tone of the period' influenced Hardy to such an extent that he became 'increasingly melancholic'.[37] Douglas Brown's commentary produces a similar reading. He writes of Hardy's pessimism harmonizing 'naturally with the movements of thought and belief in his time',[38] a view shared by G. Roppen who suggests that Hardy's pessimism had its roots in the clash between orthodoxy and scientific determinism, reflecting 'the aimless flux of evolution'.[39] In a more existential reading N. A. Scott perceives the philosophical essence of the novels to be the existential *angst* man experiences in the face of an absurd and godless universe. In Hardy, he writes, 'we encounter an extreme instance in Victorian literature of the *maladie du siècle*.... To reread his books is to be reminded that, as Paul Tillich says, "the decisive event which underlies the search for meaning and the despair of it in the twentieth century is the loss of God in the nineteenth century"'.[40]

Perhaps the most consistent interpretation of the central informing meaning of Hardy's writing, its dominant and determining idea, is that of a form of evolutionary conflict. As it would be tedious and serve no useful function to list these I shall cite only two examples. The first is a revelation of the operation of Chance, the second of historical change. If we regard these representative interpretations from a theoretical position we can see how the discourse of aesthetic ideology (re)produces writing in the image of its meaning. We find that Hardy's writing is (re)produced in the critical discourse as a copy of another discourse and that it is that other original discourse which is revealed as the literary text's essential meaning.[41] In other words, the meaning which the critical discourse reveals turns out not to be a product of the writing itself (although it is contained in it) but of another discourse which may be poetic, mythical, philosophical but in this case is scientific. Moreover, this 'original' text is itself ideologically activated by the critical discourse according to the ideological necessities of the moment of production. In the first interpretation (1932) the universal force of existence—blind Chance—is revealed as the writing's determining centre:

The Darwinian theory of 'natural selection' was generally held to be synonymous with accident, in that it proclaimed the mere freak of chance as determining who should survive and who perish; and it was natural for Hardy to see blind chance operating in every event of life.

The critic concludes that in opposition to the belief in progress which so many of Hardy's contemporaries deduced from Darwin's theory, Hardy himself 'insisted that it implied wanton cruelty and undirected accident as the prevailing force of existence'. Yet, despite that belief, Hardy hoped and believed in an ultimate progress.[42]

In the second interpretation (1954) the critic sees the determining material reality of Hardy's writing as historical change, the rape of the country by urban industrial society, the 'defeat of our peasantry and the collapse of our agriculture'.[43] But in his description of the central theme of the 'major' novels we also discover the secret text of which Hardy's writing is a copy. The critical commentary is quite clearly a reproduction of the writing, a restatement of what the novels say, but a reproduction which produces the meaning of Hardy's writing:

> His protagonists are strong-natured countrymen, disciplined by the necessities of agricultural life. He brings into relation with them men and women from outside the rural world, better educated, superior in status, yet inferior in human worth. The contact occasions a sense of invasion, of disturbance. The story unfolds slowly, and the theme of urban invasion declares itself more clearly as the country, its labour, its people and its past consolidate their presence. Then the story assumes some form of dramatic conflict, strong and unsubtle, an the invasion wreaks its havoc. Human relations and human persons are represented less for their own sakes than for the clearer focussing of the invasion and the havoc. A period of ominous waiting may follow; what the relation means becomes more evident: it is a clash between agricultural and urban modes of life. From that point the story moves to its conclusion.[44]

This reading of Hardy's major novels is a productive consumption of the writing in which Hardy's meaning is (re)produced in the discourse of criticism. The critical commentary appears as a purifying restatement in which the original, of which Hardy's writing is merely the copy, is revealed. In the discourse of aesthetic ideology that original takes many forms—beauty, truth, reality, history, God, Chance; here it is another text. Speaking of 'the great and complex battle of life', Charles Darwin said:

> We shall best understand the probable course of natural selection by taking the case of a country undergoing some ... change.... If the country were open at its borders, new forms would certainly immigrate and this would likewise seriously disturb the relations of some of the former inhabitants.... As all the inhabitants of each country are struggling together with nicely balanced forces, extremely slight modifications in the structure or habits of one species would often give it an advantage over others.... In all countries, the natives have been so far conquered by naturalised productions, that they have allowed some foreigners to take firm possession of the land. And as foreigners have thus in every country beaten some of the natives, we may safely conclude that the natives might have been modified with advantage, so as to have better resisted the intruders.[45]

In the evolutionary struggle for survival the indigenous inhabitants of rural England are incapable of resisting the onslaughts of the invading species and the 'old stable order'[46] must either change or become extinct. 'As the favoured forms increase in number', Darwin wrote, 'so, generally, will the less favoured decrease and become rare. Rarity, as geology tells us, is the precursor of extinction.... As new forms are produced ... many old forms must become extinct.'[47] Thus Brown writes of Henchard: 'John Barleycorn amid the sun and rain; the countryman of older Dorset at that moment in history when his community and way of life as they have been for generations must suffer a profound change ... this I take to be the subject ... of Hardy's saga.'[48] The meaning, however, must not only be revealed but ideologically activated. Thus, writes Brown, in the face of this historical inevitability, Hardy, having 'looked out into the wilderness' and faced despair, chaos and purposelessness, offers us the philosophical resolution of stoic acceptance.[49]

In such ways has the discourse of aesthetic ideology

(re)produced Hardy's writing in the image of its meaning. But this meaning which the critic appears to discover in the literary text is in fact generated by the critical discourse itself. The critical structure of perceptions allows the same ideology to be expressed in a potentially unlimited variety of forms each given the 'private' imprint of its individual bearers/producers. But the rich variety of its forms cannot conceal the poverty of criticism's ideological content nor, finally, its class basis. The stoical acceptance of the inevitable is a profoundly reactionary reading of Hardy's writing.

13

The Production of Meaning: 'Hardy's Women' and the Eternal Feminine

Materialist criticism conceives the materiality of literature deriving not from its status as an object or a collection of texts but from its existence as a social relation which involves a productive exchange between writing and criticism. This relation operates in and through the various material practices, both private and state controlled, which form the apparatus of the ideological/cultural hegemony of the ruling class the most important of which is the educational system. In the production of individual judgments, evaluations, discriminations, interpretations of the 'work of literature' (the 'literary text' and its accompanying commentaries), literature functions as an element in the production and reproduction of the relations of production at the ideological level. Hardy's writing, constructed by the discourse of criticism as the 'work' of the 'author' Thomas Hardy, does not exist 'outside' this relation but is rather its product.

If we doubt this we have only to imagine a person who has never heard the name of Thomas Hardy hurrying into a bookshop to buy something to read on a journey. Attracted by the brightly illustrated covers of the New Wessex Edition and taking up *Two on a Tower* and reading on the back cover that this is the tale of the love affair between an abandoned and languishing aristocrat and an Apollo-like young astronomer (just the thing for a long journey), it beats Dashiell Hammett's *The Thin Man* (dull cover) into second place and the book is bought. But as soon as our traveller opens the book she or he will find that it is quite literally enclosed in critical discourse: fifteen pages of interpretation at the front, twenty-one pages of explanation at the back as well as a list of eminent critics, a biography, a list of the author's major works, acknowledgements, the General Preface to the first Wessex Edition and a map. All of this our traveller may chose to ignore, but she or he cannot fail to be aware of the fact that as far as this particular random garnering from the field of fiction is concerned some challenging discriminations have clearly been made. Whether our reader takes any notice of it or not, *Two on a Tower* is accompanied by the discourse of aesthetic ideology and even if the interpretations and explanations are not read the 'literariness' of this text is unequivocally signalled by their presence.

Regarded simply as commodities *Two on a Tower* and *The Thin Man* stand side by side on an equal footing both produced for the purpose of realizing surplus value. But through the specific (re)production process we have been looking at, one of them has been ideologically activated, put to a definite use in the process of which aesthetic/cultural value and meaning have been added, an addition the other (as yet) lacks. As this is a social process and not a matter of an immanent value, it is clearly not impossible for their positions to be reversed. One hundred years ago, when *Two on a Tower* was written, a literary education was a classical education; only a minority of die-hards would now place Horace before Hardy. This is not because 'people's ideas' about literature have changed but because the study of dead languages is no longer adequate to the productive, political and ideological necessities of the modern state. Of course classical writers are still studied as literary texts but they no longer hold their pre-eminent position. This is why I take the term literature to signify a social relation and not some mystical and idealist notions of the inherent value or 'textuality' of writing.

Once any writing has become ideologically activated by the discourse of aesthetic ideology and produced as 'Literature' it cannot be considered by a materialist criticism apart from its interpretations and evaluations because it is precisely these commentaries which realize the writing's ideological effects. In this respect I have used the theoretical concept of the structure of perceptions to show how the reality of Hardy's writing arises not from an inviolate completeness but, on the contrary, from its openness which is betokened by the number and variety of perceptions, points of view, readings and meanings it evokes. In this sense the discourse of aesthetic ideology (re)produces writing in its own image—like ideology itself, 'Literature' knows no bounds or limits, the final word can never be spoken, the last observation never made. There is, however, a distinction between each individual critical perception and the structure of perceptions in which they are realized. While each individual critical commentary represses the contradictions in the writing it evaluates and interprets by (re)producing it in the image of its dominant informing meaning, representing it as a coherent (even if flawed) totality, the (continually expanding) sum of critical commentaries, which together constitute the discourse of aesthetic ideology, realizes the ideological effect of literature by putting these disparate and even conflicting individual points of view into play. It is in this sense that the discourse of aesthetic ideology is itself a structure of perceptions in which each individual subject has complete freedom to exercise his or her own point of view. There are two points worth noting about this overall formation: first, it produces certain ideologically determined readings which appear as dominant critical perceptions. This dominance is not imposed but appears to be freely arrived at, the product of critical consensus. Second, while these dominant perceptions are offered as a knowledge of the literary text this does not mean that any one point of view is more valuable than another. The discourse of aesthetic ideology may thus be regarded as a structure of perceptions in which all individual points of view are equally valuable, but where certain critical perceptions (because of their 'truth') appears dominant. While this is merely a provisional proposition it can be used to look at the way 'Hardy's women' have been (re)produced in the discourse of aesthetic ideology.

I have said that Hardy's writing produces a determinate view of the Victorian masculinist alter-ideology of woman as the *sexus sequior*. In this ideological construction woman appears in the image of her innate difference. Her vanity, masochism, capriciousness, her desire to be mastered, her weakness, her wiles, her 'womanliness', are all manifestations of the unfathomable mystery of her essential otherness. But this sexist ideology is not simply reflected in the writing but put into contradiction, not through images or scenes of repression, but by being activated in the structure of perceptions. Trapped and captured by the masculine gaze each of Hardy's women is enmeshed in a conflict of perceptions, a complex of visions of herself. She is constituted as the observed subject whose existence is determined by her reactions to the conflicting acts of sight of the men by whom she is observed. Interpellated as as subject, subjected to the myth of being the weaker sex, internalizing and recognizing herself in that image, she behaves accordingly. Whatever Hardy's intention, the innumerable acts of sight which constitute the structure of perceptions put the ideological construction of woman into contradiction by showing that the perception of her 'essential nature' is always conditional upon who is doing the seeing.

How is this structure of perceptions (re)produced in the discourse of aesthetic ideology? How do the female characters in Hardy's writing appear in the views of a male dominated critical discourse and how are they ideologically activated? In an attempt to answer these questions I shall look first at a random selection of critical views of woman or women in general extending over a period of approximately one hundred years, and secondly at a selection of views (again random) of just two female characters, Tess and Sue Bridehead, produced since the end of the Second World War. The reason for this selection is twofold. The first is simply the necessity to limit the field of choice which is very large. The second is that both Tess and Sue have a very strong presence in contemporary English studies. So far as students are concerned they figure among the best known characters in English writing at this time and are in consequence the source of production of an enormous number of points of view. How they are critically (re)produced and ideologically activated by the discourse of aesthetic ideology is therefore extremely important.

In the following critical views on woman the contradictions Hardy's writing produces are repressed and replaced by an ideal central idea which not only robs the writing of its reality by representing it as the reflection of something outside it, but also ideologically activates it, uses it to reproduce and reinforce a masculinist alter-ideology.

It is hardly surprising that Havelock Ellis (whose progressive *Studies in the Psychology of Sex* suffered the same fate at the hands of Dean Inge as *Jude the Obscure* at the hands of the Bishop of Wakefield: both were burnt) took an interest in Hardy's writing. What is perhaps more surprising is the way the alter-ideology of woman's essential otherness is reproduced in his views (1883) on Hardy's 'gallery of women—"Undines of the earth", they have been felicitously called—whose charm is unique'. Charming they may be, and they 'may be clever, practical, full of tact; they are always irresistibly fascinating; but veracity, simplicity, rectitude are with the men'; it is 'with the men always that the moral strength lies'. And in his 'Concerning Jude the Obscure' (1896) writing of Hardy's 'intense preoccupation with the mysteries of women's hearts', Ellis writes that 'woman has always been for man the supreme priestess, or the supreme devil, of Nature'. As this is said in the context of a perceived conflict between Nature and Society—a conflict which 'reaches its highest point around women'—the ideological construction of femaleness is quite clear. However enlightened and progressive Ellis may have been about sexual matters, we have in his view of Hardy's Undines of the earth both a repetition of Hardy's writing and its (re)production in the image of the ego-ideology of maleness and the alter-ideology of femaleness. Ellis's views clearly show the radical disjunction between ideas and ideology.[1]

I have suggested that one of the absences of Hardy's writing is the construction of woman as mystery in so far as female characters contemplated as woman are always mysterious beings, unfathomable, contradictory, illogical, capricious and finally unknowable Others. However, in the writing, the revelation of the 'essential woman' in individual women always takes place in the context of specific conflicts in which the ideological is activated so that between the subject's action and the perception of that action a relation of contradiction is revealed. In the critical discourse the absence if reproduced but the contradiction is repressed. In this purifying repetition (as Macherey has called it) woman appear simply as representative of the mysterious forces of Nature—in itself a profoundly anti-materialist and mystical notion—or Fate. Thus Abercrombie (1912) writes that 'womanly caprice, with all its tragical result, becomes at last the very type of the impersonal, primal impulse of existence, driving forward all its varying forms of embodiment, profoundly working even within their own natures to force them onward in the great fatal movement of the world, all irrespective of their conscious desires'.[2] If, as H. C. Duffin wrote in 1916, 'The *Ewigweibliche* is a book written in a strange tongue',[3] then it is a book written by men, a book in which we can read that:

> the function of child-bearing is the central idea in Hardy's view of women. The business of life is to reproduce life; existence is for the sake of existence. Nature, seeking only to prolong the species, has given this function pre-eminently to women. Hence woman's instinctive assertion of charm against which the intelligence of man revolts but to which his instincts succumb. What has been called the 'capriciousness' of Hardy's women is in reality their immediate and instinctive obedience to emotional impulse, without the corrective control of intelligence. It is one form through which the All-Mover, the Prime Impulse, works, darkly, unreasonably. What in these women seems a lack of volition, is due to their being possessed by the Will.... Hardy's women are all of one type, differing only in degree. They are essentially Cyrenaics.[4]
> (1921)

Here there are no contradictions, the writing is quite clearly (re)produced in the image of its 'central idea' of women as child-bearing life-givers, anti-intellectual creatures of instinct through whom Nature works, obedient, emotional, non-reasoning and mysterious agents of the Prime Impulse, practising hedonists. It would be possible to put this view aside were it not for the fact that the book in which it appears is in the bibliography of one of the most popular and influential series of study notes on Hardy currently available. But besides this it is a view which has a remarkable tenacity.

In such critical views of Hardy's women the repetition or simple reproduction of the writing in the commentary is always accompanied by the production of meaning. This is why I maintain that every critical reading is a productive consumption ((re)production) of the writing. To take a simple case, say Grimsditch's view (1925) of Elfride Swancourt as 'the type par excellence of Hardy's view of the educated woman'. 'Education' he writes, 'has superimposed a great deal, but has left untouched the fundamental attributes of the sex.' Can we imagine that being written about Stephen Smith or Henry Knight, Angel Clare or Clym Yeobright or Jude Fawley? Grimsditch goes on,

'She is intellectual ... but the forces which direct her actions in moments of stress are not those of reason but of primitive emotion.... Hardy conveys ... the idea that in matters of the affections there is no safety in presupposing consistent and honourable conduct on the part of woman.'[5] In the forces which direct her, in her lack of reason, her obedience to primitive emotion, inconsistency and dishonourable conduct we see an ideologically determined (re)production of Elfride in the image of the 'central idea' which she embodies or represents. In Arthur Symons's work on Hardy (1927) we find the central idea which informs Hardy's writing, his philosophy and the mystical objectification of woman, constituting the critical revelation of Hardy's essential meaning. 'In all his work', writes Symons, 'Hardy is concerned with one thing, seen under two aspects ... the principle of life itself, invisibly realized as sex, seen visibly in the world as what we call Nature. He is a fatalist, rather a determinist, and he studies the workings of fate, or law (ruling through inexorable moods, or humours), in the main vivifying and disturbing influence in life, woman'.[6]

In the critical (re)production of Hardy's central theme as the dignity, heroism, nobility, stoicism and simple humanity with which man confronts an omnipotent and indifferent Fate, the discourse of aesthetic ideology produces Thomas Hardy as a great humanist. Implicit in this construction is the idea that Hardy's 'fatalism' is the expression of an essentially tragic world view which reflects an essential humanism. In this way criticism reproduces the humanist ideology of the thinking world in its own discourse. However, it also reproduces the sexist alter-ideology of woman as the culpable Other. Whereas Hardy's writing puts these ideological constructions into contradiction, they are merely reproduced by the critical discourse with the contradictions stripped away. This is achieved by attributing the source of the idea that woman and fate are one and the same to Hardy himself. Thus Elliott (1935) argues that in Hardy's view the distinction between male and female temperaments is such that they are as divergent as different species. 'Woman must possess man', he writes, and, being 'mere vessels of emotions', they are at the mercy of their passions'. As 'instruments of Fate' endowed with 'unbridled passion', 'instability of temperament' and a 'volatile nature', they operate in the lives of men for evil, their sex being Destiny's way of trapping men: 'Man is not ruined by his sexual instinct, but by the irresponsible nature of Woman.'[7] Elliott's view of woman as the victim as well as the instrument of fate is reiterated by Cecil (1943) who writes that 'Woman's passiveness and frailty make her an especially poignant illustration of that frailty, that dependence on fate, which is the outstanding characteristic of the human lot.'[8]

Consistently the otherness of women is repeated and emphasized. Thus Cecil writes, 'to Hardy, as to Byron, love was a woman's whole existence'; J. O. Bailey (1945) that Hardy's women 'are fundamentally creatures of instinct';[9] Guerard (1949) that Hardy's women are 'irrational, impulsive, vain, fickle, dishonest, and unjust, the volatile manifestations of Fate whose actions are not rationally explicable';[10] Stewart (1971) that 'with Hardy we are in a masculine universe extremely susceptible to the attraction of women, and therefore extremely aware of their fatality'.[11] Or women are reified into the idealist category Woman, representative of a central idea. So H. C. Webster (1947) writes that 'The lives of women in general are dominated by "woman's ruling passion—to fascinate and influence those more powerful than she"';[12] Muir (1949) that Hardy 'is on woman's side against man, just as he is on man's side against nature, and for the same reason; for woman is the final victim';[13] R. A. Duerksen (1966) writing of Hardy's use of the Shelleyan ideal of womanhood says that Sue Bridehead is 'the most complete representation of the Shelleyan woman' in Hardy's work;[14] Meisel (1972) that 'it is in Hardy's conception of woman that the tension between the old order and "modern unrest" becomes real in the world of his novels';[15] and Gregor (1974) writes that 'Hardy finds woman expressive, in the purest form, of the human capacity for endurance and the steadfast refusal to be overcome.'[16]

In the purifying repetition of the critical commentary Hardy's female characters are (re)produced in the image of an ideological construction of woman. Frail, weak, irrational, dominated by her passions she appears as man's fateful or idealized Other. This construction is validated by the empiricist critical technique itself in so far as it is the discovery of the author's meaning, the 're-creating in the mind of the critic of the consciousness inscribed in the texts'. But these views of woman are always accompanied by views of specific women who exist in the imaginary world of Wessex and who are perceived by the critic in a way that is analogous to the way they are perceived by the masculine gaze of the characters in the novels in which they appear.

The theoretical value of thinking of the following randomly selected critical views of two of Hardy's characters in terms of the structure of perceptions is that it enables us to grasp the way the discourse of aesthetic ideology produces its effects. I shall look at critical discourse in terms of four major functions: (1) the free play of point of view; (2) the representation of characters as the embodiment of meaning; (3) the operation of the identification effect; (4) the production of a dominant critical perception.

(1) The first thing to be said here is that the juxtaposition of a number of critical points of view actually produces one of the primary ideological effects of the critical discourse, namely the visible evidence of the exercise of 'freedom of thought'. This freedom (which is in reality the freedom to think within ideology) is expressive not only of each individual critic's 'ideas' but also of his mastery of the writing.

(2) Through the attribution of diverse meanings to the characters the writing's aesthetic effect is realized, the number and variety of these meanings revealing the text's 'literariness'.

(3) The ideological identification effect produced by the consumption of writing can best be illustrated by an example. This is from an article written in 1849 and concerns the reading of *Jane Eyre*: 'We took up *Jane Eyre* one winter's evening, somewhat piqued at the extravagant commendations we had heard, and sternly resolved to be as critical as Croker. But as we read on we forgot both commendations and criticism, identified ourselves with Jane in all her troubles, and finally married Mr Rochester about four in the morning.'[17] The ideological identification of the 'consciousness' of the character with that of the reader is dependent for its operation upon the process of ideological interpellation of individuals as subjects. Just as in Hardy's writing female characters are interpellated in the structure of perceptions as subjects of the masculine gaze, so in the (re)production of the writing writer, character, reader are interpellated by the discourse of aesthetic ideology as subjects of the critical point of view. The identification produced in the consumption/repro-

duction process is of one subject with another—Hardy, Tess and I are identified with the Self. In the discourse of aesthetic ideology this subject is confronted by a number of universal Subjects—History, Nature, Fate, Chance, the Universal Will—variously emphasized according to the critic's perception of the writing's central and informing meaning.

(4) Finally, in the free play of points of view certain views appear as 'spontaneously' dominant critical perceptions. This spontanaeity gives these constructions of meaning a particular weight and authority.

For H. C. Webster (1947) Tess is the representative embodiment of her creator's essential humanism and the novel to which she gives her name 'a fine contribution to the war against "man's inhumanity to man" which so importantly characterized the last decade of Hardy's career as a novelist'. In the reiteration of Hardy's humanist theme it is hardly surprising that Tess's 'fight seems to have value in itself because of the nobility of her nature ... she is a tragic character in the truest sense of the word'. It is, however, in this critic's reading of Tess as the subject of two antithetical but equally powerful laws—the law of Nature and the law of society—and her status as the helpless victim of the conflict between these which constitutes the critical work's dominant perception.[18] Douglas Brown's reading of Tess (1954) emphasizes the character as the embodiment of meaning by suggesting that 'Tess is not only the pure woman, the ballad heroine, the country girl: she is the agricultural community in its moment of ruin',[19] a view which accords with Holloway's (1960) perception of Tess as 'a protagonist who incarnates the older order, and whose decline is linked ... with an inner misdirection, an inner weakness'. This weakness is a result of her heredity: 'The race is in decline ... in Tess there is something self-destroying'.[20] In these and in Roy Morrell's (1965) reading of Tess as the victim of 'a conventional idea of morality, of the condemnation of society'[21] the universal abstract Subject which confronts the subject Tess is History whereas in Tony Tanner's (1968) view it is the Universal Will. He writes that Hardy suggests 'a universe of radical opposition, working to destroy what it works to create, crushing to death what it coaxes into life. From this point of view society only appears as a functioning part of a larger process.... Hardy's vision is tragic and penetrated far deeper than specific social anomalies ... [he] reveals a Sophoclean grasp of the bed-rock ironies of existence' and he concludes that 'Tess is the living demonstration of these tragic ironies'.[22]

Irving Howe (1968) conveys the sense that the process of identification involves the recognition of an essential humanism when he writes that Tess represents something 'deeply rooted in the substance of instinctual life' and that she provides for us 'a standard of what is right and essential for human beings to demand from life'. She is, he writes, 'one of the great images of human possibility' and in responding to her 'radiant wholeness' what we respond to is Tess herself.[23] But whereas in Howe's commentary the identity between subject and subject, between author, character and reader is implicit, in that of B. J. Paris (1969) it is quite explicit. Tess, this critic writes, 'has dignity because she is loved by the author, because he enters wholeheartedly into her experience of the world, because her feelings have for him, and are made to have for the reader, an intense reality.... Tess [is] an experience and a passion for us.'[24] And in Kramer's interpretation (1975) we see both the identification process and the confrontation between subject and Subject, Tess and the Immanent Will. He writes: 'Tess, the conscious individual, becomes confronted with the great natural forces which express themselves through her.... The awareness of her that the individual reader gains through the interaction of his consciousness with hers ... permits the reader to participate in tragic vision on his own terms.' Thus we identify with Tess and consequently 'recognize' the tragic human condition which is her and our lot, subjects as we are, of 'the forces of the universe'. Again there is in this critic's interpretation of Tess the discovery of an inevitable humanism for 'despite its ostensible unconsciousness, Hardy's universe operates in such a way that man does become its centre, its measuring device'.[25] This conflict is also in Southerington (1971) who writes that the basis of Hardy's novel is 'the conflict between sentient man and insentient forces.... The basic discrepancy [is] between social laws and natural conduct.' The subject's subjection to the laws of Nature and society is reiterated. 'Tess's eventual fate', he writes, 'is caused solely by ill-adapted social ordinances ... so long as social codes fail to take account of reality, for so long does man expose himself obtusely to tragic possibilities. Heredity, economic forces, time, chance and consequence shape Tess's career and bring about her downfall. Only social convention *causes* it.'[26] In G. Thurley's reading (1975) of Tess as 'the fable of the Fall, the loss of innocence' Tess appears as the guilty victim of her own sexuality. In this psychological rendering of the relation between subject and Subject 'It is not fear of censure that dogs Tess, but her own sexual knowledge, her own sense of having fallen; and the force of this depends very largely upon her sense of having yielded out of her own sensualism',[27] whereas in Pinion's view (1977) Tess is the victim of her heredity and 'the work of others in the context of chance'.[28]

In the the critical structure of perceptions we can see ideology in operation. Functioning through point of view, aesthetic ideology activates writing and when the critical gaze is turned upon Tess then however varied the individual perceptions, Tess is produced in the discourse of criticism as the representative embodiment of an essential humanism. When Ian Gregor writes that Tess 'realizes in Hardy a feeling that we can only describe as love'[29] he points to the basic mechanism of identification. Interpellated as subjects and through the process of identification, the seer and the seen, author, character and reader/critic become fused into the single unique subject, the Self. In this figure of the observed spectator—Tess the object of knowledge and the subject that knows—we have a dominant image of humanist thought.

There exists no such empathy in the critical perceptions of Sue Bridehead for it is not the Self which criticism recognizes in Sue but the mysterious and threatening Other. Although D. H. Lawrence's view of Sue (1914) pre-dates the period of criticism we are looking at it constitutes a dominant perception. Here the writing is being activated from the position of a masculinist alter-ideology in which Sue is constructed as an aberration, an aberration, that is, in the terms of the male view of what woman should be. Lawrence writes:

> She was born with the vital female atrophied in her: she was almost male. Her *will* was male.... It was not natural for her to have children.... Whereas an ordinary woman knows that she *contains* all understanding, that she is the unutterable which man must for ever continue to try to utter, Sue felt that

all must be uttered.... [She] is the production of the long selection by man of the woman in whom the female is subordinated to the male principle.... One of the supremest products of our civilization is Sue, and a product that well frightens us.... For the senses, the body, did not exist in her; she existed as a consciousness.... Being of the feminine gender, she is yet no woman at all, nor male; she is almost neuter.... She was not a woman.[30]

In Lawrence's perception of what Sue is not we have the masculinist alter-ideology's construction of what a woman should be. It is her deviance from that ideological norm which the discourse of criticism reiterates.

Guerard's view (1949) is very close to Lawrence's and he writes that the portrait of Sue 'is one of the most impressive in all fiction of a neurotic and sexually maladjusted woman—a living portrait rather than a case study'. Her second relationship with Phillotson he reads as a symptom of hysteria in this neurotic product of the Victorian era.[31] Hawkins (1950) writes that Sue is a 'madly egocentric little sensation hunter'[32] and Walter Allen (1954) that Sue 'is a most subtle delineation of a not uncommon type of woman in the modern world and it is significant that the only writer on Hardy who has fully understood his achievement in creating her is D. H. Lawrence', but 'perhaps the key to her is in Hardy's word "intellectualized"'.[33] R. B. Heilman's view (1966) of Sue is that her apparent innocence 'masks a paradoxical double design of self-interest: she wants to be sexually attractive and powerful but to remain sexually unavailable'. She is, he says, the 'true, ultimate coquette, the coquette in nature' and it is this which is the source of her capriciousness, coquetry being 'the external drama of inner divisions.... Her deficiency in sex ... is a logical correlative of her enthroning of critical intellect.'[34] Howe (1968) sees Sue anticipating 'the modern cult of personality in all its urgency and clamour.... [She] is the first anticipation in the English novel of that profoundly affecting and troublesome creature: the modern girl.'[35] Gregor (1968) writes of Sue being 'so highly personalized that she cannot form a fully human relationship', she is 'personal to the point of idiosyncracy',[36] while Bailey (1970) sees what he calls Sue's sexual underdevelopment and her final 'madness' as the 'doom and curse of hereditary temperament'.[37] Stewart (1971) sees the basis of Sue's frame of mind as 'a terrible vanity, an unyielding self-regard',[38] and Hyman (1975) sees her as 'emotionally and morally, a child' concluding that 'she is in a word a supreme egoist'.[39]

Unlike with the construction of Tess we have here a sense of Sue being the 'unnatural' product of modern civilization, an aberrant woman. The cumulative impression produced by these views is of an hysterically neurotic, egotistical, terribly vain, self-regarding and intellectually over-developed 'troublesome creature', a sexually deficient, maladjusted and underdeveloped coquette (to use the polite term) in whom the 'vital female' is atrophied. If, as it has been suggested, 'To many a young reader *Jude the Obscure* is THE novel'[40] this ideological construction of Sue Bridehead goes a long way to answering a recently posed question as to '*why* feminists should be so interested in literature [and] what theoretical or political ends such a study might serve'.[41]

Just as the (re)production of 'Hardy's essential meaning' is based on a reading determined by a dominant class ideology, so the (re)production of 'Hardy's women' is based on a reading determined by a dominant gender ideology. Far from being neutral, open or unbiased these readings serve only the interests of certain social groups. The ultimate duplicity of the discourse of aesthetic ideology is to construct Thomas Hardy as the author of the ideas upon which these readings are based.

Exclusion and Repression: The Choric Rumination of Hardy's Charming Puppets

To think of criticism as an ideological discourse which functions as an element in the production and reproduction of the relations of production in a specific social formation is to impose upon it neither an idealist intentionality nor a spurious conformity. There is no question as to the rich variety of critical views on Hardy's writing, nor of their ingenuity and distinction from one another. Difference is a precondition of their existence in the discourse of aesthetic ideology, for it is just through the free play and expressive 'originality' of ideas that the critical discourse produces its ideological effect. In correlating these points of view I am not attempting to trace a conformity of ideas but rather the determinations of an ideological problematic.

As an ideological form the discourse of criticism is, in the final analysis, one of the ways in which the conflict between the forces and relations of production are ideologically 'fought out'. To think of it in these terms is to accord criticism a necessary social and political significance which is obscured and denied by criticism's self defence of its own necessity which is that it has a cultural/aesthetic value. Criticism is important, but not for the reasons it claims to be. In a sense it realises its ideological aim through its very 'uselessness' in an advanced technological capitalist society. Having no 'use value' it is not determined by the 'functionalism' of other discourses. In this sense it is a uniquely 'free' discourse and one, furthermore, which knows no disciplinary boundaries. Claiming for itself the inalienable right of freedom of expression, it exercises a remarkable authority, not only over writing, but over all other forms of discourse, activating them ideologically in the production of meaning. Criticism exercises this freedom through the eclecticism of 'approach', that is, by approaching its domain from a great variety of general positional points of view: aesthetic, anthropological, biographical, biological, ethical, historical, philosophical, psychological, religious and so on. Established in relation to one or more positional approaches, the critic expresses his or her 'own ideas' in the elaboration of a uniquely individual point of view. In its own view criticism is an expressive discourse the practice of which is not executive but 'creative', and the values it embodies are of a 'higher' order for they have to do not with the materiality of technology, nor with the constraining laws of science, but with human consciousness. It is in the centralizing of consciousness that critical discourse achieves its final ideological effect. In the concept of 'Literature' as the reflection, expression or registration of human consciousness we find the enunciation of consciousness as the subject of all historical development and action. It is in the study of 'Literature' that the subject is to find his or her identity, and to this end criticism produces writing as a reflexive totality centered upon an immanent meaning. To achieve this, criticism must repress and efface the contradictions produced by writing.

In the last chapters we saw how the discourse of aesthetic ideology (re)produces Hardy's writing using the techniques of separation, evaluation and revelation and the way it is ideologically activated to produce meaning. It now remains to see how the techniques of exclusion and repression are used to efface contradiction.

Conceptualized as a complex system of reality produced at a unique conjecture (the time, place, relations and means of production involved in the writing of Hardy's novels) Wessex constitutes the 'world' of Hardy's writing. That world is not the fictional representation of an external reality although that is how it consistently appears in the discourse of aesthetic ideology. This is particularly the case with those critics who discover the 'real' Dorset in Wessex, who produce a commentary on Hardy's writing which is, in effect, a Wessex travelogue. Herman Lea, for example, takes us through the novels as on a guided tour of an archaeological site which has been discovered during the course of a nature ramble. In Lea's commentary we find many passages which begin: 'We may journey in company with Oak as he walks towards Shottsford—an imitation of the town of Blandford. Leaving Dorchester by the London road, he passes

...' and so on.[1] Perhaps the most famous of these commentaries in which the reader is taken for a look over the author, a guided tour around Thomas Hardy and his rural environs, is Clive Holland's *Thomas Hardy's Wessex Scene* where we discover, for example, that:

> Not far away, and much visited, hidden in the picturesque downs, is Sutton Poyntz, the 'Overcombe' of *The Trumpet-Major* and the chief scene of that spirited novel. And hard-by is the Mill where Miller Loveday, Ann Garland and her mother lived. But the mill described by Hardy is in reality at Upwey, some four miles north of Weymouth, where there is a noted 'Wishing Well' which in summer is beautiful with its surrounding trees and many ferns.[2]

In discovering the real Dorset in the fictional Wessex and thus proposing an identity between Wessex and Dorset, between writing and reality, such commentaries, while admittedly not 'literary criticism' are analogous to literary criticism in technique and clearly show the empiricist foundations of the critical enterprise which seeks to discover the 'real' in 'fiction'. This common critical position, determined by the ancient idealist problematic of mimesis, robs writing of its reality by according it the status of an image of the real. But Wessex is not a reflection of an external reality; it is the product of a form of perception determined by conflicting and contradictory ideological readings of the history of radical separation. Furthermore, the characters who 'inhabit' Wessex derive their reality from their relation to that 'world' and the complex relations it signifies. Thus just as Wessex is not the reflection of an external reality, no more Dorset than the 'organic community', no more historical background than the 'stage of a universal drama', so the workfolk are themselves not representative of the nineteenth-century 'peasantry'.

It is my contention that the workfolk are not just important to Hardy's writing but that it cannot be understood apart from them. Far from being minor characters of peripheral importance to the central drama, their presence is constitutive because all Hardy's characters exist in relation to the experiential knowledge and customary forms of their world. It is in that relation that they achieve their reality as characters. They are also constitutive, however, in the production of contradiction. This is not a matter of the writer's conscious intention. In the conflict which the writing sets up between the customary forms of the workfolk and (bourgeois) civilization, the writing is not simply a representation, a *showing*—of the inevitable clash between town and country, urban and rural manners, folkways and educated society, the effects of 'change' and so on—but a *production*. The presence of the workfolk in Hardy's writing contributes to putting the ideology of the thinking world into contradiction, both by revealing the colonizing nature of bourgeois ideological forms, and by defining the boundaries of bourgeois ideology. As their presence defines ideology, so their language ruptures the discourse of the continuous, revealing discontinuities where it would show only harmonious passage. Again I must stress that the conflict which the writing sets up between the collectivity of the community and the differentiation and isolation of the 'conscious' individual is more than simply a showing, something we may 'see in Hardy's writing'.

The workfolk not only contribute to the production of contradiction, but their presence is also productive of a form of alienation effect (in Brecht's sense). Through the techniques of grotesque realism, through the subversive nature of their laughter and through the parodic use of their language, the writing achieves two things. In the first place it subverts the ideological identification effect, the identification of one subject with another. And in the second place it puts in question the subjective mode of perception, puts it in question because in the (re)production of the writing the workfolk are 'seen' in certain ideologically determined ways. In effect it is in the critical perceptions of the workfolk that point of view is established as an ideologically rather than a subjectively determined perception. Furthermore, the critical structure of perceptions reproduces the writing's structure of perceptions in so far as critical point of view is homologous with that of the 'bourgeois' characters in Hardy's writing itself. Clearly I am not suggesting that the views themselves are the same, but rather that they have the same repressive effect. Just as in Wessex the perceptions of the subjective consciousness displace the ways of seeing of the community of hearts and hands, so in the discourse of criticism the workfolk are marginalized and dismissed by the successive points of view of the conscious subject, the critic. In the (re)production of Hardy's writing criticism effaces the contradictions produced by the writing, producing a realignment of perceptions. This is achieved in two ways. First, consciousness is foregrounded as the centre of interest. This is achieved both generally in thematic observations, and specifically in regard to particular characters. Again, the ideological effectivity of this process is achieved through the rich variety of these different perceptions. We may read of Tess, for example, that the 'very condition of her emergence into post-adolescent consciousness is that initial infusion with the earthly, that initial divestment of innocence' and that her 'birth into Eden' is engendered by her 'drive toward an individualizing egoism'. (1962)[3] Or again that the 'tragic characters possess intensity and self-awareness; their experiences have a universality.... Emphasis on the intensity and sanctity of individual perceptions in *Tess* and *Jude* makes them among the most intimate and compelling narratives of the last century.' (1975)[4] Or, 'With *The Mayor of Casterbridge,* we arrive at a full statement of Hardy's universe ... consciousness of the inadequacy of the old order is "modern consciousness" ... [it] is a study ... in the discovery of self-alienation'. (1972)[5] Or we learn that ' in a sense [Henchard] *is* man' and in his 'passage towards self-awareness we can read the sufferings of an entire species in its struggle to master ... a destiny which demands the subjection of powerful instinctive forces'. And, from the same critic, *The Return of the Native* 'dramatises the death of older forms of perception in the struggle for survival in the modern world. It dramatises the evolution of consciousness.' (1971)[6]

More generally we may read that Hardy has a basic existentialist concern with choice and that 'His treatment of choosing and evading is indeed so exhaustive that to call it an exploration of the psychology of choice would be no exaggeration.' (1965)[7] Then again, 'Though Hardy and his characters try to place the blame for their sufferings on society, on man's biological nature, on the "crass casualty" of external nature, on absurd coincidence, or on the blind determinism of the immanent will, the secret source of pain in Hardy's intuition of existence is consciousness itself.' (1966)[8] Another critic suggests that 'Like Mill, Hardy sees as a fundamental source of value the importance of the individual consciousness ... when he looks at the cosmos from the point of view of consciousness individual subjectivity seems to be the only reality that matters. On the one hand, he sees man as insignificant in relation to an immense and indifferent cosmos.... On the other hand, Hardy exalts subjectivity, seeing the world as "only a psychological phenomenon".' (1969)[9] Another that 'according to Hegel "self-consciousness attains its satisfaction only in another self-consciousness".... Desperately searching within the confines of the natural world for some analogue of identity, self-conscious man experiences what Jude defines as "the centrifugal tendency" of life. With increased awareness of the self comes increased awareness of the other as enemy.' (1972)[10] Finally, Hardy makes use 'of every possible device for preventing, hindering, or stultifying [human communication] ... [he] associates communication with self-consciousness, and an image of consciousness evolving to its present state, to the misfortune of mankind, is one of his salient ideas.' (1978)[11]

It is not the correctness or incorrectness of these views which is in question here, but their function in (re)producing Hardy's writing as a humanist discourse in which the painful and often tragic road to self-awareness is written. The absent centre of this 'work' about which the meanings are generated is the Self with which the subjects, author, (conscious) character and reader identify. The discourse of the continuous appears here in a form with which all individuals may identify their private spiritual histories, not the social struggle into political awareness, but the evolution into self-awareness; it is upon *that* story that all eyes are focussed. It is this alignment of viewpoint which casts the workfolk in the role of 'background' figures. In this respect the history of Hardy criticism is a history of the different ways in which the workfolk have been marginalized and the contradictions their presence produces effaced.

Criticism dealt with the workfolk at the time of production of Hardy's writing in ways which were significantly different from their treatment later on when Hardy was beginning to be produced as a major author. Originally Hardy's 'rustics' were used as a stick with which to beat him, to accuse him of unreality. Middle class reviewers, firmly entrenched in their urban superiority from which they regarded the rural worker *en masse* as Hodge, often deemed their appearance inappropriate in a 'literary' discourse and resented their articulate presence. Thus one reviewer accused Hardy of putting into the mouths of his rustics 'expressions which we simply cannot believe possible from the illiterate clods whom he describes' (1874), while R. H. Hutton in a review of the same year, which has much to say about Hardy's linguistic eccentricities, wrote that 'almost all the labourers ... talk in a peculiar style, deeply infiltrated with the suggestions of a kind of moral irony mostly borrowed, no doubt, from the study of the Bible, but still applied in a manner in which neither uneducated Churchmen nor uneducated Dissenters ... would dream of applying it.' Hutton's main criticism is that the language of the workfolk is not consistent and this inconsistency is the book's (*Far from the Madding Crowd*) 'main fault', a view with which another critic agreed claiming that because the workfolk's conversations were 'inauthentic' the reality of the scenes was placed in doubt. R. D. Lang wrote in 1875 that 'The author is telling clever people about unlettered people, and he adopts a sort of patronizing voice.... The labourers are all humourists in their way, which is a very dreary and depressing way.... Shepherds may talk in this way: we hope not; but if they do, it is a revelation; and if they don't it is nonsense, and not very amusing nonsense.' In 1878 a reviewer wrote that 'The language of his peasants may be Elizabethan, but it can hardly be Victorian' and he added in some surprise that 'a curious feature of the book [*The Return of the Native*] is the low social position of the characters'. In the next decade Havelock Ellis, from an apparently much more sympathetic viewpoint, displaced the workfolk no less radically by elevating them than previous reviewers had by dismissing them as unreal. He wrote (1883) that Hardy 'has created a group of peasants, for the like of whom, we must go back to Shakespeare.... It is surprising, indeed, to see how close is the relationship between those clowns of Shakespeare and their modern representatives in Mr Hardy's novels.' The association of Hardy's 'peasants' with Shakespeare's clowns both elevates and marginalizes the workfolk as literary devices, 'great' but peripheral.[12] A decade later (1894) Lionel Johnson developed this construction, both eulogizing the workfolk as 'the material of [Hardy's] great achievements' writing that 'of these he is a master, and his work in this kind will surely stand the test of time', and marginalizing them by according them the status of a Greek chorus.[13]

I have suggested that the workfolk constitute the contradictory antithesis to the ideology of the thinking world,
'degrading' (in the Bakhtinian sense) the idealist and conscious-
ness-centered discourse of the continuous through customary
and linguistic forms deemed inarticulate by the 'lettered' and,
perhaps most importantly, by their laughter which degrades
and materializes the ideal, the abstract, the spiritual. Criticism
has responded to their subversive laughter by turning them into
comic relief or chorus. By consistently constructing them in the
image of characters in drama they are deprived of their reality as
characters in the novels. Just as Wessex appears in criticism to be
'like' Dorset, so the workfolk appear to be 'like' Shakespeare's
clowns or 'like' the chorus in a Greek tragedy; they appear, in
other words, to be reflections of something else. By being
elevated to the position of figures in a continuous literary tradition their historical reality is obliterated.

Thus we read that in his humour Hardy is like Shakespeare
and that his 'peasants have the delightful, unconscious gro-
tesqueness of pure comedy'; they are like children (1905),[14] and
'since those best enjoy life who know least about its ways, the
simple rustics form the comic relief to his tragedy'. (1925)[15] We
find the workfolk placed in the great tradition of English
humour (1929)[16] 'consciously Shakespeareanized in function ...
comic relief ... a chorus to explain and comment on the doings of
the chief characters' (1934)[17] or simply dismissed as 'period
peasants pleasing to the metropolitan eye'.[18] They have been
seen as unchanging figures who 'passively accommodate themselves to nature in the ordered ritual of their lives not rebelling
against it or attempting rash Promethean manipulations'
(1940)[19] or as 'unmistakably brittle, decorative, fictitious,
literary—as literary as Dogberry and Bottom', characters whom
it would be absurd to examine as real human beings (1949).[20]
They have been seen as 'the bridge between mere earth and
moral individuality' characters whose 'existence is colonial
rather than personal' and in whose 'fatalism lies their survival
wisdom, as against the death direction of all moral deliberation'
(1953)[21] and consistently as chorus, one critic writing of 'the
choric ruminations of the labourers' (1954), another of 'the
choruses of the rustics' (1957), a third of the 'peasant chorus'
(1959).[22] They have been constructed as 'charming puppets ...

who can go through their act whenever Hardy curls a finger' (1968)[23] and 'splendid material for a comic turn' who appear 'almost as if they were a leisure class ... quaintly discoursing in malt-houses and ingle-nooks over pots of cider or ale' (1971)[24] and relegated, in the 'minor fictio' to a 'minor role, often that of chorus or comic relief'. (1977)[25]

Seen both in the literal and in the literary sense as fools, as clods, children, peasants, puppets, rustics, clowns, the workfolk have been consistently displaced: aesthetically, ideologically and historically. As choric peasants or Shakespeareanized rustics they appear in the critical structure of perceptions as commentators upon, or comic reflief from, the tragic tale of man's developing consciousness. Thus perceived they have the same 'background' function as Wessex itself. But to construct Wessex as the 'stage' upon which the tragedy of the main protagonists is enacted and to cast the workfolk in the role of comic relief to that central tragedy is to replace the concrete historicity of Hardy's writing with an idealist universality. These interpretations not only deny the writing its historical specificity and suppress its contradictions, but also conceal the productive nature of the exchange between writing and criticism. Whatever the relation between Hardy's novels and other writing it is not one of linear descent. The line which runs Aeschylus-Shakespeare-Hardy is a *product* of the discourse of aesthetic ideology not its pre-existent given. Repressing the historically determined discontinuities and contradictions produced by Hardy's writing, criticism (re)produces it in the image of a totalizing discourse, a moment in the endless continuum of man's developing consciousness.

Perhaps the most important thing about the workfolk, however, is simply their presence. To make this explicit they should be thought of not as props 'brought in' from a stock of literary devices—clowns, comic turns, comic relief, chorus—but rather as the product of Hardy's writing, indigenous to it. It is their presence as a community of speakers which is crucial, for they are the product of the linguistic division on which Hardy's writing is based and it is this which constitutes their historical and aesthetic reality, a reality which criticism has consistently repressed. Furthermore, the presence of those linguistic practices of the community of labour which differ from those who speak 'educated' English produces one of the major contradictions of Hardy's writing. But here a distinction must be made between a linguistic division at the moment of the writing's production, namely that between two 'languages' Wessex dialect and educated English, and a division produced during the (re)production of Hardy's writing which is a matter of different practices within the same language.

15

Thomas Hardy and the Reproduction of the Relations of Production

Due to the uneven development of capitalism in the nineteenth century there still existed at the time Hardy was writing certain survivals of pre-capitalist modes of production which sustained ideological, cultural and linguistic forms which had been generally superseded. Increasingly, however, such survivals were being eradicated economically and culturally by the exigencies of the radical transformations taking place in British capitalism during the period of the 'Great Depression'. Hardy was acutely aware of the ways in which 'civilization' increasingly encroached upon and repressed the surviving cultural traditions and practices of the rural workers and small producers, believing their lives to be drastically affected for the worse by the imposition of an alien culture. Whatever Hardy's intentions, and irrespective of his own feelings of nostalgia for a vanishing way of life with which his own family was identified, the presence of the dialect speakers in the novels sets up a contradiction from which the writing cannot escape.

For the historical reasons I have given, the linguistic divisions in Hardy's writing appear as different speech practices, as Wessex dialect and educated English or, as Hardy expressed it in *The Well-Beloved*, between 'the local vocabulary [and] a governess-tongue of no country at all'. His writing shows this cultural conflict, and this 'revelation' can be identified with the writing's aesthetic intention. But the writing is not just a revelation of the process of cultural domination and submission, it is itself an agent in that very process, both showing and at the same time repressing those cultural forms and that mode of life in which the natural and individual lives of the community of labour are expressed. This is because Hardy's writing is itself determined by the 'governess-tongue of no country at all', that national common language, English. It is a language of 'no country' because it relates to no specific time, place or group but appears, like bourgeois ideology itself, ubiquitous, eternal and classless. But the production of Hardy's writing depends on the existence of that common language and, once produced, the writing itself contributes and continues to contribute (through the process of (re)production) to its maintenance and development. To take but one example of this contradiction. Tess, Hardy writes, spoke two languages, dialect and English, and in the conflict between the 'superstitions, folk-lore, dialect, and orally transmitted ballads' of the one and the 'National teachings and Standard knowledge' of the other[1] the writing shows a conflict between two linguistic practices. Try to imagine the effect of that writing on Tess herself and ask yourself this question. Although Tess has been schooled in that common language and can read and write, were she to read the text in which she herself appears, would she not be as repressed and dominated by the practice of that acquired common language, by the *literary expression* of Angel's love, as she is by that love itself?

> His had been a love 'which alters when it alteration finds'. He had undergone some strange experiences in his absence; he had seen the virtual Faustina in the corporeal Phryne; he had thought of the woman taken and set in the midst of one deserving to be stoned, and of the wife of Uriah being made a queen; and he had asked himself why he had not judged Tess constructively rather than biographically, by the will rather than by the deed?[2]

Revelation and repression: this is the inescapable contradiction produced by writing in the bourgeois epoch. To reveal Tess's oppression Hardy can only use the language of the oppressor. Wanting to see into the heart of the thing and tell the true story of the repressive nature of men's egocentric vision, language as a social event is repressed by the structure of perceptions itself, becoming 'privatized' as the bearer of the seen, an expressive medium for the subjective point of view of the perceiving subject.

With such considerations, however, we still remain on the production side of writing. But at the time Hardy was writing a radical transformation was taking place in linguistic practice, a transformation by which Hardy's writing has been radically affected. In fact it was produced at a critical moment in what might be termed the bourgeois cultural revolution. To secure its dominance, the bourgeoisie had not only to transform the relations of production but also the ideological formations. To achieve this it was necessary to develop an education system which would further the universal dissemination of the 'national language'. This revolutionary transformation which had been going on for more than a century but which had its beginnings much earlier[3] and which gathered momentum in the last decades of the nineteenth century, is characterized by making the school system the means of ensuring submission to the dominant ideology both in terms of individual submission and, even more importantly, the ideological submission of the dominated classes. Matthew Arnold was alert to the necessity for a unifying educational state apparatus writing in 1861, just ten years before the publication of Hardy's first novel:

> It is of itself a serious calamity for a nation that its tone of feeling and grandeur of spirit should be lowered or dulled. But the calamity appears far more serious still, when we consider that the middle classes, remaining as they are now, with their narrow, harsh, unintelligent, and unattractive spirit and culture, will almost certainly fail to mould or assimilate the masses below them, whose sympathies are at the present moment actually wider and more liberal than theirs. They arrive, these masses, eager to enter into possession of the world, to gain a more vivid sense of their own life and activity. In this their irrepressible development, their natural educators and initiators are those immediately above them, the middle classes. If these classes cannot win their sympathy or give them their direction, society is in danger of falling into anarchy.
>
> Therefore, with all the force I can, I wish to urge upon the middle classes of this country ... that they might be greatly profited by the action of the State....[4]

Arnold's deep concern was caused by the singularly underdeveloped state of British national education. This situation rapidly changed in the last decades of the century. In 1851 the average duration of school attendance of working-class children was two years, but by 1900 the school leaving age had been raised to fourteen. Significantly, a new subject was added to the curriculum in 1871, namely 'English Literature', which consisted of learning by heart, but which by 1880 'had become the most popular subject in the schools'.[5] By the end of the century a national system of elementary schooling had been set up but was confined to the provision of a minimum standard of proficiency in the three R's—'reading a short paragraph in a newspaper; writing similar matter from dictation; working sums in practice and fractions'.[6] But while this minimal education was provided for the working class,

> ... the old grammar schools had been widely developed, as the institutions of a largely separate class, served mainly, at the primary stage, by an extended network of preparatory schools.... The Taunton Commission of 1867 envisaged three grades of secondary school: those for the upper and upper-middle classes, keeping their boys till 18 and giving a 'liberal education' in preparation for the universities and the old professions; those for the middle classes, keeping their boys till 16 and preparing them for the army, the newer professions, and many departments of the Civil Service; and those for the lower middle classes, keeping their boys until 14, and fitting them for living as 'small tenant farmers, small tradesmen, and superior artisans'.[7]

It was, however, the Eduction Act of 1870 which institutionalized the class system in education and constructed national schooling as an ideological state apparatus. The act laid the foundations for 'a highly organized and strictly segregated system of schooling designed specifically for the working class'.[8] It was, wrote H. G. Wells, 'not an Act for a common universal education, it was an Act to educate the lower classes for employment on lower class lines'.[9] In effect, during the period Hardy was writing the novels, due in the main to the changing demands of British capitalism which was undergoing the transformation from its productive to its imperialist stage, 'the schools that came into being at opposite social poles ... were ... dedicated to the production not so much of rational individuals as of recruits to different castes'.[10] But, as Macherey and Balibar have pointed out, this division in schooling 'which reproduces the social division of a society based on the sale and purchase of individual labour-power, while assuring the dominance of bourgeois ideology through asserting a specifically national unity, is primarily and throughout based on a *linguistic division*'.[11] However, *this* linguistic division is different from that found in Wessex for it *pre-supposes* a common language. It is not founded on different speech practices, a language of 'the people' and a language of the ruling class, but upon *different practices in the same language*. It was in the education system that the contradiction between these different practices was instituted namely between a basic standard English taught in elementary schools, a training in correct usage and pronunciation, and the more advanced exercise of 'comprehension/composition' in the 'liberal education' of the secondary schools which involved the study of and writing about 'literary' texts. In fact what we see here is the institution of different ways of *reading*, different modes of consumption of writing, a process which necessitated a specific (re)production of writing by the discourse of aesthetic ideology based upon a radical *division*: between popular and great, between minor and major, bad and good, between writing and 'Literature'. This ideological necessity guaranteed that evaluation became the primary function of the practice of 'criticism'. As institutionalized in the ideological state apparatus, the consumption of writing became an agent in the reproduction of the relations of production.

Here I must emphasize once again the materiality of literature as a social relation. Produced from the exchange between writing and criticism, literature is an ideological formation realized in the common language. In this sense literature—of which the 'work of the author Thomas Hardy' is a part—is open to everybody, a universal discourse from the appreciation of which no one who can read is excluded. But the *ideological effect* of literature is one of domination, the subjection of individuals to the dominant ideology, an effect which reproduces the dominance of the ideology of the ruling class. This effect is realized in different ways, ways which are based on class division, for as Macherey and Balibar point out, for members of the educated dominant class subjection is experienced as the practice of a mastery (of the critical discourses over writing),whereas the exploited classes, while they certainly know how to read and write, find in the reading of 'Literature' nothing but the confirmation of their own inferiority. For these, subjection means domination and repression by the literary discourse of a linguistic practice which is deemed 'inarticulate' and inadequate for the expression of complex ideas and feelings.[12] This division is maintained and reinforced in the daily mass circulation tabloid newspapers (so-called) where pictures and print the size of primary reading 'flash cards' predominate.

Although his motives may have been suspect and his intentions reactionary, Hardy's writing nevertheless constitutes a prolonged contemplation of the repressive effects of education, and while it cannot be said to show any understanding of the nature of the ideological domination effect of literature, it does produce many powerful images of that effect. Yet, constituted as 'Literature', this writing contributes to the dominance of the ideology of the dominant class which is realized in the education system in which that writing now exists and where it has the effect of reproducing the dominant ideology. Produced under determinate conditions, relating to a specific moment in the history of the development of capitalism in England in the nineteenth century and to an ideological construction of that history, Hardy's writing was both produced out of, and is now a hundred years later used to reproduce, a linguistic division in education. Incorporated into the educational apparatus where it is activated in the production of discourses which enable individuals to appropriate ideology and make themselves its bearers through all those individual readings, interpretations, criticisms, commentaries and evaluations which constitute the practice of 'criticism', Hardy's writing now functions as a 'privileged agent of ideological subjection, in the democratic and "critical" form of "freedom of thought"'.[13]

It is, of course, not possible to treat these myriad (re)productions of Hardy's writing in the same way as those which exist as 'critical works' simply because of the form in which they exist in the material practice of teaching, in essay and examination questions and answers, in lectures and classroom and seminar discussions, in tutorials and so on. It is here that 'Hardy Rules O.K.'[14] for it is in the material practices of the ideological state apparatus that Hardy's writing actually *functions* as literature for those who have been selected by the education system to read him. And rules is indeed the correct word when we bear in mind just for whom Hardy is so 'overwhelmingly' popular. Given that statistically the population of this country is educationally graded at the age of fifteen on the basis of 20% achieving 'O' levels, 40% CSEs (with CSE grade four considered 'average' ability) and 40% achieving few or no exam qualifications at all, then it is obvious that Hardy is read by only an élite minority. Two things emerge from this. The first is that constituted as literature 'Thomas Hardy' exists, for the vast majority of people who live in the country where he is considered to be a great humanist writer, as a repressive absence, part of a discourse the very existence of which confirms them in their 'inferiority'. The translation of three of the novels (*Far from the Madding Crowd, The Mayor of Casterbridge, Tess*) to film and video does not alter this. Appearing on the cinema or television screen as costume drama entertainment, 'authorship' is unimportant. This only confirms the radical distinction between the mode of consumption of the 'audience' and the mode of consumption of the 'reader'. That sales of novels increase after their appearance on the screen is certainly true, but the order of precedence has been reversed. 'You've seen the film, now read the book' displaces the 'literariness' of the writing, appearing as it does as the written version of the film. For the 'audience' of *Far from the Madding Crowd* Bathsheba Everdene is Julie Christie not 'a way of dramatizing the nature of social movement, and how it works through individuals'.[15]

The second thing is that the minority who do read Hardy read him in certain specific ways, ways which are determined by the examination system. In some ways the system of public national examinations is analogous to the system of commodity production itself and 'Thomas Hardy' exists in the former as commodities do in the latter for just as in the capitalist mode of production useful articles are produced *for the purpose* of being exchanged and not for their use value, so in the examination system the novels of Thomas Hardy are (re)produced *for the purpose* of passing examinations and not for their pleasure or enjoyment value. Of course commodities *are* useful and Hardy's novels *do* give pleasure, but that is not *why* they are produced or read under these circumstances. In both cases the 'primary material' (useful article, writing) is mediated by a specific productive necessity, in the one case to realize surplus value and make a profit, in the second to realize/recognize 'literary value' and acquire a progressive certification of competency/ mastery in the practice of an ideological discourse. And in both cases the crucial determining factor is the specific mode of production in which products exist as commodities and writing as literary texts. Clearly this analogy cannot be taken too far, but it does help to emphasize that those forms of appearance (of products and writing) which we take for granted as 'natural' are in fact social products. As Marx observed, 'to stamp an object of utility as a value, is just as much a social product as language'.[16] So just as, through the process of exchange, 'the products of labour acquire, as values, a uniform social status, distinct from their varied forms of existence as objects of utility',[17] so, considered as literary texts, *all* forms of writing have a common quality, namely that of having 'literary value'. And it is this common quality which is realized in and produced by the education system.

The implications of this are considerable for it means that in the education system writing has the status of a *pretext*. The real object of the study of the 'literary text' is not writing itself but its ideological (re)productions. In effect it is the critical structure of perceptions which is being activated in the school/exam system in an increasingly sophisticated 'critical' form which enables students to appropriate ideology and make themselves its bearers and even its creators.[18] This system commences with the simple reproduction of 'Thomas Hardy' at 'O' level where students are asked to 'compare and contrast', 'consider', 'account for', 'describe', 'illustrate' and 'show', and progresses to the more sophisticated (re)production of the 'Discuss' convention of 'A' level and beyond. Research recently undertaken by Peter Widdowson has shown that 'A' level examination questions both reinforce the 'character and environment' conception of 'Thomas Hardy' and operate within a very restricted range of nature, fate, tragedy, character and the 'flaws' in his writing. From his analysis Widdowson concludes:

> Although the 'Discuss' convention 'allows' the student to contradict the quotation, the 'critical' questions are invariably negatively framed so that the student is persuaded in the first

instance to think in those terms. The underlying burden of all such questions, of course, is 'literary value' and an assumed agreement, between critic–examiner and critic–student, about a hypothetical model of the ultimately 'probable' novel, which in effect closes out any possible *positive* reading of those features that deviate from it.... What we can deduce from all this is how restricted and determined 'Hardy' is as an educational discourse ... and how this 'primary material' is reproduced within very limited parameters of intelligibility: 'Hardy' as the tragic novelist of character struggling heroically with Nature, Fate or other, pre-eminently non-social, forces. Quite clearly the Hardy who rules O.K. in school education at least, is 'primary material' in only a very dubious sense.[19]

The most significant feature of this system is the way in which the student engages with the critical structure of perceptions at *the moment of examination.* If one were ever able to isolate a moment of ideological interpellation it is this subjective test which is centred upon the articulation of point of view. What the examinee is being asked to demonstrate is his or her 'critical' mastery of the literary text on the basis of an interaction of one subject's point of view with another's to engage, that is, not with the writing itself but with its (re)production in the discourse of aesthetic ideology. Thus the student's response is not only determined by the structure of perceptions but it enters directly into the student's discourse forming the basis of his or her answer. However 'original' the individual's 'reply' it cannot escape the ideological pre-determination of the question: 'Is it true to say that Tess is unfitted for living by her moral idealism?'; ' "Tess is a murderess; and any assessment of her must take this into account." Discuss.'; ' "Despite the element of sheer bad luck, *Tess of the d'Urbervilles* has a tragic inevitability." Discuss.'; ' "Tess is the victim of those who fail to comprehend her true nature." Discuss.'. The entire period of the student's study culminates in this tense moment of 'critical' interaction. That this crucial encounter has been ideologically determined in certain specific ways is evident from the numerous and popular series of 'Study Notes'. These show how the ideological construction of Hardy's writing is reproduced in and by the education/

examination system precisely because they are 'principally designed', as the Preface to one of them states, 'for students of Hardy's major novels at GCE 'A' level and in the early stages of university study'.[20]

If we look at some of the most popular of these 'Notes'[21] we find that although their format varies they are essentially structured on the basis of a repetition of the novel (in summary form) accompanied by a commentary. This structure reveals the basic contradiction in a system based on the interaction between the critical structure of perceptions and the individual student's personal point of view. How *can* the student have an individual view in face of a Thomas Hardy who has been so massively constructed by the discourse of aesthetic ideology? And yet the whole point of the exercise is precisely to allow the free play of individual interpretations, the articulation of subjective points of view expressive of a democratic and critical freedom of thought. In an attempt to overcome this each of the Notes in one form or another is at pains to disclaim any authoritarian intentions. Brodie's has an address 'To the student' which states that 'A close reading of the set book is the student's primary task'. The Notes are intended to increase understanding and appreciation and 'to stimulate *your own* thinking about it; *they are in no way intended as a substitute* for a thorough knowledge of the book.' In the York Notes it is pointed out that the comments are intended to bring various 'different kinds of points to the student's attention ... they make no claim to completeness of any kind, but are intended to be suggestive and helpful in close reading of the text ...' Coles's extended 'Note to the Reader' claims authority but not *final* authority and suggests that Hardy's work is great by virtue of the fact that there are so many interpretations:

These Notes present a clear discussion of the action and thought of the work under consideration and a concise interpretation of the artistic merits and its significance.... The critical evaluations have been prepared by experts with special knowledge of the individual texts who have usually had some years experience in teaching the works. They are, however, not incontrovertible. No literary judgment is. Of any great work of literature there are many interpretations, and even conflicting views have value for the student (and the teacher), since the aim is not for the student to accept unquestioningly any one interpretation but to make his own.

Despite these disclaimers, however, when we actually come to the commentaries we find a Thomas Hardy who is strikingly familiar: fatalism, pessimism, human helplessness, tragedy. In Brodie's Notes on *Tess,* for example, we read 'there is only one tragic theme—the helplessness of human beings ... the general lot of man is struggle and suffering.... Life is a mocking farce, with neither sense nor reason in it.' This, of course, is represented as Hardy's view not that of writer of the Notes. They go on: 'The sense of an inscrutable fate hangs over *Tess* ... [the characters] meet life's mischances by enduring them stoically rather than by attempting to fight; they do not come out of their experiences finer than they went in.' What is interesting about these Notes is the way that the different novels are used to construct the same Thomas Hardy. With slight variations the commentaries reiterate the same theme. So *The Return of the Native* is concerned with the 'general malaise in the life of humanity. Man is a pawn in life's lottery.... Man's life avails him nothing. Men are just incidental in creation. Man may protest against his fate, but it makes no difference, he is only a plaything, he cannot master his destiny.' And at the heart of *The Mayor of Casterbridge* 'there is a sense of the cruel irony of life.... Hardy sums up his philosophy ... in the last paragraph. It is the key-note of *The Mayor of Casterbridge.* Life gives bitter blows.... The sense of an inscrutable fate overlooking man's life hangs over [the novel] it is a novel of disillusionment, of helplessness in the face of the circumstances of life.' There is a consistent emphasis on the helplessness of individuals, of the hopelessness of the human situation (H. C. Duffin is quoted to the effect that *The Mayor of Casterbridge* is 'the most hopeless book ever written. The tone of the telling, in the latter half of the story is stony despair') and of man's stoical endurance in face of the blows meted out to him by fate. And the phrase 'they do not come out of their experiences finer than they went in' is repeated like a litany, a silent accusation of Hardy's Godlessness.

The more sophisticated York Notes commentaries have a firmer authorial imprint (each being written by a different academic/critic) and perhaps by virtue of their being representative of *a* point of view rather than a distillation of many points of view they appear to be more authoratitive, more 'critical', less dogmatic. This is because we are moving into a higher and more sophisticated articulation of aesthetic ideology. A space is produced which offers students a greater freedom to think within ideology precisely by being more 'critical' themselves. Yet here too we find the familiar emphases. The 'fundamental theme' of *Tess*, writes David Lindley, is 'the inevitable struggle between mortality and the will to live.... Hardy shows in many different ways how the individual's life is determined only partly by his or her own efforts, and how much depends upon the pressure of things over which the individual has no control.' However, despite the fact that Hardy presents a gloomy picture of human life and presents 'so powerfully the operation of uncontrollable forces upon the individual and the effect of apparently chance happenings' neither his pessimism nor his fatalism should be exaggerated. Hardy also shows the will to live, real moral growth, and, in the character of Tess, 'how the flawed human being can rise to great dignity in suffering'. The construction of Thomas Hardy is still on the basis of an informing centre, the dominant themes are rehearsed but offered here in the more 'open' form of 'on the one hand ... but then on the other' which leads to the examination 'discussion'—'Critics disagree as to whether Tess is completely blameless or at least partially responsible for her own ultimate disaster. Make clear your own views on this matter ...'[22]

There is no such subtlety of approach in the Coles Notes. Here Thomas Hardy appears unmistakably as he was constructed by the discourse of aesthetic ideology up to the period of the Second World War. The 'keynote' here is fatalism/pessimism/tragedy; all the 'universal' themes are forcibly foregrounded. Nietzsche's 'agonized cry, "God is dead"' is taken as representative of the 'agony of the nineteenth century' which Hardy reflects in his novels. The key to Hardy's thinking is that 'Since there is no God to give meaning to life, Man is alone in the Universe' which is simply indifferent 'to the puny creature, Man, whose sufferings temporarily ruffle the environment. He is less a creature of Reason able to control his fate, to choose between Good and Evil, than a victim of forces within himself and outside himself.'

Tess is viewed as Hardy's attempt to write 'a classical tragedy in the form of a novel' and Hardy as a great novelist whose books are permeated 'by his great and real humanity, his personal stature as a man, his anthropomorphism, his honesty and his sincerity' and the reader reacts to them 'as he does to his life and his era'. In the major section on Hardy's philosophy which appears to be based on A. P. Elliott's *Fatalism in the Works of Thomas Hardy* (1935)[23] we read that 'Hardy fluctuates between fatalism and determinism'. And in the commentaries which accompany the chapter summaries the familiar construction of Thomas Hardy is faithfully reproduced in terms of: 'Hardy's sense of despair at the indifference of the cosmos to human pain'; his 'concept of an indifferent Nature'; his 'sense of fate and retribution'; his 'intense feeling for Nature'. This last modulates into Hardy's hatred for the machine age: Hardy 'comments on the clash between ... man, nature, and society'; to him 'the Industrial Revolution was a monster that destroyed the traditions and meaning of country life'; he shares Angel Clare's "unconquerable, and almost unreasonable, aversion to modern town life"'; 'If there is anything that Hardy despises as much as hypocritical religious concepts, it is the machine age'. This construction of Thomas Hardy is corroborated by the bibliography: Abercrombie, Beach, Cecil, Chew, Duffin, Grimsditch.

We also find the familiar treatment of Wessex as background and the marginalization of the workfolk (Brodie's suggesting that they reflect 'the failings of uneducated people generally'). So too we find the theme of 'change' and the destruction of the organic comunity, an emphasis on the collapse of religious belief and the influence of Darwin and a similar 'critical' treatment of Hardy's intellect—'It must be said that Hardy was not really an original thinker, even though later in his life he came to believe that he was.' (York Notes on *Jude*). Criticised too are those elements of 'unreality' in the novels, particularly the use of chance and coincidence. Above all, of course, Hardy's 'style' is viewed with a critical eye. Where it is praised it is in terms of its 'directness', 'simplicity', 'dignity', 'straightforwardness', 'force' in the delineation of country scenes or characters. But when Hardy attempts sophistication then he is 'verbose', 'clumsy', 'pompous', 'unconvincing', 'cumbersome', over-prone to the use of quotation and literary references. 'His is not', writes

Maureen Mahon, 'a very profound or deeply logical mind. His ideas ... now seem dated, frayed, and very unexciting ... And—a very serious defect to most modern critics—Hardy's prose style is often clumsy and laboured'. But, of course, his 'substantial virtues' are rescued from his 'glaring defects' —Thomas Hardy is 'the great delineator in prose of rural England'.[24]

And so we arrive at our point of departure. The 'essential Thomas Hardy', ideologically constructed as 'major fiction', has become the agent for the reproduction of ideology, inducing new discourses which ultimately always reproduce the same ideology although in many varied forms.[25] Produced on the basis of a linguistic division, Hardy's writing is (re)produced to maintain a linguistic division in education. It is important to realize, however, that this division does not come about 'after the event'. Hardy's writing arises out of a pre-existent division and one, furthermore, which was being instituted in the education system at the time he was writing. This division is so glaringly *present* in Hardy's writing that it has had to be excised (it could not be ignored) through the long process of critical purification which has separated the 'essential Thomas Hardy', the great humanist writer, from the 'defects' of his style. The essential quality of a 'literary' discourse written in the common language is that it should not draw attention to the contradictions inherent in a 'common language' of a society based on a radical separation of the producers from the owners of the means of production, a separation sustained by the education system. This is the basis of Leavis's rejection of Hardy for Leavis's concern was first and foremost with education. The Great Tradition is a tradition of *English,* and Leavis just could not have written about *Tess* what he did about *The Portrait of a Lady*, that it is 'one of the great novels of the English language'.[26] The linguistic contradictions in Hardy's writing are effaced by the discourse of aesthetic ideology. Represented as 'literary' failings they appear as a manifestation of some essential flaw in the writer himself.[27] It is a flaw which the education system guarantees that 80% of the population shares for their English too is 'clumsy and laboured'.

Conclusion

I have maintained that literature is not an object or a text or a 'field' but a social relation and that as such it must inevitably be in a state of constant transformation. As changes occur in the relations between the material forces and the relations of production so changes also occur in the ideological forms in which these are experienced and 'fought out'. But whatever the relations (and they do exist) between the run down of the coal industry and the number of people who study *Coriolanus*, between de-industrialization as an economic policy and deconstruction as a literary theory, they are not relations of direct determination. To say that it is not the current economic and political crises in this country which have produced the present crisis in English is to do no more than to reaffirm the relative autonomy of the ideological sphere. English is not in crisis now because of the fiscal policies of Matthew Arnold's narrow minded and mean spirited Philistines. The last time in our history when there were three and a half million people unemployed English was in a very different situation from what it is now. Then English Literature was forged as the weapon of a radical cause:

> ... the very conditions that make literary education look so desperate are those which make it more important than ever before; for in a world of this kind—and a world that changes so rapidly—it is on literary tradition that the office of maintaining continuity must rest.... We are committed to more consciousness; that way, if any, lies salvation. We cannot, as we might in a healthy state of culture, leave the citizen to be formed unconsciously by his environment; if anything like a worthy idea of satisfactory living is to be saved, he must be trained to discriminate and to resist.... It is to literature alone

... that we can look with any hope of keeping in touch with our spiritual tradition—with the 'picked experience of ages.'[1]

Taking I. A. Richards' statement that 'nothing less than our whole sense of man's history and destiny is involved in our final decision as to value'[2] as a militant manifesto, literary criticism became a radical practice in so far as the ability to discriminate between the fine and the shoddy became the key to understanding 'life' itself. But it was also more than this because the study of English was a training not only in discrimination but also crucially in resistance. Leavis and his followers saw an educated and literary élite as a species of cultural freedom fighters, inheritors of the traditions of the old English organic community engaged in a guerilla war with the forces of mass civilization. English was their chief weapon against the shock troops of the urban armies of materialism—pop culture, journalism, the cinema, television, advertising. How different the situation appears to us today.

Marx wrote that the doctrine 'that men are products of circumstances and upbringing, and that, therefore, changed men are products of other circumstances and changed upbringing, forgets that it is men that change circumstances and that the educator himself needs educating.... The coincidence of the changing circumstances and of human activity can be conceived and rationally understood only as *revolutionary practice*.'[3] This problem confronts the teacher now no less than it did half a century ago when Leavis and those who thought like him attempted just such a revolution. But while the circumstances and the people and the upbringing have certainly changed in those fifty years, the practice has remained the same and what was originally intended to function as a radical discourse has become a cornerstone of the education establishment. One might draw a parallel between the history of practical criticism and those radical and even revolutionary elements of the early nineteenth-century bourgeoisie which, after 1848, were transformed into the forces of reaction. Like the political demands of the bourgeois, Leavis's critical doctrines were based, in the final analysis, on principles not of equality but separation. Just as the political hegemony of the bourgeoisie which maintains the radical separation of the producers from the means of produc-

tion operates through the 'freedom of choice' of universal suff-
rage, so its cultural hegemony which maintains the separation of
those who read 'Literature' from those who do not operates
through the 'freedom of choice' of universal literacy.

Obsessed with the past, idealist criticism abolishes history.
Determined by an idealism of the human essence it thinks in
terms of the continuity of 'traditions': of organic culture, of
humanist realism, of Literature, art and value. Materialist
criticism on the other hand, based on a theory of social production, is concerned not with the good old days but with the bad
new ones. The necessity for a knowledge of the historical modes
of production of writing and of its social consumption and reproduction could not be more evident than now. In the year that
George Orwell's writing has been so ruthlessly deprived of its
history and (re)produced to support a political ideology which
Orwell himself would have despised, criticism can no longer conceal itself as a supra-class concern with the human essence, or
with making final decisions as to value, or the discovery of
meaning, or the search for 'signification' or the endless tracing of
the finer threads of 'intertextuality'. All such critical discourses
are profoundly idealist, self-absorbed, reactionary, and it is
important that they should be recognized as such.

There is a moment in *Nineteen Eighty-Four* when Winston and
Julia dream of escaping from the clutches of the Party: 'They
would disappear, alter themselves out of recognition, learn to
speak with proletarian accents, get jobs in a factory and live out
their lives undetected in a back-street.'[4] In order to hide themselves away in that unseen region the two would have to learn to
speak the way 'they' do, to speak in the clumsy and laboured
accents of the proletariat. It is, of course, with the plight of Julia
and Winston (the intellectual whose task it is to constantly
(re)produce history) that we are meant to identify, with their
'consciousness' and point of view, and in so doing the reader is
ideologically co-opted into the vision of post-revolutionary
society as a totalitarian hell, and into sharing the political will
that 'it shall never happen here'. Yet it is precisely in our 'free'
and 'democratic' society in the year 1984 that *Nineteen Eighty-
Four* has been used in the education system[5] in the on-going process of separating 'us' from 'them'. Criticism cannot be absolved
from culpability in the production and maintenance of that

radical separation. The task before a materialist criticism is not to liberate writing into its true meaning but to produce a knowledge of writing as a social product and literature as a social relation and to bring an end to the system in which writing is used as an ideological weapon in the furtherance of social inequality.

Conceived in idealist terms 'Literature' is immutable. Conceived as a social relation on the other hand, literature is anything but immutable. It is, therefore, possible to say (slightly changing Marx's famous declaration) that the critics have only interpreted literature, in various ways; the point, however, is to change it. As a social practice, and not an individual act expressive of a subjective will, materialist criticism can be the agency of that change and become an element in the production of a genuine knowledge. This knowledge, however, can only be produced out of the interaction between theory and practice. As Marx wrote: 'Social life is essentially *practical*. All mysteries which mislead theory to mysticism find their rational solution in human practice and in the comprehension of this practice.'[6] It is for this reason that I have retained the term criticism in the title of the present work, for while on the theoretical side materialist criticism is indeed a theory of knowledge, on the practical side it must actively engage with the material practices of an ideological apparatus the determining feature of which is precisely the act of 'criticism'.

It is important and necessary to produce a knowledge of the writing which forms the basis of study in our education system in terms of social production. It is important and necessary to understand that the Thomas Hardy who exists in the discourses and material practices which form the apparatus of the cultural hegemony of the ruling class is the construction of an ideological discourse which maintains the deep social divisions in our society. And it is important and necessary to understand literature not only in terms of the production of meaning but also the production of value, of ideology and ideological discourses, aesthetic and otherwise, and crucially the production and reproduction of the relations of production in class society. All these are important and necessary objectives. But if, at the end of the day, we are still left with the 'Valhalla of the enduring figures of literature' intact, what has really been achieved? If that 'Madame Tussaud's panopticon, filled with nothing but durable figures'[7] from the Duchess of Malfi to Tess, from Hamlet to Stephan Dedalus, continues to dominate education what effect can theory really have on practice? It is this radical contradiction which has produced the present crisis in English. The politicization of criticism has produced a situation where it has become impossible for many to teach, in good faith, English as it has been constituted as a discipline over the past fifty years. In the institutions of higher education this situation has been contained by absorbing and incorporating radical criticism as 'approaches'—psychological, feminist, Marxist approaches to—but always and inevitably, to 'Literature'. Even the most conservative English departments have their courses on Literary Theory—safely reserved, of course, for the 'brightest' students. Meanwhile these very institutions ensure that the cultural domination of English continues unabated through the maintenance of the 'canon' and the forms and rituals of the examination system.

The only way, in my view, to change this situation is to pull down the Madame Tussaud's panopticon which aesthetic ideology has constructed in order to bring an end to the cultural domination of the canon of English Literature. This is not to advocate the construction of another edifice to replace it, an 'alternative canon', but rather to build in its place a knowledge of writing as a social product and of literature as a social relation. Such a project does not mean abandoning those writings which have been constructed as 'Literature' by the discourses of aesthetic ideology. Rather it means ending their cultural *domination* by treating them, in the ways I have outlined, as cultural products, writings which can be set alongside other cultural products, other writings, other forms.

I was asked recently by someone who heard that I had been teaching a course on Popular Literature: 'How on earth do you teach Raymond Chandler?' That question, in which the distinction between 'fiction' and 'Literature' is enshrined, presupposes and unquestioningly takes for granted that there really is something in 'Literature' which can be abstracted and taught. Such teaching, which consists in the revelation of the plentitude of Wordsworth or Tennyson, has nothing to say about Chandler. Full of meaning, 'The Lady of Shalott' can be taught endlessly; about *The Lady in the Lake* on the other hand nothing can be said.

Leavis imposed just such a silence on Hardy and in that single oversight in the structure of perceptions of one of the most sincerely concerned critics of modern times we can see how the construction of canons and 'traditions' is, at bottom, profoundly reactionary for they are invariably based on some form of radical exclusion.

To study 'Literature' in order to keep in touch with our spiritual tradition, with the 'picked experience of ages', seems to be a self evidently valuable enterprise only so long as no questions are raised as to whose experience it is that is being picked and who is doing the picking. Feminist and Marxist critics have asked those questions and the answers they have suggested have not only changed the nature of the object of study but also our relation to it. What I have tried to show is that the ideological forms and institutional practices of English are, despite every attempt at concealment, profoundly political and that by understanding literature as a social relation English can be seen for what it really is, not an immutable cultural object but the site of cultural struggle. It is a struggle in which there are no neutral positions and in the present situation every reading of Thomas Hardy is an act of political commitment.

Notes

INTRODUCTION

1. F. R. Leavis, *The Great Tradition*, Pelican ed., 9.
2. In Marx's theory of value the same kind of labour may be both productive and unproductive depending on its relation to capital. Thus the labour which went into producing *Paradise Lost* was unproductive whereas that of a writer specifically commissioned by a publisher to produce a mass circulation novel titled say, *My Lost Paradise*, is productive. Clearly the relation between labour and capital is an important element in determining cultural production. See Karl Marx, *Theories of Surplus Value*, London 1969, part 1, 389–413, particularly 401.
3. Louis Althusser, 'From *Capital* to Marx's Philosophy', in Louis Althusser and Étienne Balibar, *Reading Capital,* trans. Ben Brewster, London 1975, 25.
4. J. S. Mill, *The Subjection of Women,* first published in 1869.
5. Göran Therborn, *The Ideology of Power and the Power of Ideology*, London, 1980, 28.
6. Florence Emily Hardy, *The Life of Thomas Hardy 1840–1928*, London, 1975, 335. Originally published as *The Early Life of Thomas Hardy, 1840–1891,* (1928) and *The Later Years of Thomas Hardy, 1892–1928,* (1930). Ostensibly written by his second wife this is in fact an autobiography.
7. D. G. Richie, *Darwin and Hegel*, London, 1893, vi–vii.
8. *The Life*, 148. 9. *Ibid.*, 310. 10. *Ibid.*, 346.
11. *Ibid.*, 153. 12. *Ibid.*, 229. 13. *Ibid.*, 216.
14. D. A. Dike, 'A Modern Oedipus: *The Mayor of Casterbridge*', *Essays in Criticism*, 2 (April 1952), 171.
15. Francis Mulhern, *The Moment of 'Scrutiny'*, London, 1979, 331.
16. Louis Althusser, *Lenin and Philosophy and Other Essays*, trans. Ben Brewster, London, 1971, 219.
17. T. S. Eliot, *Notes Towards a Definition of Culture*, London, 1972, 31–2. First published in 1948.
18. Louis Althusser, *For Marx*, trans. Ben Brewster, Penguin Books, 1969, 233.

19. Marx writes of the 'legal, political, religious, artistic or philo-sophic—in short, ideological forms in which men become conscious of this conflict [between the productive forces and the relations of production] and fight it out'. See *A Contribution to the Critique of Political Economy*, London, 1971, 21.
20. Therborn, *op. cit.*, 6.   21. *Ibid.*, 2.   22. *Ibid.*, 2 and 77.
23. Raymond Williams, *The English Novel from Dickens to Lawrence*, London, 1971, 98-9.
24. Antonio Gramsci, *Selections from the Prison Notebooks*, trans. Quintin Hoare and Geoffrey Nowell Smith, London, 1971, 258.

CHAPTER 1
1. *The English Novel from Dickens to Lawrence*, 116.   2. *Ibid.*, 113.
3. *The Victoria History of the County of Dorset*, 1908, 262.
4. Hardy's description in *Tess*, chapter 51.
5. A. H. Johnson, *The Disappearance of the Small Landowner*, Oxford, 1963, 104.
6. *The Victoria History*, 275.
7. Karl Marx, *Capital* III, 599. See also 806-7; 875-6 and *Grundrisse*, 587 and 713.
8. Williams, *op. cit.*, 112.   9. Karl Marx, *Grundrisse*, 276.
10. *Capital*, 1, 673.   11. *Ibid.*, 714-16.   12. *Capital*, 1, 673.
13. See D. C. Barnett, 'Allotments and the Problem of Rural Poverty, 1780-1840', *Land, Labour and Population*, ed. E. L. Jones and C. E. Mingay, London, 1967, 162-183.
14. See W. Hasbach, *A History of the English Argicultural Labourer*, London, 1908, 103 ff. Maurice Dobb in *Studies in the Development of Capitalism* notes: 'A study made by Professor Lavrovsky of parishes not yet enclosed (or fully enclosed) by 1793 led him to the conclusion that "the independent peasantry had already ceased to exist, even in unenclosed parishes, by the end of the eighteenth century"'. Footnote, 228.
15. A. H. Johnson writes that 'Whereas in the sixteenth and seven-teenth centuries the enclosures *chiefly* dealt with the commonable field, those of the eighteenth century were largely, though by no means exclusively, concerned with the wastes.' He adds that the 'indirect result of enclosure was consolidation. The poor sold and the rich bought'. See *The Disappearance of the Small Landowner*, Oxford, 1963, 86 and 101.
16. E. P. Thompson, *The Making of the English Working Class*, Penguin Books, London, 1968, 237-239.
17. G. Bourne (George Sturt), *Change in the Village*, London, 1912, 134.   18. *Ibid.*, 134.

19. *Ibid.*, 146. While Sturt was a keen observer he nevertheless presents an idealised view of the old rural community in *Change in the Village* and *The Wheelwright's Shop*. Out of such nostalgic reflections came the profoundly potent myth of the loss of the 'organic community' which Leavis put to such effective ideological use. The flavour of Leavis's petty bourgeois assault on the values of capitalist society comes out strongly in *Culture and Environment*, where we read that the loss of the organic community 'is the most important fact of recent history'. See F. R. Leavis and D. Thompson, *Culture and Environment*, London, 1933, 87 and 93.

20. *Capital*, 1, 675.

21. S. Laing, *National Distress, its Causes and Remedies*, London, 1844, 62.

22. Marx, *Capital*, 1, 692. Marx gives a lucid analysis of the history of the expropriation of the population from the land from the fourteenth century onwards (including Ireland and Scotland) and the conditions of the agricultural labourer, at the end of *Capital*, 1, 673–749.

23. E. G. Wakefield, *England and America*, London, 1833, vol. 1, 47. For the relation between pauperism and the concept of the free labourer see Marx, *Grundrisse*, 604; *Capital*, II, 245; *Capital*, III, 727–9. With regard to the term peasant, Raymond Williams correctly points out that 'Where Hardy lived and worked, as in most other parts of England, there were virtually no peasants, although "peasantry" as a generic word for country people was still used by writers.' See *The English Novel*, 100. Other terms for the agricultural labourer include 'hind', 'wretch', 'swain' and 'Hodge'.

24. F.A. Wilson and A. B. Richards, *Britain Redeemed and Canada Preserved*, London, 1850, 178–9.

25. F. G. Heath, *The English Peasantry*, London, 1874, 6.

26. *Ibid.*, 25.

27. The 'most nearly flawless of Hardy's novels' according to Michael Millgate. See *Thomas Hardy, His Career as a Novelist*, London, 1971, 50. This nearly flawless work is concerned with the passing of the 'old stable order' from agricultural life in the view of Douglas Brown. See *Thomas Hardy*, London, 1954, 45.

28. Quoted in Heath, *op. cit.*, 31–2.   29. p. 263.

30. H. Rider Haggard, *Rural England*, London, 1906, vol. 1, 268.

31. *Op. cit.*, vol. II, 540.

32. See Haggard, *Rural England*, vol. 1, 257–286.

33. Marx, *Grundrisse*, 297.   34. *Ibid.*, 589.

35. See 'Wage Labour and Capital', in *Marx and Engels Selected Works in One Volume*, London, 1970, 88–90.

36. Of this division Marx observes: 'The foundation of every division of labour that is well developed, and brought about by the exchange of commodities, is the separation between town and country. It may be said, that the whole economic history of society is summed up in the movement of this antithesis.' See *Capital*, 1, 352.
37. See *Capital*, 1, 77 and *Grundrisse*, 163.
38. The essential characteristic of commodity production is that useful articles are produced for the purpose of being exchanged. In other words, it is not the use value of the article which is uppermost in the system of commodity production but its exchange value.
39. *Grundrisse*, 511. Marx observes in *Capital* III, 667, that 'The capitalist mode of production spreads in agriculture but slowly and unevenly, as may be observed in England, the classic land of the capitalist mode of production in agriculture'.
40. *Grundrisse*, 729.   41. *Ibid.*, 497. See also *Capital*, 1, 77-8.
42. *Capital*, 1, 77-8.
43. Karl Marx, *Theories of Surplus Value*, 1, 408.
44. *Capital*, 1, 77.
45. Among Hardy's close relatives there were labourers, cobblers, bricklayers, carpenters, farm servants, journeyman joiners, servants and teachers. His maternal grandmother was a yeoman farmer's daughter and his father was himself an artisan, a self-employed mason who built up a small business (which at the height of its prosperity employed eight men and a boy) and who, at his death in 1892, left £850. See R. Gittings, *Young Thomas Hardy*, Chap. 2. We can get a good idea of the social position of Hardy's family from a statistic recorded by Hobsbawm who notes that in Cambridge in 1867 the gentlemen and clergymen at their death 'left median property to the value of £1,500-2,000; the professors and masters of colleges a mean of £26,000 each; but the local businessmen only a median of £800, the shopkeepers of £350.' See E. J. Hobsbawm, *Industry and Empire*, Penguin Books, 1969, footnote on p. 183.
46. *Theories of Surplus Value*, 1, 409.
47. M. Dobb, *Studies in the Development of Capitalism*, London, 1946, 300.

CHAPTER 2
  1. See Roland Barthes, *Mythologies*, trans. Annette Lavers, Paladin, 1973, 142.
  2. *Grundrisse*, 652.
  3. Quoted in J. Joll, ed., *Britain and Europe, Pitt to Churchill*, London, 1950, 124-5.

4. J. S. Mill, *The Subjection of Women*, M.I.T. Press, London, 1970, 7–8.
5. Matthew Arnold, 'The Popular Education of France', see *Matthew Arnold Selected Prose*, Peguin Books, 104. This essay was first published in 1861.
6. Gramsci, *op. cit.*, 260.
7. Karl Marx, *The Eighteenth Brumaire of Louis Bonaparte*, in *Marx Engels Selected Works in One Volume*, 117.
8. *Ibid.*, 118.
9. Herbert Spencer, *The Man Versus the State*, London, 1909, 7.
10. Étienne Balibar, 'The Basic Concepts of Historical Materialism', in Louis Althusser and Étienne Balibar, *Reading Capital*, trans. Ben Brewster, London, 1970, 225.
11. *The Eighteenth Brumaire*, 120.
12. Bertrand Russell, *History of Western Philosophy*, London, 1971, 696.
13. Talcott Parsons, *The Structure of Social Action*, New York, 1937, 111.
14. Thomas Robert Malthus, *First Essay on Population*, London, 1798, 194.
15. After the repeal of the Corn Laws (1846) and the collapse of Chartism (1848).
16. *Social Statics*, London, 1851, 323.
17. J. W. Burrow, *Evolution and Society: A Study in Victorian Social Theory*, Cambridge, 1966, 194.
18. Herbert Spencer, *The Man Versus the State*, London, 1909, 59.
19. *Social Statics*, 433.   20. *Capital*, III, 831.
21. *Culture and Society*, 77.   22. *Culture and Anarchy*, 226.
23. *The Popular Education of France*, 122.
24. *Culture and Anarchy*, 206.   25. *Ibid.*, 207.
26. Melvin Richter, *The Politics of Conscience: T. H. Green and His Age*, London, 1964, 137.
27. *Ibid.*, 36–7; 131; 172. Both in their idealism and their altruism Clym Yeobright and Jude are very close to this position. Of Clym Hardy writes: 'Yeobright loved his kind. He had a conviction that the want of most men was knowledge of a sort which brings wisdom rather than affluence. He wished to raise the class at the expense of individuals rather than individuals at the expense of the class. What was more, he was ready at once to be the first unit sacrificed.' (*The Return of the Native*, 196). Similarly, Jude Fawley wanted an 'opportunity of showing himself superior to the lower animals, and of contributing his units of work to the general progress of his generation'. (*Jude*, 82).
28. F. Engels, *Anti-Duhring*, Pekin, 1976, 327.

29. E. J. Hobsbawm, *Industry and Empire*, Pelican Books, 198.

30. *Royal Commission on Depression of Trade and Industry, Final Report, 1886*, xv. See also H. L. Beales, '"The Great Depression" in Industry and Trade', *Economic History Review*, V, 1924–35, 65–75.

31. V. I. Lenin, *Imperialism, the Highest Stage of Capitalism*, in *Selected Works* in one volume, London, 1969, 232.

32. *Ibid.*, 212.

33. From the time of Hardy's birth to the time he wrote *Jude* British capital invested abroad increased by a factor of almost twelve, rising from £144 million in 1842 to £1,698 million in 1893. See E. Halévy, *Imperialism and the Rise of Labour 1895–1905*, London, 1961, 13–14.

34. Perry Anderson, 'Origins of the Present Crisis', *New Left Review*, 23, 34–5.

35. Quoted in B. Simon, *Education and the Labour Movement 1870–1920*, London, 1965, 168–9.

36. *Ibid.*, 169.

CHAPTER 3

1. Florence Emily Hardy, *The Life of Thomas Hardy 1840–1928*.

2. Jean-Jacques Rousseau, *The Confessions*, trans. J. M. Cohn, Penguin Books, 17.

3. *The Life*, 50. 4. *Ibid.*, 224. 5. *Ibid.*, 376.

6. *Ibid.*, 310. 7. *Ibid.*, 333. 8. *Ibid.*, 225.

9. *Ibid.*, 416. 10. *Ibid.*, 376. 11. *Ibid.*, 335.

12. *Materialism and Empirio-Criticism*, Foreign Languages Press, Pekin, 1972, 271.

13. *The Life*, 376. 14. *Ibid.*, 310.

15. *Thomas Hardy's Personal Writings*, ed. Harold Orel, London, 1976, 56–7.

16. See Francis Mulhern, *The Moment of 'Scrutiny'*, London, 1979, 11.

17. Robert Gittings, *The Young Thomas Hardy*, Penguin Books, 15.

18. Michel Foucault, *The Archaeology of Knowledge*, trans. A. M. Sheridan Smith, Social Science paperback edition, London, 1974, 12–13.

19. *The Life*, 335.

20. Sebastiano Timpanaro, *On Materialism*, trans. Lawrence Garner, London, 1975, 17.

21. *Culture and Anarchy*, 257. 22. *Tess*, 400–1. 23. 41–2.

24. *Tess*, 156. 25. *The Life*, 137. 26. *Ibid.*, 313.

27. 'The Dorsetshire Labourer', Orel, *op. cit.*, 189. In other words, they 'degenerate' into the working class.

28. *The Life*, 131.

29. *Ibid.*, 131.

CHAPTER 4

1. *The Life,* 177.
2. This term is used as a somewhat inadequate compromise: peasant is clearly incorrect and rural petty-bourgeois does not quite fit the bill. It is meant to indicate that class where the separation of labour from the means of production had not taken place: these people both own their means of production and work themselves.
3. *The Trumpet-Major,* 47-8.   4. *Tess,* 66.
5. *The Mayor of Casterbridge,* 167.
6. Nathaniel Hawthorne, *The Scarlet Letter,* Signet Classics, 22.
7. *The Life,* 120-1.   8. *Ibid.,* 116.
9. *Under the Greenwood Tree,* 37.
10. p. 91.   11. p. 177.   12. pp. 176-7.
13. *Capital,* 1, 73.   14. See Karl Marx, *Grundrisse,* 497.
15. *Desperate Remedies,* 154.   16. pp. 119-20.
17. See *The Wealth of Nations,* book 1, chapter 1.
18. See Karl Marx, *Grundrisse,* 297.
19. *The Hand of Ethelberta,* 123.
20. *Jude,* 117.   21. p. 55.   22. p. 61.   23. p. 119.
24. p. 52   25. pp. 357-8.
26. Dale Kramer, for example, says that 'Giles is a "nature" god rather than a defender of society'. See *Thomas Hardy, the Forms of Tragedy,* London, 1975, 98.
27. *Far from the Madding Crowd,* 419.   28. *Ibid.,* 419.
29. p. 393.

CHAPTER 5

1. *The Life,* 213.   2. p. 80.
3. Mikhail Bakhtin, *Rabelais and his World,* trans. Helene Iswolsky, London, 1968, 19-20.
4. pp. 40-1.   5. p. 42.   6. p. 45.   7. p. 58.
8. p. 65.   9. p. 304.   10. p. 80-1.
11. See *Tess,* 95-7.   12. p. 284.
13. *Far from the Madding Crowd,* 313.   14. pp. 315-6.
15. *Under the Greenwood Tree,* 80.
16. See Chapter 26.   17. p. 57.   18. p. 155.
19. V. N. Vološinov, *Freudianism: A Marxist Critique,* Academic Press, 1976, 100.
20. Marx, *The Eighteenth Brumaire,* 117.   21. See pp. 256-9.
22. See *Tess,* 172-4.   23. See *Under the Greenwood Tree,* 40-2.
24. See *A Pair of Blue Eyes,* 275-8.   25. *The Trumpet Major,* 61.
26. p. 59.   27. p. 86.   28. *The Woodlanders,* 209.
29. *Tess,* 48.
30. *Desperate Remedies,* 52.   31. *Under the Greenwood Tree,* 167.

32. *Two on a Tower*, 286.   33. *The Woodlanders*, 140.
34. *Far from the Madding Crowd*, 137.   35. *The Well-Beloved*, 37.
36. p. 124.   37. *The Well-Beloved*, Hardy's Preface.
38. *Ibid.*, 36.   39. *Ibid.*, 36.

CHAPTER 6
 1. See *The Eighteenth Brumaire*, 120.
 2. Quoted in Lenin, *Materialism and Empirio-Criticism*, 395.
 3. W. H. Pater, *Studies in the History of the Renaissance*, London, 1873, 178.
 4. *Ibid.*, 209.   5. *The Return of the Native*, 98.
 6. *The Life*, 272.   7. *Ibid.*, 186.
 8. See *The Life*, 117, 177, 185, 228, 229.
 9. *The Hand of Ethelberta*, 332.   10. *The Woodlanders*, 147.
11. p. 244.   12. *The Life*, 409.   13. *The Hand of Ethelberta*, 383.
14. *Tess*, 275.   15. *A Pair of Blue Eyes*, 114–5.
16. *The Woodlanders*, 189.
17. *The Hand of Ethelberta*, 383.   18. pp. 105–6.
19. Ralph Ellison, *Invisible Man*, Penguin Books, 7.
20. Matthew Arnold's term in *Culture and Anarchy*.   21. pp. 88–9.
22. W. J. Dawson, *The Makers of English Fiction*, London, 1905. 223.

CHAPTER 7
 1. p. 287.   2. p. 71.   3. p. 43.   4. p. 115.
 5. See pp. 120–1.
 6. p. 139.   7. p. 136.   8. p. 140.   9. pp. 158–9.
10. *The Return of the Native*, 191.   11. p. 163.
12. Part 3, chap. 19.   13. p. 117.   14. p. 170.
15. See Karl Marx, *Grundrisse*, 164–5.
16. Tess 'seemed to regard Angel Clare as an intelligence rather than as a man'. p. 164.
17. Karl Marx, *Grundrisse*, 164–5.   18. p. 189.
19. p. 182.   20. *The Life*, 165.   21. *The Life*, 335.
22. See Michel Foucault, *The Order of Things*, 312.   23. p. 356.
24. Ludwig Feuerbach, *Essence of Christianity*, trans. Marian Evans, London, 1854, 268.
25. *Tess*, 254.   26. Chap. 7.
27. B. Simon, *Education and the Labour Movement 1870–1920*, London, 1965, 73.
28. *Jude*, 336.   29. p. 45.   30. p. 103.   31. p. 98.
32. p. 171.   33 p. 427.   34. p. 412.   35. pp. 170–1.
36. p. 136.   37. p. 137.   38. p. 135.   39. p. 170.
40. *The Life*, 310.   41. The Book of Job, 42, 4–5.
42. *The Life*, 216.   43. p. 41.

44. See the Apology to *Late Lyrics and Earlier.*

45. The philosophical compromise between materialism and idealism which maintains that while the thing-in-itself exists it cannot be finally known.

46. p. 34.   47. p. 40.

48. Herman Melville, *Billy Budd,* Signet Classic ed., 17.

49. pp. 56 and 57.   50. pp. 59 and 60.   51. p. 291.

52. *Ibid.*   53. p. 59.   54. p. 54.   55. p. 57.   56. p. 58.

57. See Lenin, *Materialism and Empirio-Criticism,* 235.

CHAPTER 8

1. p. 34.   2. p. 107.   3. p. 38.   4. p. 108.   5. pp. 37–8.

6. p. 104.   7. p. 116.   8. *Ibid.*   9. p. 120.

10. *Far from the Madding Crowd,* 419.

11. p. 88.   12. p. 91.

13. The following quotations are all from Book 1, chap. 7, 'Queen of Night'.

14. Like little Johnny Nunsuch who 'seemed a mere automaton, galvanized into moving and speaking by the wayward Eustacia's will'. p. 86.

15. Of Egdon she says: 'There is a sort of beauty in the scenery, I know; but it is a jail to me'. p. 118.

16. pp. 225, 96 and 233.   17. pp. 223 and 230.

18. See pp. 370–1.   19. pp. 380–1.   20. p. 35.

21. p. 273.   22. p. 35.   23. p. 196.   24. p. 198.

25. p. 215.   26. p. 223.   27. p. 197.   28. pp. 161–2.

29. p. 191.   30. p. 162.   31. p. 191.

CHAPTER 9

1. p. 288.   2. *The Woodlanders,* 68.

3. *The Hand of Ethelberta,* 331.   4. *The Woodlanders,* 69.

5. *A Laodicean,* 48.   6. *Far from the Madding Crowd,* 412.

7. *Jude,* 187.   8. *Ibid.,* 258.

9. *The Woodlanders,* 219–20.   10. *Far from the Madding Crowd,* 219.

11. *Two on a Tower,* 143–4.   12. *Jude,* 82.   13. *Tess,* 368.

14. *Jude,* 371.   15. *Ibid.,* 419.   16. p. 166.

17. E. von Hartmann, *The Sexes Compared and Other Essays,* trans. A. Kenner, London, 1895, 2. My emphasis.

18. *The Return of the Native,* 168.   19. *The Woodlanders,* 325.

20. *Jude,* 194.   21. *Desperate Remedies,* 240.

22. See *Under the Greenwood Tree,* 132–3 and 146.

23. *A Pair of Blue Eyes,* 157.   24. *Far from the Madding Crowd,* 68.

25. *Jude,* 338.   26. *Far from the Madding Crowd,* 44.

27. p. 269.   28. See p. 146.

29. *Far from the Madding Crowd*, 56.
30. John Berger, *Ways of Seeing*, Pelican Books, 47.
31. *The Return of the Native*, 183.
32. *The Mayor of Casterbridge*, 312 and 160.
33. *Jude*, 150 and 226.   34. *The Woodlanders*, 137 and 203.
35. *The Trumpet-Major*, 311.

CHAPTER 10
1. *Under the Greenwood Tree*, 82.   2. *Jude*, 82.
3. *Tess*, 197.   4. See pp. 222–3.   5. *A Laodicean*, 115.
6. *The Well-Beloved*, 31.   7. *Jude*, 59 and 78.
8. *Far from the Madding Crowd*, 52.   9. *Jude*, 45.
10. p. 85.   11. p. 143.   12. p. 197.   13. See pp. 215–18.
14. *The Well-Beloved*, 34.   15. p. 327.   16. p. 54.
17. p. 74.   18. *Ibid.*   19. pp. 80–1.
20. Hardy's Preface to *The Well-Beloved*, 25.
21. C. G. Jung, *Works*, 9, 2, p. 15.
22. *Ibid.*, 267.   23. *Desperate Remedies*, 287.
24. *Far from the Madding Crowd*, 132.   25. *Ibid.*, 161.
26. *Ibid.*, 419.
27. *Jude*, 90.   28. *Two on a Tower*, 244.
29. *The Woodlanders*, 233.   30. *Ibid.*, 147.   31. *Ibid.*
32. *The Well-Beloved*, 81.   33. p. 31.   34. *Ibid.*   35. p. 53.
36. p. 121.   37. p. 113.   38. p. 75.   39. p. 67.

CHAPTER 11
1. *A Theory of Literary Production*, 16.
2. *The Great Tradition*, 9.
3. *Ibid.*, 34.   4. *Ibid.*, 9.
5. See Pierre Macherey and Etienne Balibar, 'Literature as an Ideological Form: Some Marxist Propositions', trans. Ann Wordsworth, *Oxford Literary Review*, vol. 3, no. 1, p. 9.
6. *The Great Tradition*, 27.
7. John Bayley, *An Essay on Hardy*, London, 1978, 201.
8. These quotations are taken from R. G. Cox, ed., *Thomas Hardy. The Critical Heritage*, New York, 1970.
9. Lionel Johnson, *The Art of Thomas Hardy*, London, 1894. 56.
10. See pp. 87 and 192.   11. See pp. 58–60.   12. p. 275.
13. See the General Preface to the Wessex Edition of 1912.
14. W. J. Dawson, *The Makers of English Fiction*, London, 1905, 202.
15. See pp. 223–5.
16. H. B. Grimsditch, *Character and Environment in the Novels of Thomas Hardy*, London, 1925, 75.

17. Virginia Woolf, 'The Novels of Thomas Hardy' (1928), *Collected Essays*, London, 1966, Vol. 1, 262.
18. *Ibid.*, 266.   19. *Ibid.*, 258.   20. *Ibid.*, 265.
21. Bonamy Dobrée, *The Lamp and the Lute*, London, 1929, 31-2.
22. *Ibid.*, 25.
23. Frank Chapman, 'Hardy the Novelist', *Scrutiny, III* (June 1934), 30.
24. T. S. Eliot, *After Strange Gods*, London, 1934, 54-5.
25. William Rutland, *Thomas Hardy: A Study of his Writings and their Background*, Oxford, 1938, 176.
26. *Ibid.*, 211.   27. pp. 256-7.   28. pp. 86-7.
29. David Cecil, *Hardy the Novelist: An Essay in Criticism*, London, 1943, 12.
30. p. 13.   31. p. 85.   32. p. 123.   33. p. 126.
34. p. 146. 35. pp. 148-9. 36. p. 150. 37. p. 126. 38. p. 146.
39. Albert J. Guerard, *Thomas Hardy — The Novels and Stories*, Oxford, 1949, 8.
40. Edwin Muir, *Essays on Literature and Society*, London, 1949, 117.
41. Desmond Hawkins, *Thomas Hardy*, London, 1950, 87-8.
42. Douglas Brown, *Thomas Hardy*, London, 1954, 29.
43. Frank O'Connor, *The Mirror in the Roadway*, London, 1957, 241-2.
44. David Daiches, *A Critical History of English Literature*, London, 1960, 1073-4.
45. David Lodge, *The Language of Fiction*, London, 1966, 188.
46. Irving Howe, *Thomas Hardy*, London 1968, pp. 18 and 59.
47. J. I. M. Stewart, *Thomas Hardy: A Critical Biography*, London, 1971, pp. 180, 144 and 77.
48. N. Page, *Thomas Hardy*, London, 1977, 36-7.
49. *op. cit.*, 98.
50. J. Hillis Miller, *Thomas Hardy, Distance and Desire*, Oxford, 1970, 261-2.
51. Merryn Williams, *Thomas Hardy and Rural England*, London, 1972, 200.

CHAPTER 12
1. *Reading Capital*, 35-6.   2. *Op. cit.*, xii.
3. *A Theory of Literary Production*, 76.
4. Helen Garwood, *Thomas Hardy: An Illustration of the Philosophy of Schopenhauer*, Philadelphia, 1911, 6, 30, 38 and 68.
5. *Op. cit.*, 33.
6. A. P. Elliott, *Fatalism in the Works of Thomas Hardy*, New York, 1935, 11 and 46-7.

7. *Op. cit.,* 1073-4.
8. Ian Gregor, 'What Kind of Fiction did Hardy Write?', *Essays in Criticism,* 16, 1966, 242.
9. Ian Gregor, *The Great Web: The Form of Hardy's Major Fiction,* London, 1974, 33.
10. F. B. Pinion, *Thomas Hardy: Art and Thought,* London, 1977, 10, 36, 114, 148, 43 and 45.
11. Lascelles Abercrombie, *Thomas Hardy: A Critical Study,* London, 1912, 13, 14, 17, 18 and 99.
12. H. Child, *Thomas Hardy,* London, 1916, 18 and 117.
13. H. C. Duffin, *Thomas Hardy: A Study of the Wessex Novels, the Poems, and The Dynasts,* 1916, 186, 126, 257.
14. S. C. Chew, *Thomas Hardy, Poet and Novelist,* New York, 1921, 32.
15. H. B. Grimsditch, *op. cit.,* 139.   16. Dobrée, *op. cit.,* 25.
17. Pierre D'Exideuil (Georges Lasselin), *The Human Pair in the Work of Thomas Hardy,* trans. F. W. Crosse, London, 1929, 67.
18. R. E. Zachrisson, *Thomas Hardy's Twilight View of Life: A Study of an Artistic Temperament,* Uppsala, 1931, 12.
19. A. P. Elliott, *op. cit.,* 35.   20. Rutland, *op. cit.,* 149.
21. *Ibid.,* p. 56.   22. Cecil, *op. cit.,* 19, 26 and 35.
23. H. C. Webster, *On a Darkling Plain,* Chicago, 1947, 213.
24. Daiches, *op. cit.,* 1073-4.
25. F. R. Leavis, *For Continuity,* Cambridge, 1933, 15.
26. F. R. Leavis and Denys Thompson, *Culture and Environment: The Training of Critical Awareness,* London, 1933, 85, 86 and 87.
27. Michel Foucault, *The Archaeology of Knowledge,* trans. A. M. Sheridan Smith, London, 1972, 12.
28. Guerard, *op. cit.,* 18-30.
29. Hawkins, *op. cit.,* 14 and 16.
30. Brown, *op. cit.,* 30.
31. John Holloway, *The Charted Mirror: Literary and Critical Essays,* London, 1960, 95.
32. Howe, *op. cit.,* 5, 19, 21 and 24.
33. Ian Gregor, '*Jude the Obscure*', in *Imagined Worlds,* London, 1968, 245.
34. P. Meisel, *Thomas Hardy: The Return of the Repressed,* London, 1972, 40.
35. L. Lerner, *Thomas Hardy's Mayor of Casterbridge: Tragedy or Social History?* Sussex, 1975, 89-93.
36. Page, *op. cit.,* 63.
37. Webster, *op. cit.,* 47-8, 139 and 140.
38. Brown, *op. cit.,* 20.
39. G. Roppen, *Evolution and Poetic Belief,* Oslo, 1956, 297.

40. N. A. Scott, 'The Literary Imagination and the Victorian Crisis of Faith: The Example of Thomas Hardy', *The Journal of Religion*, XL (Oct. 1960), 280.

41. Macherey says something very similar. See *A Theory of Literary Production*, trans. Geoffrey Wall, London, 1978, 75.

42. L. Stephenson, *Darwin Among the Poets*, Chicago, 1932, 276–7, 291 and 291–2.

43. Brown, *op. cit.*, pp. 32 and 36.   44. *Ibid.*, p. 30.

45. Charles Darwin, *On The Origin of Species by Means of Natural Selection*, Thinker's Library edition, London, 1929, 60–1.

46. Brown, *op. cit.*, 45.   47. Darwin, *op. cit.*, 81.

48. Douglas Brown, *Thomas Hardy: The Mayor of Casterbridge*, London, 1962, 41.

49. *Thomas Hardy*, 134.

CHAPTER 13

 1. See *Thomas Hardy: The Critical Heritage*, 104, 111, 310.

 2. Abercrombie, *op. cit.*, 51.   3. Duffin, *op. cit.*, 217.

 4. Chew, *op. cit.*, 184–5.   5. Grimsditch, *op. cit.*, 109.

 6. Arthur Symons, *A Study of Thomas Hardy*, London, 1927, 6.

 7. Elliott, *op. cit.*, see pp. 90–7 and 57.

 8. Cecil, *op. cit.*, 31.

 9. J. O. Bailey, 'Hardy's "Imbedded Fossil"', *Studies in Philology*, XLII (July, 1945), p. 671.

10. Guerard, *op. cit.*, 132.   11. Stewart, *op. cit.*, 72.

12. Webster, *op. cit.*, 129.   13. Muir, *op. cit.*, 119.

14. R. A. Duerksen, *Shelleyan Ideas in Victorian Literature*, London, 1966, 162.

15. Meisel, *op. cit.*, 42.   16. Gregor, *The Great Web*, 203.

17. Quoted in Gregor, *The Great Web*, 26–7.

18. Webster, *op. cit.*, 176–80.   19. Brown, *op. cit.*, 91.

20. Holloway, *The Charted Mirror*, 98.

21. Roy Morrell, *Thomas Hardy, The Will and the Way*, Singapore, 1965, 36.

22. Tony Tanner, 'Colour and Movement in Hardy's *Tess of the d'Urbervilles*', *Critical Quarterly*, X, 1968, 219–239. This appears in the Coles Notes on *Tess*.

23. Howe, *op. cit.*, 111.

24. B. J. Paris, '"A Confusion of Many Standards" Conflicting Value Systems in Tess of the d'Urbervilles' *Nineteenth Century Fiction*, XXIV, (June 1969), 76.

25. Dale Kramer, *Thomas Hardy: The Forms of Tragedy*, London, 1975, 134.

26. F. R. Southerington, *Hardy's Vision of Man*, London, 1971, 131–3.

27. G. Thurley, *The Psychology of Hardy's Novels: The Nervous and the Statuesque*, St Lucia, 1975, 153 and 170.
28. F. B. Pinion, *Thomas Hardy: Art and Thought*, London, 1977, 135.
29. Gregor, *The Great Web*, p. 203.
30. D. H. Lawrence, *Study of Thomas Hardy*, (written 1914), *A Selection from Pheonix*, Penguin Books, 236, 237, 242-3 and 252.
31.. Guerard, *op. cit.*, 109.   32. Hawkins, *op. cit.*, 84.
33. Walter Allen, *The English Novel*, Penguin Books, 257.
34. R. B. Heilman, 'Hardy's Sue Bridehead', *Nineteenth Century Fiction*, XX, (March, 1966), 313-19.
35. Howe, *op. cit.*, 111 and 138.
36. Gregor, '*Jude the Obscure*', *Imagined Worlds*, 251-2.
37. J. O. Bailey, 'Heredity as Villain in the Poetry and Fiction of Thomas Hardy', *The Thomas Hardy Year Book*, eds. G & J Stevens Cox, Guernsey, 1970, 9-18.
38. Stewart, *op. cit.*, 201.
39. V. R. Hyman, *Ethical Perspectives in the Novels of Thomas Hardy*, London, 1975, 170.
40. Coles Notes on *Tess*, 9.
41. Michèle Barrett, *Women's Oppression Today*, London, 1980, 84.

CHAPTER 14
1. Herman Lea, *Thomas Hardy's Wessex*, London, 1913, 34.
2. Clive Holland, *Thomas Hardy's Wessex Scene*, London, 1948, 123. See also D. K. Robinson, *Hardy's Wessex Reappraised*, Newton Abbot, 1972.
3. A. Brick, 'Paradise and Consciousness in Hardy's *Tess*', *Nineteenth Century Fiction*, XVII, (Sept. 1962), 120 and 123.
4. Kramer, *op. cit.*, 23 and 165.
5. Meisel, *op. cit.*, 90, 102 and 108.
6. Southerington, *op. cit.*, 104 and 94.
7. Morrell, *op. cit.*, 114.
8. J. Hillis Miller, 'Implications of Form in Victorian Fiction', *Comparative Literature Studies*, 3:2 (1966), 117.
9. Paris, *op. cit.*, 73.
10. L. J. Starzyk, 'The Coming Universal Wish not to Live in Hardy's "Modern" Novels, *Nineteenth Century Fiction*, XXVI, (March 1972), 427.
11. Bayley, *op. cit.*, 34.
12. See *Thomas Hardy: The Critical Heritage*, 19, 23-5, 36-7, 46, 104-5.
13. Johnson, *op. cit.*, 275 and 134.   14. Dawson, *op. cit.*, 219-22.
15. Grimsditch, *op. cit.*, 27.   16. Dobrée, *op. cit.*, 39.
17. Chapman, *op. cit.*, 29.   18. Eliot, *op. cit.*, 57.

19. D. Davidson, 'The Traditional Basis of Thomas Hardy's Fiction', *The Southern Review,* VI, (Summer 1940), 175-6.
20. Guerard, *op. cit.,* 123 and 119.
21. Dorothy Van Ghent, *The English Novel: Form and Function,* New York, 1953, 205-6.
22. Brown, *op. cit.,* 71; O'Connor, *op. cit.,* 242; J. Paterson, '*The Return of the Native* as Anti-Christian Document', *Nineteenth Century Fiction,* XIV (Sept. 1959), 124-5.
23. Howe, *op. cit.,* 61.   24. Stewart, *op. cit.,* 131.
25. Page, *op. cit.,* 36.

CHAPTER 15
1. See Chapter 3.   2. p. 419.
3. See Raymond Williams, *The Long Revolution,* Penguin Books, Part Two, chap. 1, 'Education and British Society' and chap. 4, 'The Growth of "Standard English"'.
4. *The Popular Education of France, Selected Prose,* 121-2.
5. R. D. Altick, *The English Common Reader,* London, 1957, 161.
6. R. Williams, *The Long Revolution,* 157-8.   7. *Ibid.*
8. Simon, *op. cit.,* 112.
9. H. G. Wells, *Experiment in Autobiography,* London, 1934, Vol. 1, 93, quoted in Simon, 97.
10. Simon, *op. cit.,* 120.
11. Macherey, Balibar, 'Literature as an Ideological Form', *O.L.R.,* 6-7.
12. See 'Literature as an Ideological Form'.
13. *Ibid., O.L.R.,* 12.
14. The title of an article by Antonia Byatt in *The Times Educational Supplement* (2.1.1981) concerning the favourite reading of prospective candidates to University College, London. Two things emerged from this: first, the 'huge popularity of novelists compared with poets or even dramatists' and second, the fact that the most popular novelist was 'overwhelmingly Thomas Hardy'.
15. John Lucas, *The Literature of Change: Studies in the Nineteenth Century Provincial Novel,* Sussex, 1977, 138.
16. *Capital,* vol. 1, 73.   17. *Ibid.,* 73.
18. See Machery, Balibar, 'Literature as an Ideological Form'.
19. Peter Widdowson, 'Hardy in History: A Case Study in the Sociology of Literature', *Literature and History,* vol. 9, 1, (Spring, 1983).
20. Maureen E. Mahon, *Thomas Hardy's Novels: A Study Guide,* Heineman Educational Books, London, 1976, 5.
21. Brodie's Notes, Pan Study Aids, first published 1966 by James Brodie Ltd.; Coles Notes, Coles Publishing Co. Ltd., Toronto, 1981; York Notes, Longman York Press, 1980, Notes by David

Lindley. All three are notes on *Tess* to which I shall broadly limit my observations.
22. Joint Matriculation Board 'A' level question, 1981.
23. Although this is not acknowledged and the book does not appear in the bibliography.
24. Mahon, *op. cit.*, 106 and 110.
25. See Macherey, Balibar, 'Literature as an Ideological Form'.
26. *The Great Tradition*, 187.
27. So Henry James's 'later style' was seen by Leavis as evidence that 'there really was incapacity, essential loss of power, that something had gone wrong in his life'. *The Great Tradition*, 192.

CONCLUSION

1. F. R. Leavis and Denys Thompson, *Culture and Environment: The Training of Critical Awareness*, London, 1933, 1, 5 and 82.
2. I. A. Richards, *Principles of Literary Criticism*, London, 1976, 230. First published 1924.
3. The Eighth Thesis on Feuerbach, *Selected Works* in one vol., 30.
4. George Orwell, *Nineteen Eighty-Four*, Penguin Books, 125.
5. As a set book for 'O' level examinations.
6. The Third Thesis on Feuerbach. *op. cit.*, 28-9.
7. Both these expressions were used by Bertold Brecht in his essay 'Against Georg Lukács'.

Index